THE
OUTER SHORES

PART 2
Breaking Through

From the papers of Edward F. Ricketts,
introduced and edited by
JOEL W. HEDGPETH

Dr. Joel W. Hedgpeth has taught at Scripps Institution of Oceanography, University of the Pacific, and Oregon State University. He has been a visiting professor at Woods Hole Oceanographic Institution, University of Wyoming, Stanford University (*Te Vega* Cruise 17), San Francisco State University, and Brigham Young University. He now resides in Santa Rosa, California where he works as an independent consultant on problems of marine ecology and teaches an occasional course on the history of marine biology.

MAD RIVER PRESS INC.

© 1978 Joel W. Hedgpeth
and Edward F. Ricketts, Jr.

Published by Mad River Press, Inc.
Route 2, Box 151-B
Eureka, California 95501

Printed by Eureka Printing Company, Inc.
Eureka, California 95501

ISBN 0-916-422-14-3

Ein Verkundiger der Natur zu sein, ist ein schönes und heiliges Amt.

Novalis: *Die Lehrlinge zu Sais*

And this I believe: that the free, exploring mind of the individual human is the most valuable thing in the world.

John Steinbeck: *East of Eden*

ACKNOWLEDGEMENTS: PART 2

My indebtedness to all those mentioned and thanked for assistance and permissions in Part 1 applies to this part in equal measure.

In addition, I wish to thank George Robinson for his letter about Steinbeck's disposition of Ed Ricketts' papers and his own letters.

For illustrations used in this part I am especially indebted to Lynn Rudy for five drawings prepared for a forthcoming book about the marine life of the Gulf of California by Paul and Lynn Rudy, Nick Carter for several photographs taken around Loreto about 1960, and William Shepherd for two recent photographs near La Paz. Gary Brusca assisted with illustrations, and Richard Brusca likewise, one of these with the permission of the University of Arizona Press. The Viking Press is duly thanked for permission to use a photograph from *The Forgotten Village*. The John Steinbeck collection of the Salinas Public Library is thanked for permission to reproduce the full view photograph of the *Western Flyer* (probably taken by Fred Strong). I have been unable to locate B.J. Roberts, from whose thesis of 1941 I have used two diagrams. I cannot at this time remember how I came by the photographs of W.C. Allee; I suspect they were supplied some years ago by Ralph G. Johnson.

Several short quotations from Robinson Jeffers used by Edward F. Ricketts have been revised according to *The Selected Poetry of Robinson Jeffers* (Random House, c. 1959). Brief quotations and phrases from various works in print, all duly acknowledged in the text, fall under the fair use provision for citation in a critical review.

ERRATA AND ADDENDA FOR PART 1

p. viii, first line: existance should read existence.

p. x. For J.B. Phillips read H.B. Phillips.

p. 6, Par. 2, line 15: undoubtably should read undoubtedly.

p. 22, end. The quotation is the concluding paragraph from:
Lewis, John R., 1968. "Water movements and their role in rocky shore ecology." *Sarsia*, vol. 34, pp. 13-36.

p. 43. The child in the photograph is not Kay but Ritchie Lovejoy's son John.

p. 85. Unfortunately the scale was omitted from the map of Graham Island. The straight line distance between Masset and Port Clements is 25 miles (40 kilometers).

pp. 109-110. Among the list of photographs that Ricketts hoped to obtain for the Outer Shores was the Edenshaw house, abandoned after the death of the Chief. The photograph below was obtained from a member of the Edenshaw family through the courtesy of H.B. Phillips of Masset. At the time of this picture the house was still occupied. I regret that this was mislaid during the preparation of Part 1. J.W.H.

TABLE OF CONTENTS

CHRONOLOGY

1897.   May 14. Edward Flanders Robb Ricketts born, Chicago, Illinois.

1914.   Graduated from John Marshall High School, Chicago.

1915-1916.   Attended Illinois State Normal.

1917-1918.   Employed at various jobs in the Southwest.

1918-1919.   Sept.-March. Served in U. S. Army.

1919-1922.   Attended University of Chicago, with emphasis on zoology.
(Absent Spring Quarter 1921 through Summer, 1922).

1921.   November-December. Walk, from Indianapolis to Savannah.

1922.   August 19. Married Anna Macker.

1923.   Sept. Established in Pacific Grove with A. E. Galigher as partner in
Pacific Biological Laboratories.

1930.   Met John Steinbeck.

1932.   June-July. Boat trip to Sitka and Juneau in Jack Calvin's *Grampus*
with Joseph Campbell, Sasha Calvin and Xenia Kashevaroff. Took up
full time residence on Ocean Ave. (Cannery Row)

1936.   November 25. The fire.

1939.   *Between Pacific Tides,* by Edward F. Ricketts and Jack Calvin, published. John Steinbeck becomes partner (and Vice President) in Pacific
Biological Laboratories.

1940.   March 14-April 18. Voyage of *Western Flyer* to Gulf of California with
John Steinbeck.
June-July. To Mexico City, with John Steinbeck and film company
working on *The Forgotten Village.*

1941.   Began relationship with Toni Jackson (Antonia Seixas).

1942-1943.   Second hitch of duty with U. S. Army, at Presidio of Monterey.

1944.   *Cannery Row* written, copyright 1945 but released in December.

1945.   May-July. Collecting and observing trip to west coast of Vancouver Is.

1946.   May-July. Collecting etc. to west coast Vancouver Island, Masset,
Queen Charlotte Islands and Prince Rupert.
June 21. Divorced by Ann(a) Ricketts.

1947.   Nov.-Dec. Separated from Toni Jackson.

1948.   Jan. 2. Married Alice Campbell (not related to Joseph Campbell).
May 8. Hit by train.
May 11. Died as result of injuries.

I

BREAKING THROUGH

IA. Ed Ricketts and John Steinbeck Journey
to the Sea of Cortez and beyond

The expedition to the Gulf of California began as a plan for John Steinbeck to accompany Ed on one of his annual trips to the coast south of Ensenada. Then John talked of buying a truck, and perhaps renting some fishing boat out of San Felipe. Then it was to be a drive to Guaymas. John would help Ed write up the trip. And so on. Probably it was John who suggested they charter a boat in Monterey and go all the way by sea. This would not only be doing something for Ed, it would also enable Steinbeck to escape for a while from the publicity over *The Grapes of Wrath*.

Ed was working on his three philosophical essays, *The Philosophy of Breaking Through; A Spiritual Morphology of Poetry;* and *Non-teleological Thinking*, and by August 1939, he had them in shape, at least in his own opinion, to send to editors. Concerning these essays, Ed wrote to Joseph Campbell, resuming correspondence after a seven year gap: "In continuation of the things we discussed, I have worked up three essays that pretty well sum up the world outlook, or rather the inlook, that I have found developing in myself more and more during the years." (EFR to Joseph Campbell, August 25, 1939) A few weeks later, Ed wrote that they had been rejected by Harper's in spite of the intervention of John Steinbeck and Paul de Kruif, and that he was planning to send them to other magazines. He never quite gave up on these essays. Even after *Sea of Cortez* was published, he wrote to Joseph Campbell about Henry Miller's favorable reaction, that he "apparently liked very much and praised very highly those three essays of mine." (EFR to Joseph Campbell, December 31, 1941)

Steinbeck's offer of literary collaboration was doubtless stimulated by Ed's lack of success with the editors, who were rejecting his essays by return mail, as well as by conversation with Ed. Quite possibly he did not realize how large a camel was going to follow the nose into his tent. Steinbeck was in an expansive mood those days. He gave his Pulitzer Prize money from *The Grapes of Wrath* to Ritchie Lovejoy so he could work on his long poem.[1]

Ed loved to plan expeditions; and he was happy as the proverbial

---

[1]Extensive extracts were apparently printed in the *Pine Cone*; one poem, "The Swamp", was published (on the same page with one by Kenneth Rexroth) in the *New Republic*, Aug. 9, 1939. This publication was probably what Ed had in mind when he wrote to Joseph Campbell that Ritchie was becoming "a consequential poet." I have been unable to verify the publication of Lovejoy's poem "Hands"; it was supposed to have been printed in England and praised by Auden.

clam at high tide, planning for the trip on the *Western Flyer*. He did forget, however, to measure the spaces aboard and designed an elaborate combination bookcase and desk that unfortunately would fit nowhere inside and had to be lashed to the top of the cabin, where it was covered with tarpaulin and took some time to get at. Ed also wrote his will, a holograph document dated February 28, 1940, bequeathing royalties "from any books now in the offing with John" to his wife and three children and his notebooks and papers that were to be the basis for a system of metaphysics to John, in the obvious hope that John might bring them together in a book. His books of poetry he left to Jean Ariss. The will concluded with the statement: "So here it is. I have practically nothing to bequeath—except a few prospects." While Ed planned the collecting side of the trip, John and their attorney-friend, Webster Street, took care of arrangements for the boat, ship's supplies, and the like.

The *Western Flyer* left Monterey on the afternoon of March 11, 1940. Almost everybody in town knew about it. Ed had told them all. He was always talking to his friends about what he planned to do, and it was no secret that Ed and John planned to write a book about this trip. Or, for that matter, that Ed had hoped to make a trip like this for years. For him, it would be the sequel to his 1932 trip to Alaska with Jack Calvin and Joseph Campbell. According to the newspaper account, the book about the trip would be by Steinbeck: "Actually a compilation with Ricketts, it will be a readable account of the trip with all their scientific findings included in a form valuable to the scientist and interesting to the layman." (Lead story by Jimmy Costello, *Monterey Peninsula Herald*, March 11, 1940.) Aside from the stories in the *Peninsula Herald* and the *Carmel Pine Cone* and, a few days after their departure, two pictures in the *San Jose Mercury Herald* of Carol Steinbeck as a local girl off on a cruise, there was not very much publicity. During the trip, a few installments of a running account of the trip, by Sparky Enea of the *Western Flyer*'s crew, appeared in the *Monterey Peninsula Herald*. The return of the expedition also received due notice, and again the prospect of the forthcoming book was mentioned. In a United Press release from San Diego for April 19, Steinbeck is quoted as saying that he "planned to study the sociological aspects of marine life . . . I don't pretend to know much about biology, but it seems that some of the broader, more general aspects of the tie-in of all animal species with one another has been lost since Darwin went out of the picture. We are trying in our small way to get back to a phase of that broader view."

The original plan, evidently, had been that both Ricketts and Steinbeck would keep journals for the material for the book. But it turned out that only Ricketts kept a journal.[1] A number of people

---

[1] In a letter to Elizabeth Otis written aboard the *Western Flyer* on March 26, 1940, Steinbeck wrote: "We've been working hard, collecting, preserving and making notes. No log. There hasn't been time." (*A Life in Letters*, p. 200)

Portrait of John Steinbeck circa 1941.

Ed Ricketts, circa 1938. Courtesy Ed Ricketts Jr.

remember Steinbeck saying that Ricketts' original was too question-
able to save, yet the typescript "verbatim transcription" requires no
editing for propriety. This typescript was made immediately after
the trip, apparently. The decision was made, evidently after some
preliminary writing, to omit Carol Steinbeck from the book; possibly
this was in deference to the fisherman's mystique which considered
women tabu on fishing boats or, perhaps, as Ed's philosophical ideas
grew into the book, there seemed to be less place for a woman. Also,
Steinbeck's marriage was in difficulties; the divorce was not far off.
There is also that querulous passage on page 237 of *Sea of Cortez*
about the prejudice against the manner in which the wife aboard an
expedition is mentioned; perhaps this is Steinbeck's *ex post facto* ra-
tionalization. But there were a few discrepancies as a result of the decision to omit Carol from the account: the ship was provisioned for
seven people but only six are mentioned and there was an extra piece
of pie. In a memorandum about the writing of *Sea of Cortez*, Ed
wrote:

> Originally, a journal of the trip was to have been kept by both us, but
> this record was found to be a natural expression of only one of us. This
> journal was subsequently used by the other chiefly as a reminder of what
> actually had taken place, but in several cases parts of the original field
> notes were incorporated into the final narrative, and in one case a large
> section was lifted verbatim from the other unpublished work. This was
> then passed back to the other for comment, completion of certain chiefly
> technical details, and corrections. And then the correction was passed
> back again. (Memorandum from Steinbeck-Ricketts to Pat Covici, Aug-
> ust 25, 1941.)

The actual writing of the book that became *Sea of Cortez* did not
begin until perhaps January of 1941, however. In the interlude,
Steinbeck went to Mexico to work on a documentary film *The
Forgotten Village*, and Ed joined the company in Mexico City for
most of June and part of July of 1940. He brought along with him a
young lady named Faun, a bookstore clerk who offered to go along
after hearing Ed talk of his plans. It turned out for once that both
parties had misunderstood each other about the travelling arrangements, and after a few days Ed put her on the train back to California. It appears from the extant letters that Ed spent much of his
time in libraries, seeking out material about the Gulf of California;
and he filled several notebooks of abstracts of this reading in his
careless pencil scrawl. He also worked on his essays, weighing carefully the suggestions made by Joseph Campbell, expressing the hope
that eventually they might be made into a book after he became
famous enough from his collaboration with John. He found time to
observe and comment in letters to friends about the people and their
ways of living. To him, there was something special in the Mexican
way of life, of accepting a timeless pattern of being, of coming into
equilibrium with fate. He did not believe that such a pattern
should be abandoned in favor of the modern industrial syndrome and

Elwood Graham's portrait of Steinbeck in Ed's living quarters at the lab.

he did not like the implication of social improvement in Steinbeck's work on the documentary film. Sometime in April of 1941, when both he and Steinbeck were working hard on *Sea of Cortez*, John presented Ed with a copy of *The Forgotten Village*. Ed did not like it. He probably told John he did not like it. He wrote to Toni Jackson: "I don't think it's much good. And I cannot imagine even that the movie from which the scenes and captions are selected is much good." Later in the year, after *Sea of Cortez* was safely out of the way, Ed returned to his brooding over *The Forgotten Village*, stimulated perhaps by the article on China in *Life* Magazine for November 24, 1941; the quotation from this article used in the script is entered on page 89 of Ed's 1941 notebook under the title "Materials for a script on Mexico." Then he wrote it all up and sent it to John. What Steinbeck thought of this "anti-script" is not available, although one of Ed's letters indicates that it was discussed in their correspondence.

In all probability the anti-script had some bearing on the final version of *The Pearl*, which became a much more involved and elaborate tale than the brief parable recounted on pp. 102-103 of Sea of Cortez.

It is still amazing to realize how much Ed got done in the matter of curating, shipping and writing about the collections, and how quickly he got replies. Between the time the *Western Flyer* returned late in April of 1940 and submission of the manuscript of *Sea of Cortez* in August, 1941, Ed had managed to get dozens of specialists to identify the specimens collected on the trip.

In a summarizing letter to John Steinbeck (August 22, 1941), Ed wrote:

> When complete data comes to hand, I think we shall have collected more than 600 species, of which 60 will have been undescribed at the time they were taken.
>
> It would be an understatement for me to say that this little trip of ours is growing to be an important expedition, and that out of it are coming some fairly significant contributions to invertebrate zoology, to marine sociology and even—I wouldn't be surprised—to human thought.
>
> This is all the more remarkable when you consider that: (1) we worked solely in a small, but natural, subdivision of a single geographical province; had we taken specimens along the way, from here on down there, as the average expedition, interested solely in numbers, would have done, we could have collected in three provinces, with a corresponding increase in the number of species taken; (2) we took shore animals solely—since we didn't even have any dredging equipment on board—and 95% or more of the material was strictly intertidal; and (3) we paid very little attention except incidentally, to (a) such pelagic materials as jellyfish, ctenophores, micro-crustacea and other planktonic elements; (b) fishes, except for the commonest shore species which were important elements in the sociology of the region; and (c) rarities, small animals, or obscure forms.
>
> The average expedition takes material indiscriminately by dredging, seining, tow-netting both in deep water and on the surface and usually far from land, and pays special atention to rare or unknown forms. We operated on the opposite plan: the commoner the animal, the more atten-

tion we devoted to it, since it, more than the total of all rare forms, was important in the biological economy. Instead of operating on any hit and miss plan, we had merely the one coordinated objective: to become as familar as we might, in our limited time, with the short biology of the region—to make a survey of the common and obvious animals of a restricted area.

I think we not only succeeded, but that we succeeded beyond our hopes. If even we had no limited objective and if we had worked without any geographical or ecological restrictions whatever, still we'd have done well to get such a bunch of material. And getting it all whipped into shape for a thorough report within less than two years is almost unprecedented. I think we have done a good job by any standards. and furthermore, said he, we few, with no decent facilities, and with the laboratory, library and office difficulties incident to a small boat, and with no coordinated force of specialists and clerks, collected, prepared (usually well), sorted, labelled, dispatched and kept our records straight on this enormous bulk of material without any grave confusions, whereas many a pretentious expedition got back with lots of their specimens poorly preserved, unlabelled, mislabelled, or lacking field notes.

It seems gratifying to reflect on the fact that we, unsupported and unaided, seem to have taken more species, in greater number, and better preserved, than expeditions more pretentious and endowed, as we were not, with prestige, personnel, equipment and financial backing. As Toni says: "Two guys in a small boat, with enthusiasm and knowledge."

John Steinbeck wrote part of *Sea of Cortez* while sitting for his portrait in Ellwood Graham's studio; Graham has told Richard Astro that he remembers Steinbeck had Ed's typescript journal and was writing from that, while Graham worked on the portrait. The portrait, as it turned out, distressed many people. But it was published in color as a cover of a local magazine and the original sketch has been reproduced as an end page in the recent book, *John Steinbeck: the Man and His Work*. The whereabouts of the original is uncertain at this time. Ed had no reservations about Steinbeck as an artist and happily wrote to Toni: "I have just been reading what Jon wrote today. It's so damn beautiful I can hardly stand it. He takes my words and gives them a little twist, and puts in some of his own beauty of concept and expression and the whole thing is so lovely you can't stand it." (EFR to TJ, February 28, 1941.) Covici's reaction to the completed text was even more ecstatic; he dashed off an undated pencilled note on two slips of copy paper:

Dear John:

It is four o'clock in the morning. I just finished your book, and I say it is a great book. I feel as if I were among some distant stars, bewildered, amazed with the mystery of it all. Why am I here, and where am I floating?

Yours is gigantic thinking and it takes gigantic reading. I don't claim that it is all clear to me but I want to read it again and again till it becomes part of me. I don't remember another reading experience like this.

Love
Pat

Shortly after Ed began to correspond with Toni Jackson (Antonia Seixas), she came to live with him on Cannery Row and did the typing for the book. Ed assumed responsibility for most of the details, obtaining illustrations of his cherished invertebrates, having references checked in the University library at Berkeley by Virginia Scardigli, and carrying on an involved correspondence about the project with Pascal Covici of Viking Press and with John's literary agents, McIntosh and Otis. John was often away and was not concerned in any event about the details of the appendix or the illustrations. Ed's concern for meticulous arrangement, various sizes of type and the like, which could give even a University Press qualms, evidently caused some anguish at Viking. Ed was very unhappy about the quality of the illustrations, especially at the proof stage. He had wanted to bleed plates and had gone to a great deal of time and trouble supervising the photography and drawing of the plates, and he felt that the Viking people had let him down. In the midst of all this, Covici sent Ed a copy of *The Viking Book of Poetry of the English Speaking World*. Thanks to a quirk of lighting or an out-of-focus glance, Ed misread the dust jacket as "the English Speaking Bulldog." This stimulated speculations and conversations about how it would be if such a mistake had actually been made, or what would happen if somebody deliberately played a practical joke with the printers. Everyone was getting a bit punchy from the struggle, and Toni wrote a pastiche about a book *Sea of Pizzaro* by R.E. Fickert and Steinberg and how the great author, distracted by his contract to produce so many thousand words, arranged a misprinted dust jacket by R.E. Fuckert.

Sometime before the agitation over bleed cuts, collotypes, various type fonts and all the other details Ed struggled with, Pascal Covici questioned the matter of joint authorship and suggested in a letter of May 20, 1941, that Ed's name be relegated to authorship of the appendix only:

> I have been wondering whether the by-line as you have it isn't quite leading. The first part of the book is distinctly John's, just as the Appendix, the scientific portion of the book, is distinctly yours. No reader with the widest stretch of the imagination could possible mistake the authorship of one for the other. No matter how much John helped in writing your part or you his, it is still unquestionably obvious that the writer of *The Sea of Cortez* is not the author of the Appendix. Undoubtedly the two parts complement each other, but they are two distinct entities. Then why not say so? Why confuse the reader?

On the back of this letter, in John Steinbeck's handwriting, is the telegram he sent to Covici: "I find your suggestion outrageous. This book is the product of the work and thinking of both of us, and the setting down of the words is of no importance. I not only disapprove of your plan but forbid it."

A later note to Covici makes it plain that Ed was out of town at the time and probably did not see the letter of May 20 at all. For that matter, he may not have seen Covici's reply (dated May 22) to John's reaction:

It shall be done as you and Ed say, but be it on your heads. I still think you are wrong and that you will regret it. One of these days you will consider our judgments more favorably.

Modesty and self-effacement are often true characteristics of greatness; but come, John, when you say the setting down of words is of no importance you completely deny the art of writing. The work and sweat you suffered all these years learning the setting down of words denies your gallant assertion.

Surely in your introduction you could give Ed full credit for his ideas and the help he undoubtedly was to you, and Ed in turn could honesly tell of the inspiration and assistance you were to him on his end of the job. Neither of you then could be accused of assuming the other's particular talent. However, it is your book and I shall do as you say.

Sea of Cortez was published at an unfortunate time. Few people probably read the reviews published in most of the newspapers on December 7, 1941, or, if they did, gave them serious attention. Most of the reviewers were as confused as Covici about the authorship, as Ed suspected they would be,[1] and perhaps as both authors hoped they would be. It is now somewhat disconcerting (Ed would certainly have been upset) to realize that few readers of the version known as *The Log From the Sea of Cortez* are aware that it is not the whole book. The big green first edition with the scientific appendix and the color plates became a collector's rarity. Covici finally had his way, for the title page of the *Log* version suggests that this is really John's part of the book, an impression he did little to discourage in the preface, "About Ed Ricketts."

Obviously, several of the reviewers did not know quite what to make of the book. Joseph Henry Jackson, arbiter of literary fates for the *San Francisco Chronicle* did not like it at all. He refused to write a personal review for the Sunday section, but instead farmed it out in two parts. The narrative part was condescendingly reviewed by Scott Newhall as a sort of yachtsman's journal, and I commented on the more factual half as a contribution to science (anyhow, I got a review copy for my pains). Joe Jackson had no patience with mysticism and made it plain in his radio comments and personal remarks that he did not think this the sort of writing that Steinbeck ought to be doing. But then he had a proprietary feeling about Steinbeck's career. Donald Culross Peattie, that mellifluous nature writer of the times, was quite aware that it was probably Ed who was teaching Steinbeck philosophical tricks, although he slipped badly when he remarked that Ricketts' friends would be surprised to know how much beer he drank. His approach to the book was that of a parochial nature writer, with little knowledge either of the authors or the sea. (*Saturday Review*, December 27, 1941.)

[1]In a letter, EFR to JWH, Nov. 18, 1941. Later John Steinbeck persuaded EFR Jr. in a letter (Dec. 13, 1950), to relinquish his father's copyright for the "Log" version of *Sea of Cortez*: "You will remember that I did what I could while I could." In later editions of *The Log from the Sea of Cortez*, copyright on behalf of EFR Jr. was reinstated.

In his review of *Sea of Cortez* for the *New Republic* of February 16, 1942, Stanley Edgar Hyman blames the whole thing on Steinbeck, for as he wrote:

> One of the arbitrary nuisances in this book is the conscious merging of the collaborators' personalities so that it is almost impossible to tell who wrote what, an important question if one is using the book as a key to Steinbeck's other writing. The only way to solve the puzzle is to assume that anything Steinbeck didn't write he is willing to take responsibility for—or he would not have permitted the editorial 'we'—and to pin everything on him.

Of course, he realizes that this makes Steinbeck responsible for "a great deal of pretentious mysticism, a small-boy or Hemingway glory in vulgarity . . . and some of the corniest gags on record." This is perhaps more unkind than necessary, a seeking for quotable words. But the spirit of the review might profitably have been heeded by several Steinbeck critics lately come upon the scene. Those readers who think this is a great book are not bothered by philosophical shortcomings. They are tone-deaf to the tradition of formal philosophical writing and what they find in *Sea of Cortez* makes them feel like philosophers. This opinion is not unanimous. Even at the outset, some readers outside the literary and philosophical demesnes had little use for the book. Walter K. Fisher of Hopkins Marine Station thought it all a bunch of rubbish except for the solid material of the appendix. However, it must be noted that as a frustrated artist who took up painting in his retirement, he was not an unbiased critic.

As might be expected from his acquaintance with the authors, Joseph Campbell recognized the fundamental unity of *Sea of Cortez* and its relation to Ed's "holism," that bringing together of all threads of thought and experience:

> I simply have to tell you how much I enjoyed reading *Sea of Cortez*. In the first place, of course, there were my own grand recollections of our epochal voyage of a decade ago: so many of the moments I recognized again; and so many of the charming little intertidal personalities returned with their timeless physiognomies!! On the level of personal reminiscence, the book was enormously enjoyed. And I was glad to see that the marvellous form of living which we met during those weeks on deck, namely, a form directly in touch with the mother zone between the tides, and with the innumerable little children of the teeming shallows; and a form at the same time moving along the shoreline of contemporary society and contemporary thought, languid and lazy from the standpoint of megalopolitan busyness, deep and terrifically impelling, nevertheless: —I was glad that this form had at last received its book-form; for I am still the man who hardly believes in a thing until it has gotten itself between covers. And I think that the book form discovered by you and John is perhaps as close to the life form itself as a book could possibly be to life. The on-and-on carelessness of the first two hundred pages with the cans of beer and vague chewing of the fat; and then, emerging out of all this, the great solid realization of 'non-teleological thinking'; and then again, that moment just before the entering of Guaymas, when a realization of

two realistic worlds, in the most moving way, presents itself; gradually, meanwhile, the dominant theme of the work is emerging and, from this remark and from that, we understand the society itself is an organism, that these little intertidal societies and the great human societies are manifestations of common principles; are themselves units in a sublime, all-inclusive organism, which breathes and goes on, in dream-like half-consciousness of its own life-processes, oxidizing its own substance yet sustaining its wonderful form. Suddenly, then, the life goes out of the trip and we are on our way back to the laboratory to follow this great thing through in a more exact set of terms, linking it into the fantastic thought-net of the modern scientific workers, whose thoughts somehow (as mysteriously as possible) duplicate the marvels of the fact world, and reveal in their own way the prodigious yet profoundly intimate mysteries of 'that which simply is because it simply is'. Ed, it's a great great book—dreamlike and with no end of implications—sound implications—all-sustaining implications: everything from the beer cans to the phyletic catalogue is singing with music of the spheres. (Joseph Campbell to E.F.R., December 26, 1941.)

Ed's reply to this emphasized Steinbeck's part as the artist:

You got the gist of what was intended, not only better than everyone else, but as no one else . . . I was very charmed with the book. Jn certainly built it carefully. The increasing hints towards purity of thinking, then building up toward the center of the book, on Easter Sunday, with the non-tel essay. The little waves at the start and the little waves at the finish, and the working out of the microcosm-macrocosm thing towards the end. I read it over more than I do lots of other things still. Well, it's nice to like something you have a hand in. I figured you'd like it too. Right down your alley. And doubly so because you had a hand in some of the ideas and collecting details both. (EFR to Joseph Campbell, December 31, 1941.)

Nobody was doing much travelling around for several years after December 7 and *Sea of Cortez* lapsed from print and remaindered copies were available for a time.[1] It was Ed who suggested that the narrative part be published separately, first in a letter to Stanley Cronquist of the Stanford Press in February of 1942 and later, in June, to McIntosh and Otis, Steinbeck's agents. He hoped, nevertheless, to keep the appendix in print, perhaps with Stanford Press, as part of his proposed trilogy of works on the Pacific shores. But we were in the middle of a war and by the end of 1942, Ed was back in the army. During the duller moments of military existence as a medical technician he wrote a journal about the inanities of life on an army post.

Ed took this tour of duty philosophically. He considered himself unfit to be a soldier and regretted the effort it took to conform into the social structure of barracks life as a somewhat superannuated medical technician. It was an uninspiring routine of dispensary

[1] Good second hand copies were commanding prices of $80 to $100 in the 1970's when the book was reproduced in facsimile (including the color plates) by Paul P. Appel, Mamaroneck, New York, 1971. The reproduction is excellent and the binding superior to that of the original edition.

duties, but he found the various personalities interesting and could not resist commenting on the human condition in his journal. He became something of a privileged character at the Presidio, at least within the little sub-world of his unit. He contrived to simplify his duties as short arm inspector of returning privates by placing his cot conveniently near the dutch door of the dispensary. When a soldier presented himself on returning to base, Ed could turn on his flashlight and order the subject to drop his pants at the open door, thereby conducting his examination without getting out of bed. He thought it "very likely" that his commanding officer considered him a good soldier, but as he reflected, "my being a good soldier is at a cost so great that all my thot and effort has to go into it which might otherwise be poured into more suitable things more profitable to the successful prosecution of the war."

Then he remembered how things were the first time:

> During World War One I had one consuming desire: to kill my top sergeant. And this choice hatred lasted for months after I had received my discharge from the army. He seemed to me then an unnecessarily brutal man. Now I understand better. He may have been merely one of those many whose latent sadism push them aggressively into superior positions in the handling of men.
>
> Now in World War Two again I have been kicking against the pricks. But more philosophically this time. The things I have been beefing about I find also in myself.
>
> Potentially, I am the first sergeant who wisecracks at the expense of frightened recruits. I am the ogre colonel who checks on each shined button and polished shoe. I am the C2 who rejects the hospital corner of the bed I've just spent half an hour in making.[1]

Nevertheless, in spite of "all its ridiculousness" he clung to the warmth of the army, "to the companionship of 30 squadroom men in equal misery—who are moved to their not inconsiderable depths by the unity of the unpleasant circumstances into which all of us are thrown."

Writing a journal was not Ed's only way of accepting fate; many of the entries were rewritten as letters to John Steinbeck and others. Occasionally he would try a frontal attack on the Establishment; his letter about the defective Ingersoll watch concisely summarizes many of the frustrations of life on the post:

May 8, 1943

The Ingersoll-Waterbury Co.
  (Division of Waterbury Clock Co.)
Repair and Service Dept.,
Waterbury, Conn.

Attention: Mr. Ingersoll (or Mr. Waterbury)
Dear Mr. Ingersoll:
I am in a difficult situation and I think you should know about it. It's on

---

[1]EFR journal, Jan. 4, 1943. (also other quotations on these pages).

Ed Ricketts during World War II. Courtesy Ed Ricketts Jr.

Ed Ricketts during World War I, 1918. Self photo.

account of one of your watches. The top sergeant is a good guy. A little bit touchy maybe, but not nearly so bad as the guy at Headquarters co. And the Captain is fine. A good bunch of men I say. On the whole. But it naturally arouses their baser instincts when I get in a little bit late. Or a whole lot late. Or too early like the other morning when the boys said I disturbed their best sleep. I was just bored, it being so quiet and all when I got there an hour early everything very dark and nothing to do.

Anyway my wife gave me this watch for Christmas. Because after I got in the army I needed a watch more than ever to keep time. In the army things are very punctual. I am a married man, Mr. Ingersoll and sleep home as you probably do with Mrs. I., but only 4 nights a week as they say in the army, not enough but what can you do? And probably you know that you can't buy alarm clocks for love or money. Or maybe your house is full of them and you wouldn't know. You being a manufacturer of clocks so to speak. And not very good ones if I do say so.

So after Christmas I thought "Now I can get to reveille and retreat on time and maybe not get into so much trouble". Well, the watch didn't keep such good time. It's your Warrior KI, and very G-I khaki-colored. So we took it to the dealer and he fiddled with it, and still it didn't run so good. So my wife sent it to your S F branch, though how she found out the address is more than I understand. She is certainly a livewire that woman. And they sent it right on back, and for a while I used it and it only gained or lost about 5 or 10 minutes per day but you can easy allow for that. Until it got so it would stop. And maybe during the night, with you waking up and looking at its luminous dial but then not knowing the real time any better than if you didn't look in the first place. So we sent it back again, and this time they sent it clear back east and it finally came back all nicely repaired or so we thought, silly fools that we were. Well hell what's the use. It wouldn't even start to go this time. I say if a watch won't run at all it's no good; it's just simply no god dam good at all Mr. Ingersoll, no matter if you did make it or if it's very pretty G-I khaki-colored and looks swank as hell on your wrist or on anybody's wrist I don't care who. And now I think my wife is pregnant though you can't blame the watch for that, directly, anyhow. So you can see how it is. Now what I was thinking is this. If you can surely fix it so it'll run for say a year or even for a few months fine and good, I'd like that fine. But if you can't, let's not kid ourselves either of us. I hate to be sending it back and bothering you, and giving you quarters (25c) and paying postage and getting somebody to typewrite a label, and with your men probably busy too and wartime scarceness of labor and your man working on a hopeless thing.

Just don't send it back at all. Hell its no good if it won't tell time. Let it be a present to you from a soldier far away in California on the shores of sunny Monterey Bay. And no hard feelings on either side Mr. Ingersoll, those things just happen sometimes.

Yours very respectfully

CPL E F Ricketts 39108601
Dispensary S C U 1930

Presidio of Monterey, Calif.

Ed served 18 months as a medical technician in the Presidio of Monterey, and while he was not far away from Cannery Row and often went home on week ends, the business of the Pacific Biological Laboratories was suspended. It never did recover. Even after Ed's release from service, collecting on the seashore was a suspicious activity in those days of blackouts and restricted areas. Ed was losing interest in the business anyhow. In the months between Pearl Harbor and when he was caught by the draft, Ed studied the literature of the Mandated Islands, the territories held by Japan after World War I. Most of his reading was in zoology and anthropology, especially the technical papers published by investigators at the Palau research station. From all this material, a significant amount of information of military significance could be gleaned. Ed approached the Naval Intelligence people about preparing a report for them on this literature. John Steinbeck wrote a letter to Secretary of the Navy Knox about it. As far as they were concerned, nothing came of it; and in his retrospect of Ed, John wondered whether the Navy ever did get the information together.

They did. Somewhere in the woodwork of course the importance of all these things was realized and people were doing just about what Ed was suggesting. But it was not always obvious. For example, somebody classified Dampier's *Sailing Directions* because an admiral requested the book from the library on the assumption that whatever an admiral was reading had military value. Two scientists, who knew each other personally, were assigned highly confidential tasks they could discuss with nobody. One was supposed to prepare a summary of the nearshore oceanography, currents, tides, etc., around Japan from published documents of the British Admiralty (some of them based on Japanese sources). The other was supposed to do the same with Japanese data. The two reports eventually arrived at the same desk and the authors were summoned in to explain why they had not collaborated, at which time they learned what each other had been doing for the last several months.

Ed, who always hoped to make something of all his reading and note-taking, proposed a book about the Mandated Islands to Steinbeck's agents and began as essay on the subject. He wrote an article, "One man's approach to international understanding". It was a somewhat diffuse and rambling article about Germany, Hitler, Italy and Japanese bushido that apparently came back from *The Atlantic* by return mail.

In 1943, after 18 months, Ed was released with the rank of corporal; but the war was still on and he went to work for California Packing Corporation as a chemist in the cannery, a job he held intermittently most of the remaining years. In those times, the sardines were abundent. Landings at Monterey were among the highest in history and things looked so bright that one of the canning companies took out an option on Ed's lab. He began negotiating with Stanford University to build his establishment on the grounds of Hopkins Marine

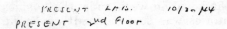

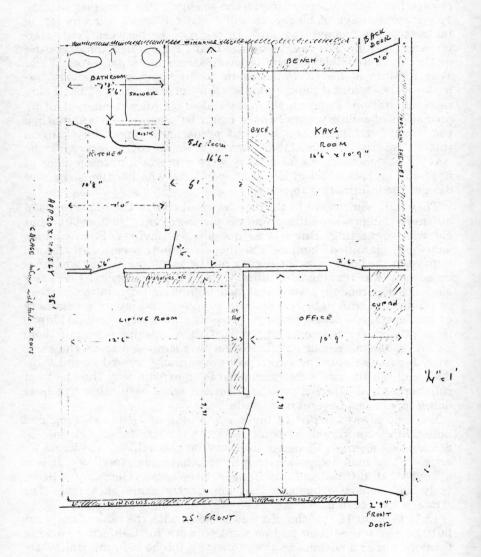

Ed's drawing of the second floor of the existing lab, 1944.

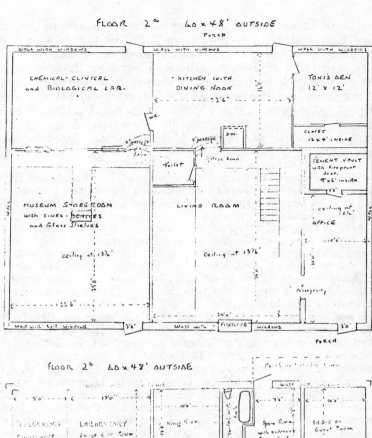

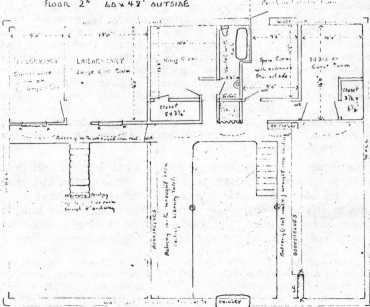

Ed's drawings of two versions of the second floor of the proposed new lab.

Station, to be financed with the proceeds from the sale of the lab on Cannery Row and with support from John Steinbeck. The original idea seems to have been Ed's, as he first made some notes about it in 1939-40. Stanford's motives in seriously discussing the idea were not altruistic. Steinbeck had married a second time and was living in New York (when not travelling as a war correspondent) and was obviously not quite sure what Stanford had in mind, although he may have acquiesced to Ed's idea. According to a letter from Ed to L.R. Blinks, then Director of Hopkins Marine Station, dated November 11, 1944:

> If we were to erect a substantial and appropriate building, would H.M.S. be willing to dollar-a-year-lease to me and John Steinbeck a portion of its unused land, on condition that the improvements passed to Stanford University at our deaths?
> We have in mind a combination establishment, research, residence, biological supply house, which shall serve as headquarters for our explorations and investigations into the fauna of the Pacific during the next twenty years or so (I am 47, John a few years younger). Of the three-part faunistic study projected some years back, two parts have been completed and published. The plan is to complete this by an investigation and report on the extreme North Pacific, then to build up a working collection of specimens and the necessary library, and finally to work up a fairly comprehensive manual of the marine invertebrates—something on the order of Pratt, but restricted to Pacific coast species from the Bering Sea to Panama, and from shore to 25 or 50 fathoms.[1]
> This would require an establishment of which the first building, a 2½-story structure about 50' x 50', comprising library, laboratories, museum shelf room, offices, living quarters, etc., can already be envisioned after the war. This could be substantially constructed so that it could be converted to your uses with a minimum of remodelling. Under such an arrangement, these improvements, together with equipment, specimens, biological library, and whatever commercial establishment remained still in operation (by that time probably leased out) would revert to H.M.S. at our deaths.
> I should think such an arrangement might provide a desirable extension of the Hopkins Marine Station programme, and it could in fact be planned so as to work that way.

On the same kind of paper as the copy of this letter and probably of the same date are sketches of the front elevation of the proposed building and floor plans, showing that Ed proposed to have his living quarters at the left end of the front, so that facing the building he would go up the identical flight of stairs to the right and enter his office by turning left. At the end of the office, however, there would

[1]The work referred to is H. S. Pratt, 1935, *A Manual of Common Invertebrate Animals*. Blakiston's, Philadelphia. The manual to the east coast fauna, hoary with age (the original edition dates to the 1920's) still turns up as a reference and not long ago was used to identify animals found in a sewage investigation in San Francisco Bay. Time has rendered it utterly useless and copies should be recycled. The manual projected by Ricketts was never done, and would involve an impossible number of species to be of any value.

Ed's living quarters at Pacific Biological Laboratory.

be a fireproof vault. As in the old quarters on Cannery Row, the living room would be entered by turning left. There would be no windows on either side, just as if the proposed building were sandwiched between canneries. Like a hermit crab, Ed obviously wanted a newer and larger shell, but of the same species of snail as before. Of course, Cannery Row in those days was not a place to go to look at the sea. Even the few feet of shore behind the lab was hardly worth a second glance. For Ed, the orientation was to other shores—increasingly far away. It would seem that he viewed his project for Hopkins as a base for expedition across the oceans, probably outward to the far Pacific and its coral reefs, or possibly inward, within the familiar walls of his own place and its books, music and thoughts.

Among the undated papers relating to this matter is one titled "Argument for S.U. selling me home-lab space:"

> The program which I am engaged on has I think some social value. I am going ahead and will go ahead on it anyhow, but a suitable location and building will certainly facilitate things. I need very urgently some compact and ready at hand museum space in which, during the balance of my life-time at least, the beasts I'm working on can be stored for instant accessibility. Whoever inherits my library will profit by having them stored decently in the meantime. I keep collections of highly desireable specimens, identified by specialists, & bound & unbound collections of reprints of great regional & coastal value, under fire & loss hazards that appall me. Before my life is over I shall have assembled complete or nearly complete collections of literature in the groups I am working on, carefully bound together and well indexed.

Ed continued to discuss the matter with the people at Hopkins and Stanford's lawyers worked up a formal agreement. Steinbeck evidently took little part in the matter, as he was away from New York and left negotiations up to his agents. The idea that he was to build an aquarium somehow got into the discussions; and while it is obvious that Stanford hoped for great things from John Steinbeck, he was a bit disingenuous in writing to Joseph Henry Jackson that Stanford was after him to build an aquarium for Hopkins Marine Station. "If I can, I will. It would amuse me. And I love aquaria." (JS to JHJ, Spring, 1945.) He had evidently made it plain, however, that his interest was contingent upon Stanford's "treatment of a friend, Mr. Edward F. Ricketts." (L.R. Blinks to Mildred Lyman of MacIntosh and Otis, October 2, 1945.) But the whole plan fell through when the cannery withdrew its option to buy the Pacific Biological Laboratories.

The real event during these negotiations with Stanford University was the writing and publication of *Cannery Row*. Ed saw the book in manuscript and galleys and apparently knew about it some time before that, for he wrote to his son that "I approved the writing of it and OK'd the MS." (EFR to EFR, Jr., January 26, 1945.) Earlier, he had described the book for young Ed:

It's very funny, exceedingly funny, sort of *Tortilla Flat*-ish, but has a better architecture and an undertone of sadness and loneliness. It's mostly about me, and the "Western Biological" and Wing Chongs (Lee Chongs) and Flora Woods (Dora Flood) and the bums. Because I occurred in it so obviously and so frequently, Jn wanted me to OK it, and tho it makes me out to be a very romantic figure and I'll practically have to leave town after publication until things quiet down, still it's a fine job and I approved thoroly. (EFR to EFR, Jr., October 23, 1944.)

In writing *Cannery Row*, John Steinbeck made use of his best friend; much of the humor and good-heartedness that is part of the book is Ed, as is also the sadness and loneliness. But John kept himself out of the story completely.[1] In that sense, the book like the later preface, "About Ed Ricketts," is patronizing and a bit proprietary. Of course, it is a one-sided portrait, fairly true in spirit to one set of Ed's ideas of himself. It might be protested that there was no place in *Cannery Row* for the hopeful philosopher and the earnestly serious zoologist; the concept of the book required a portrait close to caricature. Nevertheless, it is a portrait based on a real person, and it is the only full treatment of a marine biologist in English fiction. In the popular imagination, Ricketts has become Doc, a loveable character who lived just as he wanted to live, getting enough to drink, eat, listen to and go to bed with, and in the end, to read. In the minds of some students, all this is what you do when you are a marine biologist and the learning comes just as easily as the wine, women and song. Of course, there is also *Between Pacific Tides*; and the combination of such a detailed reference book and Steinbeck's romanticized version of its author may indeed have recruited some students to the ranks of marine biology. And, many readers who would never have otherwise been confronted by such words as tunicates, cephalopods and bryozoa have learned to speak them almost as casually as biology majors after their first invertebrate class.

Many critics consider *Cannery Row* to be Steinbeck's last really successful book, and some have suggested that when he left California he left his talent behind. Perhaps there is something to this: *Cannery Row* is still a California book, about a California scene and people. The flavor of that earth had not faded from his writing memory. And of course it was about Ed, when he was still alive to react to it. Later when Steinbeck tried to recapture the *Cannery Row* mood in *Sweet Thursday*, he failed. To me, *Sweet Thursday* is a parody of an

---

[1]Among the untold stories, the hilarious episode of the plaster life-mask might have been more appropriate for *Sweet Thursday*, however. Steinbeck had volunteered to be the subject for Ritchie Lovejoy's first attempt, but Ritchie had forgotten or not read carefully enough about the procedure and failed to grease John's face beforehand, with painful results to John, including loss of his mustache. The episode resulted in a hilarious scene that forced a chance caller at the height of the clamor to retreat in confusion; the caller happened to be our old friend, the chiton expert mentioned in *Sea of Cortez* notes, the Reverend Elwood Hunter. Yet, after he recovered and Ritchie was willing to try again, so was John. The life-mask turned out successfully and still exists.

original already dangerously close to caricature and the only true thing in it is the reference to the name Webster F. Street, whether or not he actually concocted the drink named after him. From the viewpoint of Steinbeck criticism, however, *Sweet Thursday* is Steinbeck's parting statement on the old days, his valedictory to the theme that the rosebuds have been gathered and time indeed has flown. The sardines are gone, Ed and his friends are gone, there is nothing left but the shell of the Lab and memories: "...Steinbeck's transformation of Doc from a holistic marine biologist and genuine lover of nature into a lonely and love-lorn sentimentalist seems a most bitter comment on the tragic destiny of the heroic figure in a thoroughly unheroic age."[1]

In another sense *Cannery Row* is a prophesy of the shape of lives to come, an unintended prediction of an alternate way of living based on Ed's life style. In this context some parallels between *Cannery Row* and the *Tao teh Ching* have been discussed by Peter Lisca in a somewhat disingenuous way, although in implying that John Steinbeck may have had an interest in the Tao independently, he does state "significantly, Ed Ricketts...was much attracted to Taoism and refers to it several times in his letters and unpublished papers."[2] Lisca suggests that Steinbeck was most probably familiar with the Lin Yutang version, of the several that were available. However, the version that Lisca quotes is that of Witter Bynner, one of several, and the least expensive, available in paperback. It was first published in 1944. However, it is more probable that Steinbeck was familiar with another, less well-known version possessed by Ed Ricketts. This version, by Dwight Goddard, is much closer to the original than Witter Bynner's (Bynner clearly stated that he could not read Chinese). The first line, for example, is rendered by Bynner as "Existence is beyond the power of words to define", but the Wai-Tao and Goddard version has it that "The Tao that can be tao-ed cannot be the infinite (or ultimate) Tao." The version often quoted by Ed in conversation was "The Tao that can be tao-ed is not the true Tao." There are many possible translations or interpretations; Alan Watts lists eight, but not Bynner's, nor the Carus version (also currently available in paperback), "The Reason that can be reasoned is not the Eternal Reason."[3] In the foreword to Watts' book, Al Chung-liang Huang writes this simply as "The Tao that can be tao-ed is not the Tao." This appears to be a sort of Chinese pun: "The Way that can be waylaid is not the Way." In any event, Ed quoted the Goddard version in his essay "The Philosophy of Breaking Through"

[1]Richard Astro, "Steinbeck's Bittersweet Thursday." *Steinbeck Quarterly*, 4 (2), pp. 36-48, 1971.

[2]Peter Lisca, "Cannery Row and the Tao teh Ching." *San Jose Studies*, 1 (3), pp. 21-27, 1975.

[3] See: Alan Watts. *Tao: The Watercourse Way*. With the collaboration of Al Chung-liang Huang. Pantheon Books, New York, xxvi + 134 pp., 1975.

and gave John Steinbeck a copy of the essay in 1939 or 1940. The concepts and ideas in this essay were discussed among Ed and his friends for years before that.

After the destruction of his library in the fire of November 1936, Ed kept a record of library replacements, including the purchase price when he bought them. Everyone gave him books for Christmas that year, and among them was the Goddard version of Lao Tse, privately printed in Santa Barbara in 1935, a gift from Jim Fitzgerald.[1]

Among the books Ed purchased in 1937 were D.T. Suzuki's *Essays in Zen Buddism* (at that time the only book on Zen available in English), and two books by C.G. Jung, *Two Essays in Analytical Psychology* and *Modern Man in Search of a Soul*. In December of 1937 he bought a copy of S. Obata's *The Works of Li-Po*.

John Steinbeck often looked at Ed's books; and if John read Lao Tse, it was probably Ed's copy. My first sight of John Steinbeck was as he was standing beside a bookshelf in Ed's place with a book in his hand.

Ed did not just stock his shelves with books, he read them carefully, often making annotations in the margins and listing passages of particular interest by page number on the front leaves. He made these annotations in pencil, as a reader who respects his books should. Many of these marked passages were part of his conversation and of his philosophical essays; and it is from them, especially the essay on "Breaking Through" with its clear quotation of the Tao that can be tao-ed is not the ultimate Tao, that Peter Lisca became aware of the relationship of the *Tao teh Ching* to *Cannery Row*. There are many other themes still lying in wait for literary critics in need of articles. John Steinbeck did not quite understand what Ed was driving at in his ideas of "breaking through," nor did he realize that Ed was a mystic at heart. Ed found that his ideal of the complete, transcending experience was approached most closely in music, although he thought that Bach had not quite made it. Yet, he would have agreed with that passage in Steppenwolf about the music of Bach and Mozart: "In this music there was a feeling as of time frozen into space, and above it there quivered a never-ending and superhuman serenity and equal, divine laughter." All the threads that led to Hesse's view of life as the mirror of our inner self were known to Ed Ricketts: the mystic theologian Jakob Boehme (whose *Signature of All Things* was on Ed's shelf), the poetry of Novalis, the writings of Jung and the essence of Zen. And, by association, John Steinbeck was exposed to most of them. Certainly the genesis of *Cannery Row* is not in the *Tao teh Ching* as Steinbeck may have read it, but in the personality, conversation, and writings of Ed Ricketts. The humor of

[1]There were several editions of Goddard's book; Ed's copy was the "second edition" of one published in 1919, privately printed in Santa Barbara in 1935. The second, revised edition by Bhiksho Wai-Tao and Dwight Goddard, greatly expanded with critical commentaries and an essay on Taoist Philosophy and Religion by Kiang Kang-Hu was printed for Dwight Goddard in Thetford, Vermont in 1939.

Cannery Row, its essential lighthearted awareness of the ridiculous nature of man, was not Steinbeck's view of life, but Ed's.

Ed's favorite bit of advice, "When you are caught by the tide, don't fight it, drift with it and see where it takes you" is pure Zen, the essence of the Tao: "The course, the flow, the drift, or process of nature, and I call it the Water Course Way because both Lao-Tzu and Chuang-Tze use the flow of water as its principal metaphor." So wrote Alan Watts in his last book, *Tao: The Watercourse Way*, a book which would have found an honored place in Ed Ricketts' library. But the Tao is not for everyone, and for John Steinbeck the watercourse became the western arroyo, its water trickling out and lost in the dry channels of the long summer.

After John Steinbeck moved to New York City in 1943, he made many trips back to the Monterey coast. Ed kept up a steady flow of letters, and John must have replied to many of these in enough detail so that whatever was in them was of some concern to him after Ed's death. It was in the midst of their planning for a joint trip to the outer shores of the Queen Charlotte Islands that Ed had his fatal accident.

An accident, by definition, is an unplanned, unpremeditated event that should not have happened. Nobody was prepared for or anticipated Ed's encounter with the train. Certainly it was not planned by Ed, although suicide was suggested in some accounts of the event. Steinbeck said he found and destroyed evidence in Ed's papers that he planned suicide. But Ed knew too much about ending life painlessly as a matter of his business of preparing animals for dissection to choose such a painful and uncertain way out of life. And was he not philospher enough to prefer a more dignified end—like Socrates? Ricketts was a careful reader of *Crito* and *Phaedo*. Steinbeck's *The Moon is Down* derives from a session of "speculative metaphysics" with Ed, and the book's closing scene evokes the trial and death of Socrates.[1] Steinbeck's sense of loss after Ed's death may have clouded his memory of his friend's philosophical attitudes.

Another version of the accident is that Ed was drunk or had at least reached a stage of mellowness that made him careless. Unfortunately, the police record has disappeared so there is no objective account of the circumstances. It was (and is) a bad corner, that Drake Street crossing. After the accident a flashing light and bell were installed there. Now the train no longer runs and only the rusting tracks remain.

In his tribute to Ed, John Steinbeck concludes with a last picture of Ed all by himself, finishing a day's work, and leaving the lab: "I

[1]For the relation of *The Moon is Down* to these conversational sessions (or games) with Ricketts, see R. Astro's *John Steinbeck and Edward F. Ricketts*, p. 157. The only reference to suicide I found in Ed's notes was a long journal entry (Feb. 28, 1946), concerning the impending breakup with Toni in which he discussed the possible implications of suicide especially the effect on the act on others. It sounds like Ed's usual way of exploring all possibilities; subsequently he married Alice and planned for *The Outer Shores*.

Pacific Biological Laboratory, 1947. Courtesy Ed Ricketts Jr.

see him go out and get in his beat-up old car and slowly drive away in the evening." John, of course, must have been told that Ed was not alone the day he was hit. It was a Saturday afternoon; Rick Skahen, then a medical student from Berkeley, had arrived earlier in the afternoon and remembered a long concentrated discussion about the statistics of the sardine fishery. Other people began to show up, including Ritch and Tal Lovejoy. It was going to be another one of those friendly conversational evenings. Only a few days before, Ed had returned the proofs, at long last, for the second edition of *Between Pacific Tides* to the Stanford Press; and he had finished transcribing his journal of the Queen Charlottes for John. It was a relaxed, yet anticipatory time, and obviously there was not going to be enough food in the house. So, as he often did, Ed quietly slipped out and went to the store.

What seems significant is the manner in which John reconstructed that final afternoon. He surely heard all the many versions of the accident and knew that people had gathered, but he wanted to remember Ed for himself. That was his privilege and I do not quarrel with it except that it does not quite meet Ed's idea of presenting the "*toto* picture" of a person or an event. And, somehow, it subtly suggests a sense of purpose, this mental picture of Ed quietly arranging his dissecting tools and driving slowly away.

John Steinbeck tried to rush to Ed's bedside from New York, but the plane was delayed. It would have done no good; Ed was barely conscious after the first shock. John was badly upset; he wanted to tear the town apart because he had been delayed and because Ed had been allowed to die before he got there. He threatened to burn down the lab and a student from India, Raghu Prasad, appealed for help to hold Steinbeck down while he confiscated all combustibles. The person he appealed to was Sarah Wheatland, who talked to John and distracted him while Raghu sought out all the matches. Sarah also remembered that not long before, Ed in a morbid mood, still regretting the departure of Toni, had talked about death and the need for a funeral to symbolize the reality of death to the survivors.

Few of the people who knew Ed wanted to attend any sort of service, however. Somebody—was it John or Virginia Scardigli—or someone among the group waiting at the Lovejoys that afternoon—said, "Ed would not have gone to this." But many of them went to the chapel, looked in for a moment from the back, and went out to the beach, the wonderfully beautiful rocks and sea, and sat there for a long time, looking at the sea in the bright sunlight and not saying anything. Others were at Ed's lab, playing records.

John, in first pain of grief, resented some of these people he had not met before, and in that bad time asked, "Who are you? What right have you to be here at all?" Each one felt that he had the right to be there, to be part of the sad contemplation of becoming adjusted to a way of life without Ed and Cannery Row. They scattered, but many of them came back for some bit of something from the old lab for remembrance—a book, a record, a plate, or anything. John went immediately to the safe and took custody of Ed's papers, once he got it open.

As a partner in Ed's business, the Pacific Biological Laboratories, John had a personal interest in the property. He was also entrusted with Ed's papers. In a holograph will dated February 28, 1940, Ed bequeathed:

> To John Steinbeck. My personal notebooks, papers and Mss in progress. These contain a great deal of . . . conceptual material for a system of metaphysics. Also lots of good dope and probably some plain crap on human relations, etc. This could be sorted out by one competent and sympathetic mind, such as John's, into quite significant work, altho such work would take deep discipline in the old-fashioned or (living) sense of "prayerful watching and waiting." Also, if he wants, my scientific library, which, when it became significant enough, I had planned for Hopkins Marine Station eventually.

In a codicil dated October 22, 1945, he specified that all biological books, records, etc., were to go to Hopkins Marine Station, especially the Queen Charlottes material.

Steinbeck's first concern was for the correspondence between Ricketts and himself. Whatever his motives were, he evidently did not want this record of their friendship to survive. He wrote in *Log from the Sea of Cortez*:

> Once a week or once a month would come a fine long letter so much in the style of his speech that I could hear his voice over the next page full of small elite type. It was as though I hadn't been away at all. And some times now when the postman comes I look before I think for that small type on an envelope. (p. liv).

Steinbeck's replies and all Ed's carbon copies of his letters were neatly filed, as were the rest of Ed's papers. Now most of them are gone except copies from *Sea of Cortez* correspondence. Only two Steinbeck letters to Ricketts could be found for inclusion in *A Life in Letters*.[1] Steinbeck did not believe in records or biographies; he believed that his writing should stand for itself, and he lost no time in cleaning out Ed's files. George Robinson, then a manager of one of the canneries, helped John clean out Ricketts' lab:

> John was involved with one of his plays in New York—casting—rewriting—not sure just what but he was in a great hurry to get back and wanted to be sure that none of his letters to Ed were left in the lab. I went to Wing Chong's grocery and got as many empty cartons as we needed and John went through files and boxes of papers and passed on to me anything that should be tossed out and I filled the empty cartons. I remember that he called for a special garbage pickup because they normally only took one can a week. Many of the papers thrown out were John's letters to Ed. A number of galley proofs were also discarded. I recall that one proof was for "A Russian Journal." There were stacks of leaflets from

[1]Elaine Steinbeck and Robert Wallsten, *Steinbeck: A Life in Letters.* Viking Press, New York, xv + 906 pp. 1975.

the Dept. of Agriculture and Dept. of Labor and I assumed that they were studied in preparation for *Grapes of Wrath*. Much that was tossed out was in John's handwriting and I assume you know it as well as I do. You cannot mistake it. John took a number of Ed's black notebooks back to his little house in P.G. I did not see him go through them nor tear anything out. I, too, have heard the story. (George Robinson to J.W.H., June 9, 1978)

Yet he could not destroy everything. Ed wanted his papers and his library to go to Hopkins Marine Station, and John as executor of the estate took most of what he found to the Stanford laboratory for safekeeping and eventual permanent deposit. Ed was a zealous accumulator of papers. He never threw anything away, and he often made several carbon copies of his letters and other writings. Many things escaped the hand of the executor: scattered letters, copies of the "essays" and, most significantly, of the long, closely typed transcriptions of the "log" of the trip to the Gulf of California and the journals of his trips to Vancouver Island and the Queen Charlotte Islands.

For a while all this material—letters, business records and typescripts of books—was piled on tables at Hopkins. Nobody knew quite what to do with it. When I passed by I told them that something should be done about the typescript for *The Sea of Cortez*, tied up in brown paper bundles; and this, I think, was sent to the Smithsonian. Later an eager young graduate student from the University of Washington came by and declared himself a Steinbeck scholar. Partly on my recommendation, alas, he was allowed to cart off significant parts of the accumulation. For many years he apparently never looked at these files until I examined them at Gainesville and inadvertently betrayed their value. Ed would not have approved of the jealous sequestration of these files, much less of the failure to read them carefully.

Now, what is left, along with the original manuscript of *Cannery Row*, has gone to the Stanford University library, where despite the grossly anti-Steinbeck attitude of the Stanford University Press, it has been received with honor.

Despite all this, however, Ed's papers have fared better than many other accumulations that have fallen into unsympathetic hands. What has survived substantiates the careful analysis by Richard Astro, in his book, *Steinbeck and Ricketts, The Making of A Novelist*. Papers do somehow survive the holocausts of well intentioned and interested parties (save us from widows like Isabel Burton!), even before the days of tape recorders and copy machines. Ed would have loved the xerox copies. One can imagine him making dozens of copies of his best thoughts and sending them to his correspondents. After all, he believed in communication.

Within the month of Ed's death I was requested obviously too soon, to ask John if he could write something for *Pacific Discovery* about Ed. His reply, unfortunately mislaid, did not come to light until after the collection of Steinbeck letters was published:

Ritchie Lovejoy, 1948. Courtesy Ed Ricketts Jr.

May 24, 1948

Dear Joel:

I have your letter and I am answering it right away. There is nothing to say about Ed, not yet anyway. That might take a very long time. I know the impulse is to make some kind of celebration and requiem but I can't do that. It is going to take time for rearrangement. I shall try to put his collecting notes in order for the outer shores and in long range, and shall edit his intimate journals for some future use. As you may know, he wanted his library to go to Hopkins and, although that cannot be done legally until the court so orders, I did have all the books, separates, indexes and notes moved over there where there is less danger of fire. There are many things that do not occur in Hopkins library. They are planning to make a section of their library in his name.

As for the laboratory itself, I think it will in a time have to liquidated. As you may know, it was a corporation and its only asset outside of Ed was the real property on which it stood. It is ridiculous to think that any of us could run it or keep it going. Alice and young Ed will want to stay in it for a time anyway.

It is fortunate that the second edition of *Between Pacific Tides* was completed and is in the press now. Also Ed had ordered that his Plankton paper should be made up into some separates one of which I know he would want you to have. It is a brilliant paper. The whole of it of course is included in the new edition.

As for the personal loss, that is something we all have to work out for ourselves and this time without help. And of course our thinking will have to be rearranged and that is not a quick process. I do not think I could do the piece for the California Academy of Sciences. It is much too soon.

I am glad you wrote and I hope I will see you before too long. I do not know when I will next be in Monterey but should imagine that it would not be too far in the future. All kinds of things are likely to happen and they are very vague to me now.

Thank you again.

Sincerely,
John

On that same date Steinbeck responded to an enquiry from Floris P. Hartog of Stanford University Press about the possibility of preparing Ed's journal of the Queen Charlottes for publication:

I wish I could complete the work on *The Outer Shores* but I do not feel able to do that. However, I do have all of the collecting notes for the two previous years and it is my intention in time to edit them and to put them into some kind of form. I am promised by Dr. Blinks of Hopkins that they would then give the necessary help in preparing some little shadow of what the book might have been. I will not be able to do that right away but it is my intention to do it in the future and I think you might be interested in such a volume in spite of the fact that it will be incomplete. Further, although this is an even greater long-range proposition, I intend to edit Ed's journals for the last twelve or more years which contain his thinking in all directions. This seems a valuable thing and I do not know how long it will take. Thank you for your kind letters. (JS to FPH, May 24, 1948.)

On June 3 Steinbeck wrote again to Mr. Hartog, who expressed interest in John's comment about editing Ed's journals:

I have your letter of May 26 for which thank you. It will be a very long time I am afraid before I can get to work on Ed's journals. Indeed I should like to leave them for some future leisure when I can go over them in quiet and also when some time will have given me more perspective than I now have. I think these journals will prove to be almost the clinical development of the best mind I have ever known. It was a mind that knew itself and yet was apart from itself. Its observations of its own times and of the events that went on about it will be of value I am sure. But that is something I am not going into in a hurry.

You may be sure that when it is done, Stanford Press will surely have a look at it. Always, you must remember though, this mind took in all things and took them in order of their importance. Thus sexual development both in thought and in practice will have a part in direct relation to their actual importance to the human organism.

I look forward in the not too distant future, to going back to Pacific Grove and sitting quietly and going over these journals, commenting where necessary biographically or perhaps critically. Ed's mind had no reticences from itself. It was extremely healthy in that respect and yet it was the most complicated affair. In a great many ways I understood it and I am sure (as must be with all associations) in many ways I did not. But all that is for the future. Be sure only that when it is done, you will have a first refusal of the material. It might be a little too strong meat for the average University Press. We will see whether it is for Stanford.

A few days before Steinbeck wrote a revealing letter attempting to console the Lovejoys:

There's been a lot of thinking to do. By some intelligence greater than our own, we were able to stay drunk enough or withdrawn enough during the immediate thing. But that comes to an end and I have been sitting alone in my hotel room for some days now. Impact is not sharp now—all dulled out. It would be interesting if we all flew apart now like an alarm clock when you pry off the main spring with a screwdriver. Wouldn't it be ineresting if Ed *was* us and that now there wasn't any such thing—or that he created out of his own mind something that went away with him? I've wondered a lot about that. How much was Ed and how much was me and which was which? And another strange thing, I have a great feeling of life again. It's not the same but it is vital and violent. Almost as though I were growing new tissue. Do you feel that at all? There were times of cold terror about doing it alone but now the prop is out I have a feeling that I can. It won't be the same but it will be done. Do you feel that at all? You know how sometimes candle light, the room darkens and then lights up again and seems to be brighter? Its's kind of like that. I haven't yet got used to the unreality of this new reality but I am sure now it is going to be all sorrow and all happiness possible. They are ready when they are needed.

Then there's another thing. The rock has dropped into the water and the rings are going out and God knows where they will go or for how long or what patterns they will change obliquely. I have to tell this to someone and I guess you are the ones to tell. Nothing about me is the same. It is all changed. Tightening up now but in a different way. Almost a relief to be alone. As though some kind of conscience were removed and a fierceness I have not had for many years restored. I'm going to work now as I have never worked before, because, for the time anyway, that's all there is.

. . . .

I've been going back over everything. Surprising how many things you can remember—gestures, attitudes, words, expressions, and a million incidents. I have wanted to do them once more and then put them away for good and let go.

Don't tear yourselves to pieces so. That's not good nor useful to anyone.

Summer is coming. There's heat in the air today. And I haven't really anything to say, I know.

So long,

John

(JS to R&TL, May 27, 1948.)

All that came of Steinbeck's intentions to do something with Ed's papers was the 67 page introduction to *The Log from the Sea of Cortez*. He wrote that he had to remove many entries from Ed's notebooks because they were explicitly about women: "I removed the notes but did not destroy them. They have an interest, I think, above the personalities mentioned. In some future time, the women involved may lovingly remember the incidents." Steinbeck must have been referring to another set of notebooks, as those I have seen are almost entirely intact. While there are references that some people living would not care to see printed, I could find no entries that Steinbeck called "blackmail material on half the female population of Monterey." In the summer of 1949 when I saw Steinbeck in Pacific Grove, I got the impression that John had destroyed all this materiai. Perhaps this reference to a hoard of spicy notes was simply a literary one.

I imagine that there are as many Eds as there are friends of Ed's. And I wonder whether there can be any parallel thinking on his nature and the reason for his impact on the people who knew him. I wonder whether I can make any kind of generalization that would be satisfactory.[1]

R.D. Laing said it better: we know only our own experience of another person, or the experience of his experience. By that reckoning, Ed had several more levels of experience for others to experience than most people. What Steinbeck was trying to say was that Ed had a way of talking and being with people that made each person who knew Ed feel that his relation with Ed was a special one. His lively and thoughtful interest in the human condition and his willingness to let his mind run free gave you the impression you were with someone significant and important; many people came back to talk

[1]John Steinbeck, *The Log of the Sea of Cortez*, p. lxiv.

to Ed because talking with him was a good experience. And there was always the unexpected: you never knew what he might want to talk about today: why one century seemed to run to artists, another to musicians, or about Robinson Jeffers as a poet, or why pycnogonids seemed so scarce in the Sea of Cortez. His voice had a vibrant, interesting quality that was pleasant to listen to in conversation and he had a sure sense of pitch and musical memory, so acute that he could recognize fragments of Gregorian chants through a closed door. A small man, of my own size (5'6" or so), bearded when I first met him, he liked to move among his friends at a party in a quick and graceful way, now and then walking lightly on his toes, a mannerism John Steinbeck described as his "tippy-toe mouse dance."

Ed did not like to be alone very much, although he obviously spent long hours reading, thinking and writing, always keeping his mind active; and I remember now that when I found him alone at the time of our first meeting that I had a feeling this was not the usual state of affairs for him, or it may have been that he was expecting someone anyhow. If you found him alone, it was seldom for long; someone else would show up soon. Many have remembered how Ed would not argue with people but hear them out, agree with them for the sake of listening to their ideas or perhaps just experiencing their personality. His instinct was to communicate and participate, and because of this he made people feel that he was interested in them for their own sakes. "There are some people who have the quality of 'built-in awareness' of others as a special talent or special gift ... Their presence in the midst seems to activate in others a contagion of good feeling towards the world in general."[1]

Ed was interested in bright people especially. For a long time, he wondered about the incidence of genius in various times and countries and compounded a long chart on graph paper showing the incidence of great artistic and scientific creativity—how in some epochs artists—painters, flourished and in other periods, composers or writers—and how there seemed to be plateaus of creativity at various times.[2] Several of the group around him were subjects of the study of gifted children being conducted by L.M. Terman of Stanford University. Most of these Terman "geniuses" or "termites" took this in their stride, but Ed was perhaps unduly impressed because they were people who had been classified and summarized in terms of test scores. Toni was one of them. At one

[1]Howard Thurman, *Mysticism and the Experience of Love*. Pendle Hill Pamphlet 115. It was after I selected this quotation that I learned that Howard Thurman and Ed had actually met, introduced by Virginia Scardigli (an old college classmate of mine, to tangle the web further), but at that time Ed still had some residual xenophobia. Toni thinks he was beginning to overcome this.

[2]A study resembling this, on a smaller scale, is that of the incidence of biologists by D.M. Ross; "Some national features of the history of biology in Europe", Actes VIIIe, *Congress International Hist. Sciences*, 3-9 Sept., 1956, 99. 657-667, 6 figs.

time, evidently before Toni came upon the scene, Ed tried to classify his friends according to Jung's psychological types. He considered himself to be "Intuition-thinking" and John Steinbeck to be "Intution-feeling."

One of Ed's particular friends was Evelyn Ott, a practicing psychiatrist who had studied under Jung. Ed was often at her house discussing Jung and psychology in general. Ed, always fascinated by his dreams, would note them down for discussion with Evelyn. Dr. Ott was one of the more generous contributors to the book party held for Ed to provide him with a library after the fire; but there is no record of the extent, if any, to which Ed analyzed his friends with Evelyn.

Ed did not cultivate only bright alert and interesting people; he observed all sorts and conditions of men and found something of interest and significance in people with whom he had little in common:

> . . . I had lunch today with an old acquaintance who in the years became a banker. In thought we've diverged about as completely as any two people may; I don't suppose there's one single economic or intellectual or cultural pattern we have in common. Except that we like each other quite genuinely. He thinks different than I on most important questions. But the fundamentally important thing is that he's a good sweet man and I love him. I guess if you love your enemy, you're alright, you'll work something out. But if you hate and fear him, you can really get into a mess. Part of the complex which is everyone, comprises xenophobic elements that make us regard with extreme suspicion everything we're not familiar with. It's an emotional thing, and it spreads to other emotions, both in me and in the other guy. If I permit those elements to take charge of my action, I get to thinking that he's *bad* thru being *wrong* (i.e. different from me who am a known and *right* factor), and therefore not meriting my love. Then I'm sunk, and the situation is sunk, and we're in for bitter nationalistic warfare. Directed love instead of directed hate—and neither the love nor its direction need be unreal—could have prevented this. (From an undated letter to John Steinbeck, about 1946)

Ed may have had an unexpressed concern that his talent for friendship with his own sex might have been latently homosexual or that he was not adequately masculine. Consequently his need for relations with women might have had a trace of *machismo*—he needed to love women. At the same time—or did the egg come before the hen?—women were attracted to him. In discussing this aspect of Ed's character, John Steinbeck overstated or at least over-emphasized the physical aspect of Ed's relations with women and left us with the implication that it was basically physical, a case of "hot pants." This phrase, incidentally, fascinated Steinbeck; it was what he wanted to talk about most when remembering Ed on the occasion of our last meeting in 1949. He also characterized Ed as "concupiscent as a rabbit." In a notebook entry for February 29, 1946, Ed wrote of himself: " . . . I am interested in work & sex; I get pepped up quickly, & quickly over it." Nevertheless, sexual intercourse was a lovely and holy thing to Ed, an expression of body and spirit, that "divinely superfluous beauty" for which almost any price was not too great. But it was not the simple matter of the afternoon of a faun in some carefree glade: The faun might die or fall asleep, but Ed would remember for years with a sharp nostalgia for the irretrievable past, and try again. Like Goethe, whom he much admired, Ed was a dilettanteish existentialist who loved many women; but, unlike Goethe, he did not leave them so easily, and he never put an old love completely out of mind. This sometimes distressed his later lovers, for, like Benjamin Franklin, he tried to remain on friendly terms with his past.

Not in the same ways and not equally Ed did love all his girls. He built up the emotional relationships and of course projected his own idealization of the other person into the relationship. He was quite aware of this, remembering how things had once been, scrawling down his thoughts in soft pencil on cheap paper, while on duty at the Presidio one evening:

> I closed my eyes for a minute and Jean went by, dressed in that black and white tweed coat, and with overalls or jeans. I got that strong flash of nostalgia. Curious that that should have gone wrong somewhere. The mutual biochemistry was so fine! That breakup was the only really bad thing that ever happened to me. A pity she couldn't have been what I found in her. Or, maybe, a pity conditions weren't otherwise. Because that had for me a really essential rightness. Maybe she herself didn't conform to my picture of her, but the *picture* had essential rightness. I wonder what's the answer in a case like that. I still *know* that my forsaking that thing is somehow, somewhere, forsaking some very essential thing in me. But what does a person do? I face the fact that my love was a projection, and a projection may be on an unsuitable medium . . . and I face the fact that it's over. And do nothing to keep her or get her back, altho sometimes the temptation is very strong (and very right in myself at least) to get in touch with her again. And make a life elsewhere. Which is a good life. But there's some essentialness, something that's essentially mine, that I can't seem to crystallize. And that Jean did crystallize. Or rather, her fitting into my picture of her crystallized it. Well, maybe somehow I'll understand how my intuitions, which are usually good, led me into that which seemed essential, but which couldn't be fulfilled.

Ed's view of life and love is very similar to that of Ortega y Gasset; he would have enjoyed reading the essay, "On Love," and would have found, perhaps, some explanation for his own ability to love so many, sometimes several at the same time:

> Almost all men and women live submerged in the sphere of their own interests (some, without doubt, beautiful and respectable) and are incapable of feeling the migratory urge toward what is outside themselves. Whether treated well or badly by the landscape that surrounds them, they live definitively satisfied with the line of their horizon and do not miss the vague possibilities which they might realize only at a cost. This limited range is incompatible with deep-seated curiosity, which is, finally,

"Buddy and I." Ed and early friend, Easter, 1919.

an untiring instinct for migration, a wild urge to depart from oneself to the other.[1]

Granted this curiosity and instinct towards others which Ortega considers rare among people—especially the Spanish—frequent love is possible. It requires a vitality of mind which Ed certainly had: "The ability to interest oneself in a thing for what it is in itself and not in view of the profit which it will render us is the magnificent gift of generosity which flourishes only at the peaks of the greatest altitudes of generosity." (p. 184) Ed understood this very well:

> ...humans suffer mostly from being only human; they suffer from death and from separation; if they were infinite, their love could be everywhere, wherever it wanted to, wherever it had to go, and it could be endless and deathless. I should be two people, many people, all of us should; there's the Alice thing, the Toni thing, even still the Jean thing; they're all true. But human limitations and finiteness necessarily cut the proliferations of deeply good things as it does all things. We should be God Whom we're a part of. That's the enigma of all enigmas: how we can be truly part of God and therefore partakers of the whole, which is in fact indivisible, and yet have the limitations of being not-God. Perhaps only a logical enigma. Times when we truly participate, that doesn't apply. But the limitation then is still there: time. The square root of one is impossible; to go from a minus to plus infinity isn't possible, yet we do it in fact all the time, and because we're familiar with it, we forget its mystery. Just as you never think of the fabulousness of the infinite images—the reflections—in a rain-washed pavement, the number and the position of the images being entirely a function of the number and positions of the observers. (EFR to TJ, December 22, 1947.)

From Steinbeck's account of Ed's sex life, it is obvious he did not understand; but then John never wrote about love or women in a way that indicated understanding. It has often been pointed out that the women in his books were either whores or neurotics: a reaction, perhaps, to the formidable matriarchal dominance of his family. Ed's frankly open sex life was not the best example for increasing John's understanding, if we are to judge from the manner in which he translated his observations into writing. According to Walter Fuller Taylor in his essay, "*The Grapes of Wrath* Reconsidered," the interior meanings of the book include "an elaborately illustrated and reiterated philosophy of casual sexual indulgence" that is based on the idea of sex as "a simply natural appetite that involves no responsibilities for possible children or for the feelings of one's sexual partner."[2] This attitude certainly does not characterize Ed, who was more than an intellectual rabbit. Steinbeck reacted to this aspect of Ed's life out of a very conservative, conventional background of small-town American morality. It was Steinbeck's interpretation

[1]Jose Ortega y Gasset, *On Love*. Meridian Books, World, 1957, p. 185.

[2]*Modern Fiction Studies* lv (Summer, 1958), pp. 177-178, reprinted in *A Casebook on the Grapes of Wrath*, ed. by Agnes McNeill Donohue, Thomas Y. Crowell, 1968, pp. 185-194.

that the basis for Ed's approach to sex was exclusively physical.[1] Ed apparently did not think of its primarily this way and, in fact, considered that his physical need was quickly and easily satisfied. Perhaps the difference between Ricketts and Steinbeck was that described by Ortega y Gasset:

> . . .there are two irreducible kinds of men: those who experience happiness as a feeling of being outside themselves, and those who, on the contrary, feel fulfilled only when self-possessed. From alcohol to mystical trances, the available means for getting outside of oneself are plentiful; similarly, there are many ways—from a shower to philosophy—to produce a state of self-possession. These two classes of men go different ways in every area of life. (*On Love*, p. 69.)

But it is, of course, not quite that simple and clear-cut; Ed was seeking fulfillment and he reached out towards women who were receptive to his need to expand, to find the "deep thing." They were women either willing to subordinate their own selves—given they had any well-developed personality, or they were much younger and impressed by his knowledge and wisdom or superior years. Ed may well have believed with Goethe that it is through the finer essence of women that man achieves deeper understanding and acceptance of life. (Das Ewig-Weibliche zieht uns hinan.) Yet at the same time it was not easy for him to accept women on their own terms as equally intelligent or as persons in their own rights.

Many have envied Ed, or Doc of Cannery Row, as a person who lived as he wanted to in spite of the mundane requirements of society, an impression of his way of life that *Cannery Row* has conveyed far beyond the community in which Ed had found his place. This place was between the interfaces of old style American suburbia and the vanished seacoast of Bohemia in one direction, and between the formal learning of the hermitic scholars of Hopkins Marine Station and the unlettered (be they paisanos or college graduates of zoology) in the other direction. Ed was not a rebel against society. He simply ignored much of it; and when necessary, as during his time with the army, conformed in his own way. He did not ask much more than a place to live (he would have liked a better place, free from the constant worry about another fire, however), food and drink, books, records and friends, and in his last years, employment that was not so demanding that he could not take leave for his trips to distant seashores. His way of life then, was not defiance of convention but compromise, on his own terms for the most part, with society and its institutions. Inevitably the only mark in his copy of Plato is a pencil

---

[1] "John's memoir of Ed. . .is in many respects an embarassing essay on sexual envy. Ed got the women. But Steinbeck seems wholly unable to realize that Ed got the women as a substitute—largely unsatisfactory—for getting what he wanted but could not get." William Appleman Williams, "Steinbeck and the Spirit of the Thirties," in *Steinbeck and the Sea*, Oregon State University Sea Grant College Publ. ORESU-W-74-004, April 1975.

line alongside: "But why, my dear Crito, should we care about the opinion of the many? Good men, and they are the only persons worth considering, will think of these things truly as they occurred."

But love of women, philosophy, and simple delight in the animals of the seashore was not all. Ed was by instinct and intellectual commitment a biologist; he found in zoology "a symbol of the deep thing" and, in taking stock of himself, some time in 1942, he considered his alternatives (today's word would be options) for a "real deep true life" to be through a relationship with some understanding woman (and he considered two possibilities), or "externally through zoology and construction of deep true manuals." Later, in 1946, he was not certain he was up to the task:

> In the remote field of marine biology, I have been distressed at being able to contribute so very little to a world structure that obviously needs so much...Mostly, I have to do biology; perhaps out of that, even, light can be got on the public events that are now so overwhelmingly important as to threaten our world of science, and art, and book publishing and making airplanes.

Yet loneliness and unfulfilled expectation were never very far away in his own mind. Often he thought of himself as neurotic; obviously he either did not need much sleep or could not sleep so he spent hours writing in his journals, or transcribing notes, writing letters and drawing up plans for things he intended to do or write about. He hoped to have himself psychonalyzed to learn more about what kind of a person he really was. He wanted to write, to make some sort of mark in the world as a philosopher, but he did not know how to turn words so that anyone but his friends could read his essays. He eagerly accepted criticism and tried to improve his writing. Always he believed his best hope was to write "deep, true" manuals of zoology. Through them people would learn about the "good, kind sane little animals," and share his insights of the life of the shores.

In many of these attitudes and ways of looking at himself Ed was like the unfortunate "W.N.P. Barbellion," (Bruce Frederick Cummings, 1889-1919) who despite chronic illness, secured a post as zoologist in the British Museum (Natural History) and made some modest contributions to science.[1] His best known work is *The Journal of a Disappointed Man* which records the details of his slow decline from multiple sclerosis. In his sympathetic introduction H.G. Wells reminds us that most of us are egotists, "and our desire is to think and if possible talk and write about this marvellous experiment of ourselves, with all the world—or as much as we can conveniently assemble—for audience."

For many of his years Barbellion lived in poor health and knew that

[1]W.N.P. Barbellion, *The Journal of a Disappointed Man*, with an introduction by H.G. Wells. George H. Doran Co., New York, viii + 312 pp., 1919.

W.N.P. Barbellion, *A Last Diary*, with a preface by Arthur J. Cummings. Chatto & Windus, London, xlviii + 148 pp. 1921.

his last years were numbered. Ed was not so unfortunate, he was not "tragically caught by the creeping approach of death" as H.G. Wells put it, but his notes and his journal are similar to those of Barbellion in this respect:

> He is attracted by natural science, by the employments of the naturalist and by the thought of being himself some day a naturalist. From the very beginning we find...the three qualities...'Observe me he says to himself, I am observing nature...But he also says, I am observing nature!' And at moments comes the clear light. He forgets himself in the twilight cave with the bats or watching the starlings in the evening sky, he becomes just you and I and the mind of mankind gathering knowledge.[1]

He would undoubtedly have been a kindred soul to Ed Ricketts; he did have a startling resemblance of manner, as indicated by his brother's description:

> He had a musical voice, which he used without effort, and when he spoke, especially when he chose to let himself go on any subject that had aroused his interest, the energetic play of his features, the vital intensity which he threw into every expression, had an irresistable effect of compulsion upon his friends. His hands were strong and sensitive, with a remarkable fineness of touch very useful to him in the laboratory, and it was always a pleasure to watch them at work upon a delicate dissection.[2]

Barbellion had his book of essays accepted, although he died before they were published. Ed got his best essay rewritten and published by his friend and expected the critics to be confused by the authorship, as they were. At last he and John were equal collaborators, on a project dear to Ed's heart. While John did write *Sea of Cortez* "for Ed" he did not believe in collaboration. It is debatable whether he would have gone through with the idea of still another book with Ed, or with the dream on the back burner that Ed Ricketts and John Steinbeck might someday go to the tropical Pacific and collaborate on a book about coral reefs. After all, Ed had been a character, or part of a character in several of John's books, so it was natural that Ed should dream of moving closer in to the creative process. Steinbeck took his craft very seriously and probably was growing a bit weary of Ed's hopes for collaboration. Perhaps he felt he had done enough with and for Ed and it was time to go to other things. He did, for a time, play with the idea of making something of Ed's notes and journals; but Steinbeck was not the sort to work with papers and without Ed the stimulus was not there. So Steinbeck went on to play with research on the stories of King Arthur, and to write such books as *Travels with Charley* and *The Winter of our Discontent*. His last attempt at a big book, to be the story of his people in the valley and the California of his memory, lost direction and

[1]H.G. Wells, intro. *The Journal of a Disappointed Man* p. vi.

[2]Arthur J. Cummings, in *A Last Diary* p. xxiii-xiv.

became *East of Eden.*

Both Ed and John had lost direction: Ed in his own sight and John in the opinion of the critics. Nevertheless, Steinbeck had made Ed unforgettable as his most famous character, Doc of Cannery Row; and Ed's philosophical ideas have become widely popular among readers who never read formal philosophy because Steinbeck took them over and blended them with his considerable literary skill into *Sea of Cortez.* It was the kind of book Ed wanted to write himself. The ultimate price Ed paid for his friendship was to become the proto-type—or perhaps the archetype—of the serious biologist of the counter culture, the memorable guru of the motley social milieu of Cannery Row, another Steinbeck symbol.

John Steinbeck had little patience with the dust dry aspects of scholarship. It mattered little to him if a date was wrong or a circumstance not quite right if the alteration improved the story or made for better sentence rhythm. Nevertheless, John did play very seriously at being an Arthurian scholar. The snide impeachment of his authority by George Frazier (who is he?) in "John Steinbeck! John Steinbeck! How still we see thee lie—and lie—and lie" (Esquire, November 1969) because Steinbeck had never heard of George Maynadier who "good God, was perhaps the outstanding authority on Arthurian legend" is both unkind and unjustified. Maynadier's book on the use of the Arthurian theme by English poets was published in 1907 and he did nothing else in this field. His book is used as a source of quotations. Maynadier was a judge of college essay contests, one of which was won by Frazier. Steinbeck was, however, not scholarly in his approach to matters, often got dates wrong, and sometimes garbled things. It is uncertain, for example, whether his curious misinterpretation of the creation of Lleu Llaw Gyffes' wife from flowers was because Ed had not told it straight or Steinbeck garbled the idea from memory, in reference to Ed's idealization of women in the essay "About Ed Ricketts." (The lady had been conjured out of flowers by Math's sorcerer men folks because he had been cursed not to have a wife born of women—the lady from the flowers turned out to be such a schemer the sorcerers turned her into an owl—hence the Welsh word for owl is *blodeuedd*—flower-face.) Quite possibly Steinbeck had not read the *Mabinogion* for himself.[1] As for literary artifice, how about that episode in *Travels with Charley* at Johnny Garcia's bar in Monterey? Did it really happen?

Although there is some suggestion that Steinbeck at one time considered an original extension of the "Matter of Britain" in his own way (in a sense he had already done this in *Tortilla Flat*). His was to be vastly different from the interpretation by T.H. White and C.S. Lewis in *That Hideous Stength.* But instead Steinbeck confined himself to a retelling of the stories. His incomplete manuscript has fi-

---

[1]For a clear English version see Patrick K. Ford, *The Mabinogi and other Medieval Welsh Tales*, University of California Press, 1977.

nally been published, but even this appears to be only a part of it with hundreds of pages discarded, perhaps among them the parts Eugene Vinaver though so highly of.[1] Somehow Steinbeck's heart did not seem to be in *The Acts of King Arthur and his Noble Knights*. Merlin enters the stage like a tired grocery clerk rather than the quintessence of the Celtic undertone of all England even beyond the border marches, sensed so strongly by the English for whom the "Matter of Britain" has become their great folk myth.[2] Although much of our land, especially the west, is barren of myth for those who have come here to live these last few centuries, perhaps this "Matter" cannot be transplanted to landscapes were no one speaks of moors or downs or ruins of great castles by the sea.

From his first published writing Steinbeck disturbed the critics. He was a writer with a lovely, polished style, writing often about unpleasant things in a detached, pleasant way: "...the enchantment of his style, of that liquid melody which flows on and on until even such experience as a man's dying of thirst in the morning sunlight among the remote and rocky hills can seem not altogether ugly, because it was become a legendary thing that happened once upon a time."[3] This appraisal by T.K. Whipple was written in a review of *The Long Valley*, published soon after but written before *In Dubious Battle*, which Whipple considered "by all odds Steinbeck's best book because it is far and away the best written. Perhaps for once his material ran away with him; at any rate his style disappears into the material and they become indistinguishable." At the time this was written, Steinbeck was working on *The Grapes of Wrath*, but it remains the opinion of many critics that *In Dubious Battle* is his best work. Ironically, it is possible that he may have got the idea for it from his brief encounter with Daniel Mainwaring.[4]

[1]See Roy S. Simmons, "The Unrealized Dream: Steinbeck's Modern version of Malory" in *Steinbeck Society Monograph Series* no. 5, 1975, pp. 30-43

[2]See Geoffrey Ashe, *Camelot and the Vision of Albion*, Heinemann Ltd., 1971.

[3]T.K. Whipple, "Steinbeck, Through a Glass Brightly", in *Study out the Land*, University of California Press, 1943.

[4]Daniel Mainwaring, *One Against the Earth* (Ray Long and Richard R. Smith, New York, 1933, 305 pp.), and "Fruit Tramp" (a short story), Harper's July 1934. For an account of the coincidences and comparisons, see Richard Astro, "Steinbeck and Mainwaring: Two Californians for the Earth," *Steinbeck Quarterly*, 3 (1): 3-11, 1970.

One Against the Earth was written by Mainwaring as a student at Fresno State College; Mainwaring and Steinbeck made a joint appearance at a class in writing conducted by W.W. Lyman at Los Angeles City College in 1933 just after the appearance of Mainwaring's book and Steinbeck's *Cup of Gold*.

Dan's mother had no reservation in her opinion that Steinbeck was a literary thief. Dan himself was more restrained about the matter. He had to support himself and his family and turned to writing detective stories and movie scripts under his middle names, Geoffrey Holmes. Constance Mainwaring was my mother's sister-in-law and dearest friend; and it was on the occasion of my mother's visits to her in Pacific Grove that I visited Ed's place on Cannery Row. Both mothers were born story tellers. Too bad we did not have tape recorders then.

Fishing boats moored at Monterey Harbor.

Be that as it may, Joseph Henry Jackson, the literary lion whose roar sold books among the San Francisco literati, regarded John Steinbeck as our homegrown white hope to pick up the torch dropped by Frank Norris—and to carry on in the tradition of *The Octopus*. His review of *The Grapes of Wrath* was ecstatic. Edmund Wilson however, would never allow Steinbeck in the pantheon of great American writers. Steinbeck is, in fact, omitted from many comprehensive treatments of American writers.

Ed always thought that Steinbeck would win the Nobel prize, eventually; and he was right, although the award near the end of Steinbeck's writing career was somewhat of an anti-climax, or as Steinbeck himself suggested, an epitaph. Now Steinbeck's posthumous works, the collection of letters and the rewriting of the stories of the Round Table, have been promptly issued in paperback. They are universally available—along with everything else he wrote—in paperback emporiums and even in the dreary caves of Greyhound Bus stations. Despite the reservations of many critics, John Steinbeck continues to be an admired and popular author.

Steinbeck himself once referred to *The Grapes of Wrath* as a tract, in an encounter with William Saroyan. William Everson, in commenting on this remark, points out that Steinbeck's tendency to simplify his themes and to produce stereotypes rather than characters, along with his "oft reiterated 'non-teleological' premise" are reflections of Steinbeck's divided self.[1] Perhaps it is appropriate then that Steinbeck should still be so popular. His native land was an emotionally divided, schizophrenic state of mind and his writings still speak to all manners and conditions of men. After all, Steinbeck remains in print; and the critics stew in their own juice. Who reads them anyway but other critics, mostly professors of English looking for material for lectures.

When we talk of a truly western writer, a Californian, native to the hot summer valleys and familiar with the people and representing them (sometimes to their violent objections), we must recognize that John Steinbeck wrote from a background inadequately considered by his critics. His life grew out of more than serene valleys of "the pastures of heaven" and beyond the boyhood experience of the "red pony." These are, of course, the stories that Californians who read Steinbeck like best. And whether Steinbeck would have been a better writer without "non-teleological thinking" and other overtones of his friendship with Ed Ricketts, no one can say. Ed represented the influence of eastern culture (in the sense of somewhere remotely east of the Sierras) that colors all western writing. In ways that John Steinbeck did not always realize, his friendship with the philosophical Chicagoan Ed Ricketts greatly influenced the course of his work as a writer. Some of us knew Ed as a biologist, others as a neighbor and counselor, and others still as "the man who knew Steinbeck."

[1]William Everson, *Archetype West: The Pacific Coast as a Literary Region*. Oyez, Berkeley, 1976. Chapter 12.

The lab, the place where so many of these things happened, is still there; but it is an empty shell. The Row itself is being metamorphosed into all sorts of fashionable tourist traps—restaurants, souvenir shops and little theatre efforts. Nothing like Flora's establishment remains; such places are no longer in style anyhow. A bookstore across the street from the lab has been in trouble for not conforming with the spirit of these latter times. Years ago, about 1957, when it was first suggested that Cannery Row should be developed into a "first class resort or residential neighborhood," John Steinbeck said it should be torn down, and replaced by something better,

> . . .it should not be a celebration of a bunch of mud houses, not a vague memory of something that happened in the past. . . I've always thought it could be the most beautiful place in the world. The coast line would be perfectly lovely once you got the fish scales out of it and put up some pleasant looking places. Man's greed killed off the fish. Now they've got to 'kill off' some tourists to make up for it.[1]

But it is in keeping with the Cannery Row of Doc and the boys that it should no longer be a real place, something not much different from the enormous shopping center over the hill, and that John Steinbeck should stand over it in bronze, blindly staring at the passing scene. It is symbolic of the town's self-conscious tourist trapping syndrome that "Doc's Birthday" is a happening planned for October 31. What does it matter if Ed was born on May 14? At least this occasion was celebrated on May 14, 1978 by the christening of the Research Vessel *Ed Ricketts* at Monterey by the Moss Landing Marine Laboratories.

With each successive Sunday supplement article or piece in the giveaway airline magazines Cannery Row retreats further from the poem, the stink and the reality of the days when the sardines were caught and canned and people lived there. As Tom Weber has put it in his poem-like book about the "ecology" of Cannery Row,

> Cannery Row, drunk with the 'glory' of the past, is limping through the present with Steinbeck as a cane—and uncertain of the future.[2]

Recently the most blatant part of the tourist trap element of Cannery Row was destroyed by fire (which did not reach Ed's old place). Concerning policies of the California Coastal Commission that would obviously control if not prevent a resurgence of the developers syndrome on Cannery Row, one indignant critic remarked at a public hearing in Monterey that if there had been a coastal commission in the old days there would have never been a Cannery Row at all, and, of course, no John Steinbeck.

[1]From an undated newspaper clipping found in a bookstore copy of a first edition of *Cannery Row*.

[2]Weber, Tom. *All the Heroes are Dead*: The ecology of John Steinbeck's Cannery Row. Ramparts Press, San Francisco, 1974. xv + 163 pp.

Much of the countryside not far away is still there to be seen and sensed beyond the ever creeping slurbs of undisciplined towns, and the shore of Jeffers' austere thoughts is still there; both are suitably memorialized in handsome coffee table books.[1] But the best way to find out what it was like in those days is to get up before dawn to meet the summer tide in the fog along the shore of white sand and granite, when the waves are quiet among the rocks and the harbor bell sounds now and then in the surge, and the smell of seaweed, sponges and other creatures enriches the air. Then, as you sit on the rocks while the fog thins out and the sun regains its strength, is the time to remember the enquiring minds that have enriched these shores, and with whom, in retrospect, we may also go down to experience the sea.

[1]Crouch, Steve. *Steinbeck Country*. Photographs and words by Steve Crouch. American West Publ. Co., Palo Alto, 1973. 191 pp.

Not Man Apart. Lines from Robinson Jeffers. Photographs of the Big Sur Coast. Sierra Club, San Francisco, 1965, 159 pp.

48

W.C. Allee. Photo courtesy Ralph G. Johnson.

On a biology field trip. Allee is the figure on the left. "[Ricketts] was a member of a small group of "Ishmaelites" who tended sometimes to be disturbing, but were always stimulating. I am pleased, particularly, that Mr. Ricketts lived up to the promise he showed in those years of having real ability." [W.C. Allee to J.W.H., Sept. 18, 1950.] Photo courtesy Ralph G. Johnson.

II

RESEARCH AND ESSAYS

IIA. Ricketts as a Biologist

Ed Ricketts was always writing once he came to the Pacific Coast. By nature a thoughtful observer, his collecting trips on the seashore stimulated him. First he was impressed by the differences in abundance of intertidal life on exposed and sheltered shores and attempted an essay on wave shock as a factor in littoral ecology. This he completed sometime around 1932 after a trip up the Inland Passage as far north as Sitka. This journey is described in the first volume of Ricketts' papers where they are more appropriate to the context, especially since Ed had hoped to use the ideas on wave shock for his proposed book about the outer shores of British Columbia.

Ricketts was also interested in the relations between tidal levels and the occurrance of plants and animals between the tidal levels on the rocky shore. He began to examine this relationship in the 1930's and came to most of his conclusions about these observations without much outside help. In the days before computers, data—especially tidal data—was hard to come by. Ed laboriously posted numbers from the raw data of the actual time of tides at San Francisco. From his analysis of these numbers, he recognized the changes in gradient of tidal elevations that he associated with the heights of observed occurrence of plants and animals at Pacific Grove and, by extension, on other parts of the Pacific coast.

He also began to add those dimensions of thought and speculation that shed light on great problems, if not directly, at least by stimulating a reader's mind. His unpublished paper on the tides was completed about 1934. It consists of 45 double-spaced pages in elite type. Evidently several copies of this paper circulated around Pacific Grove; but when the original and all the illustrations and tabulations were lost in the fire of 1936, Ricketts did not have the energy to reconstruct them. By that time, however, the manuscript had been made available to several students at Hopkins Marine Station, including Willis G. Hewatt, who acknowledged its usefulness in his work on the intertidal zonation of the rocks at Hopkins Marine Station. At the end of Ricketts' copy, after the closing sentence, "One hopes that a comprehensive study . . . can be carried through and published soon by some competent observer," there is a note in Ricketts' handwriting: "It was, by Hewatt, & confirmed the ideas."[1]

Another student at Hopkins who apparently studied Ed's paper (but without clear acknowledgement) was B.J.Roberts. He conducted pioneer experiments in removal and transfer of intertidal animals, especially sea anemones. His Master's thesis, submitted in 1941, was titled "A survey of the methods employed by intertidal organisms in resisting desiccation."

The critical level idea; namely, that at certain stages of the tide there are significant differences in the duration of exposure or submergence to organisms that control their vertical distribution, became common currency around Hopkins Marine Station in the 1930's. Visitors from distant lands, as well as students, discussed it with Ed and the staff and read Ricketts' paper. Rolf Bolin wrote a brief paper for the 13th International Zoological Congress in 1948 in which he discussed critical levels and remarked that some intertidal organisms "have come not only to tolerate, but to require periods of exposure." His concept of intertidal distribution as a one-dimensional or peripheral distribution which "increases the chance for the survival of mutations and gives the organisms with a linear distribution a high evolutionary potential" was evidently original with him.[2]

The critical level concept which was also suggested by J.S. Colman in England was examined by Max Doty who later made an experimental test of the hypothesis.[3] However, for those situations where there seem to be distributions governed by critical levels, there are as many that are obviously not so related, and the critical level concept has become one of several explanations for intertidal zones. The world-wide studies of the Stephensons added little to the theory of zonation (if indeed the matter has a "theory"); and if we view the seashore—especially the rocky shore—as a region of the three interacting factors of air, water and salt content, a tripartite arrangement seems inevitable and the influence of both tide and

[1]Hewatt, W.G. 1937. Ecological studies on selected marine intertidal communities of Monterey Bay, California. *Amer. Midl. Nat.*, 18: 161-206. This paper by Hewatt is the published version of his doctoral thesis; the work was done at Cabrillo Point from late 1931 to June 1934. At the time, George MacGinitie was Assistant Director of Hopkins Marine Station (Hewatt remembers that Dr. Fisher "rarely visited the labs, lived in a new home up Carmel Valley") and became Hewatt's professor and taskmaster. But Hewatt soon met Ed and "accompanied him on many collecting trips and he taught me about as much as did MacGinitie." (WGH to JWH, 21 May 1970.)

[2]Bolin, R.L. 1949. The linear distribution of intertidal organisms and its effect on their evolutionary potential. *XIII Congres International de Zoology*, 1948. Paris, 1949. p. 459-460.

[3]Colman, John. 1933. The nature of the intertidal zonation of plants and animals. *Jour. Mar. Biol. Ass. U.K.*, n.s., 18: 435-476.

Doty, Maxwell S. 1946. Critical tide factors that are correlated with the vertical distribution of marine algae and other organisms along the Pacific coast. *Ecology*, 27 (4): 315-328.

Doty, Maxwell S. and Justine G. Archer. 1950. An experimental test of the tide factor hypothesis. *Amer. Jour. Bot.*, 41 (6): 458-464.

Ed Ricketts collecting in the intertidal. Courtesy Ed Ricketts Jr.

wave action are subordinate to the gradient pheonomena between air, water, and salinity.[1] Biological interactions add yet another complication to the system.[2] A careful reading of the "Conclusions and derived discussions" of Ricketts' 1934 essay indicates that Ed realized these aspects of intertidal distribution, although he was diverted by the not entirely unrelated issue of the possible origin of sexual cycles from lunar influences and ancient tidal rhythms. His comment about "the rupture of turgid sacs of sexual products" brings to mind some speculations by his professor, W.C. Allee, about the origin of sex:

> ...it seems quite possible that sex arose originally from the beneficial stimulation received as a result of the aggregation of two, or more, simple asexual organisms. Sex, once originated, became one of the integrating factors in further social development. In sex-conditioned society, the offspring of one pair or of one parent may have remained in association with their parents for the immediate mutual benefit of all concerned, or there may have intervened a sexually promiscuous horde life from which the consociation of off-spring with their individual parents arose as a further protective evolution.[3]

Ed's speculations sound strikingly modern, especially his use of the word "imprint" in reference to the well-timed response of some marine organisms to tidal and lunar cycles. He used this word before behavior had become a recognized branch of biology, and apparently before the term "imprinting" had come into wide use. How this imprint may be transferred to the next generation is still as much of a puzzle as it was forty years ago.

Students of intertidal ecology will note that many of Ricketts' theories, as he summarized them in his "Conclusions and derived discussions" still confound researchers. Not many theorists, however, have been as explicit in emphasizing that "with littoral associations we are dealing with marine animals pushing upward toward land, rather than with land animals colonizing downward."

Since those halcyon days at Pacific Grove, studies on intertidal zonation and the interactions of animals on the seashore have blossomed into a formidable "literature" (the word used for scientific papers, without respect to readibility).[4] I attempted to review the main trends of these studies in an essay titled "The Living Edge," published in a journal not usually consulted by marine biologists or seashore aficionados, and can do no better here than repeat the con-

---

[1] den Hartog, C. 1968. The littoral environment of rocky shores as a border between the sea and the land and between the sea and the fresh water. *Blumea*, 16 (2): 374-393.

[2] Connell, Joseph H. 1972. Community interactions on marine rocky intertidal shores. *Ann. Rev. Ecol. & Syst.*, 3: 169-192.

[3] Allee, W.C. *Animal Aggregations*. Univ. of Chicago Press, 1931, p. 350.

[4] A good summary, as well as field exercise guide for the present way of looking at the seashore, is the text by Thomas Carefoot: *Pacific Seashores. A Guide to Intertidal Ecology*. Seattle, University of Washington Press, 208 pp., illus., 1978.

Because of the large format, this book is actually much longer and comprehensive than its pagination suggests.

cluding paragraphs of that review:

> More than a hundred years ago, Edward Forbes remarked that there is "a deeper interest in the march of a periwinkle and the progress of a limpet" than in the episodes of man's secular history. In a sense, he anticipated our own environmental concern, and its implicit admonition that "thou shalt protect endangered species." It is natural then that we should be concerned with periwinkles, limpets, and barnacles, and with attempting to understand the processes under which they prosper or perish. It would seem that no one approach to the problems of the shore, descriptive, analytical, or philosophical has more validity than the other. The motivation for studying the seashore is not to produce scintillating ideas win prizes or gain admission to academies, but to gain fresh understanding, further insight into the orderly jumble of processes and interactions on the world's most active and significant interface, the edge of the largest of living spaces on our globe. And so we hope, along with Carl Sauer, that the seashore will still be worth visiting "when all the lands are filled with people and machines."
>
> The moral of this review is not that since nobody seems to be altogether correct, there is therefore no use in doing anything, but that, to the contrary; each student of the seashore has contributed some vital element to our understanding, and that of course we need much more of this scientific beachcombing (and well-designed field experimentation) if we are to understand the seashore as a habitat and interface of ecological interactions. Unfortunately, it has come to pass that the hubristic self-esteem of to many university departments mitigates against such beachcombing in favor of what seems the most likely highway to laurel wreaths in Stockholm. The result is that some of this essential work is being sponsored by those whose interest is too immediate and limited in time and supervised by people who consider beachcombing or field experimentation as unnecessary diversions, under the direction of administrators poorly qualified to judge the results. Time is, above all, the most expensive and essential ingredient, time to spend observing and taking data, time to think things over and put the right questions, but most of all, just time spent in the environment, time "to go down and experience the sea."[1]

As a marine ecologist Ed Ricketts did as well as anyone else in his time, although I am not sure his idea of comparing numbers of species per trip or time observed would have produced the hard sort of data to hold up against subjective appraisals. Yet this is precisely the method now being used by the many consulting biologists who have sprung up like toadstools after the first showers of our environmental consciousness. (They count the species seen on one trip as contrasted with another, or creatures scanned while drifting by in a diving outfit.) Ed's technique of comparing shores by percentages of exposure, then calculating such percentages in order to compare localities of greatly different tidal ranges might also be useful; but no one has tried this approach in quite that way. Recent efforts have been made in South Africa—appropriately enough—to make objective measurements of differences in wave shock on rocky shores, this

[1]Hedgpeth, Joel W. "The Living Edge." *Geoscience and Man* 14, pp. 17-51, 20 figs., 1976.

being a complicating factor with reference to differing tidal heights. Such measurements have required tedious and destructive sampling and reliance upon sophisticated computer programs.

It is interesting to note that Ed also mentioned counting "test squares." He never had time or inclination to pursue this notion. One must remember that, in the early years especially, the seashore was also his source of livelihood and he could not afford to divert too much time from the collection of material for his business. Even today, counting and measuring is undertaken with reluctance by most seashore observers.

It is obvious that Ed had an ecological mind. He was forever turning over ideas and putting idea and observation together, as he did with the concept of "competitive exclusion." This idea has since become one of the irreducible essences of ecology, according to Garrett Hardin.[1] Ed Ricketts first encountered this concept in *Biological Abstracts*. For years afterward few other biologists appreciated the hypothesis. Eventually Evelyn Hutchinson at Yale urged students to consider the idea and examine its first expression by such theoretical ecologists as Lotka and Gause.[2] These gentlemen did not state the concepts clearly, though today it is often called Gause's hypothesis.[3] In 1932 Gause did indicate that in a given ecological situation, niche, set of requirements or whatever, there can be only one species, or that there cannot be two species of the same ecological requirements in the same ecological place. Evelyn Hutchinson renamed this ecological place a "hyperspace." The Argentinian zoologist, Angel Cabrera, seems to have made a similar inference independently and more concisely. Perhaps it should be called Cabrera's Rule instead of Gause's hypothesis since Cabrera's abstract was the first clearly stated expression of the concept:

In the same locality and same geological period, directly related animal forms always occupy different habitats or ecological stations. This leads the author to formulate the following law: related animal forms are ecologically incompatible, and their incompatibility is the more profound, the more directly they are related. The relation of this law, illustrated by

[1]Hardin, Garrett. 1960. The competitive exclusion principle. *Science*, 131: 1292-1297.

[2]Lotka, Alfred J. *Elements of Physical Biology*. Baltimore, Williams & Wilkins, 1925.

Gause, G.F. *The Struggle for Existence*. Baltimore, Williams & Wilkins, 1934. Both books have recently been reprinted by Dover.

[3]Gilbert, O., T.B. Reynoldson and J. Hobart. Gause's hypothesis: an examination. *Jour. Anim. Ecology*, 21 (2):

numerous examples from zoogeography, paleontology, and taxonomy, to epharmony and speciation is discussed.

(Biological Abstracts, 1935: No. 4488.)[1]

It is a pity that there was not someone to encourage Ed to continue in the direction he was thinking, to call his attention to Lotka's *Elements of Physical Biology,* to Gause's *The Struggle for Existence,* and to other gathering clouds of the coming ecological storm. W.C. Allee might have helped him; but Chicago was too far away. Nevertheless, Ed came very close to a break-through in ecological thinking. He saw the relationship between Cabrera's principle of competitive exclusion and Allee's idea of cooperation as "demonstrating survival value for the primitive tendency toward aggregation." It would not have been many more steps to the concept that aggregations of different kinds of organisms act as a system which tends toward an adjustment with its environmental resources.

---

[1]Cabrera, Angel. 1932. *La incompatibilidad ecologica. Una ley biologica interesante. An. Soc. Cient. Argentina* 114 (5/6): 243-260. This journal is not generally available; the only library in the United States which has it is that of the Franklin Institute. Had it appeared in a more accessible journal, it might have been noticed long since. It was not cited in *Biological Abstracts* until 1935, and I seem to be the first person in this country to look up the original paper, thanks to finding the reference in Ricketts' papers. Cabrera's paper is listed in the terminal bibliography ("References Cited") of Lee R. Dice's *Natural Communities* (Michigan, 1952), but is not discussed in the text.

IIB. Ricketts as a Philosopher

Ed was very serious about his philosophical essays. They were part of the core of his life, and he never quite gave up the hope that someday they would be published as a separate book. He was always asking friends to read them and he thought over their comments carefully. But somewhere he got the idea that to be profound one had to be difficult, and that to use old words in his personal context or to twist them to his own use (e.g. finishedly) was part of being profound. He must have read some bad translations of German philosophy. John Steinbeck said Ed Ricketts was the most profound person he had ever known, but he was over fond of that word himself.

The essay on non-teleological thinking, as revised by John Steinbeck in *Sea of Cortez,* has attracted many readers; and passages have often been quoted, usually as if they were Steinbeck's own ideas. John did not fully understand what Ed was trying to say. The version included in this book has been placed with the other *Sea of Cortez* material where it belongs, although Ed intended it to be part of an essay series. As for the other essays on "breaking through" and poetry, John read them or discussed them with Ed, and had copies. As Richard Astro has shown in his book *John Steinbeck and Edward F. Ricketts: The Shaping of a Novelist,* many phrases and ideas from these essays may be traced in John Steinbeck's writing.

All of them are hard reading; and as Desmond King-Hele has said of the verse of Erasmus Darwin, they are "too indigestible to absorb in a continuous reading, and are best taken like meals, at intervals." Yet by the same token, they provide unexpected insights and diversions and point the way along interesting pathways. In another sense they are the remains of conversations recorded on a reluctant machine.

As with so many other terms that Ed attempted to use in a philosophical sense, "non-teleological" had a private meaning for him, a suggestive implication of "anti-teleological." Alongside the passage in *Studs Lonigan* where the atheist asks: "God, why do you create men and make them suffer and fight in vain...why do the beautiful girls you create become whores, grow old and toothless...etc.," Ed wrote in his copy: "good example of teleological thinking on a very low level." It is apparent from this that Ed's view of teleology goes back to his Sunday school experience.

Perhaps more words than necessary have been spilled over the matter of "non-teleological" thinking and the "biological way of life." Biology, or life, is perpetually teleological in the sense that it seems to be going in some direction. As some wit put it, "Teleology is a mistress no biologist can acknowledge but still cannot get along without" (or some such). Things always seem to be going in some direction or another; and if that be teleology, so be it.¹ If you are philosopher enough, there are ways out of all dilemmas:

> The denial of the doctrine of final causes involves the denial that a goal casually determines the actions that may realise it, but does not deny (or affirm) that the goal may determine prior activities in the second, episto-mological sense of 'determine!'. This distinction suggests that we might interpret the position of the defenders of teleology as involving no more than the assertion that the goal of purposive activity determines, in the epistomological sense, the purposive activity itself. Under such an inter-pretation, teleology is stripped of its suspicious trappings.
>
> (Beckner, p. 140.)

It ought to be said that Ed Ricketts was not exactly a rigidly "pure" biologist because he was always trying to bring other ideas and disciplines to bear, at least within his own mind; hence, Jospeh Needham's remark, "To treat sociological problems with purely bio-logical concepts is to add oneself to the long list of humanity's false prophets," would be too severe. Ed was a prophet or spokesman for nature; one always felt when talking to him that there were reserves beyond the conversation of the moment. And so there were. It is ob-vious that in his essays Ed tried to express these greater dimensions.

The three philosophical essays, "Non-teleological Thinking," "The Philosophy of Breaking Through," and "A Spiritual Morphology of Poetry" were considered to be phases of an examination of "the pure thing" which Ed called "Participation," and he thought this word would be a suitable title for the finished work.

> Participation is, if not the most dramatic, at least the most deeply inter-esting thing in the world. To the degree of its intensity or depth, it's 'all things' not superficially disseminated or spread out—diffused, but deeply, participatingly, all things, and so, in its absolute sense, beyond life, but often glimpsed nevertheless . . .

In his account of Ed in *The Log of the Sea of Cortez,* John Stein-beck does not mention these essays and all the effort Ed went to in discussing and re-writing them. Of the idea of breaking through, Steinbeck did write:

> He was walled off a little, so that he worked at his philosophy of 'break-ing through,' of coming out through the back of the mirror into some kind of reality which would make the day world dream-like. This thought ob-sessed him. He found the symbols of 'breaking through' in *Faust,* in Gregorian music, and in the sad, drunken poetry of Li Po. Of the *Art of the Fugue,* he would say, 'Bach nearly made it. Hear now how close he comes, and hear his anger when he cannot. Every time I hear it, I believe that this time he will come crashing through into the light. And he never does—not quite.'

---

¹Readers who may wish to dive deeply into this subject are referred to: Morton Beckner, *The Biological Way of Thought,* Univ. Calif. Press, 1968, esp. Chapter VII, "Teleological systems, behavior, and explanation."

And of course it was he himself who wanted so desperately to break through into the light.

(*The Log of the Sea of Cortez*, p. liii.)

This idea of "breaking through," perhaps beyond the bonds of humanity, as Robinson Jeffers had it: "humanity is...the crust to break through," was one of Hermann Hesse's major themes. Hesse found this essence in Bach—and also in Mozart while Ed did not listen much to Mozart until his last year or so.

But "breaking through" is also escape into the past, to go home to times before we learned that our share of the world is not ours forever but must end with time. Perhaps this is a mood of our own times, because we are changing the world so rapidly with the stupidities of material progress and the catastrophes of war and genocide that we have been a part of in this most terrible of centuries. In his later years, as his parents died and he absorbed the implications of being the subject of such a book as *Cannery Row*, Ed had more thoughts about nostalgia, and began gathering material for an essay on the subject. Some of these notes are included at the end of this section.

One of the curious aspects of Ed's essay on "The Spiritual Morphology of Poetry" is that he never quite comes to grips with the nature of poetry itself. Why do people try to express themselves in poetry; this high use of language in obviously structured terms? What are they really trying to do? Make us feel that the Chinese girl of long ago at the turn of the road will indeed receive her lover, or that time will stand still on Dover Beach? Not exactly. Language is being used as a means of defining the poet's relation to the world as he understands that world. If he is a poet. Otherwise he is a versifier simply reducing experience to formal structure. The "morphology" of poetry is that a structure is conformed to, yet transcended. Through composition the poet has interacted with his mind, his language and his world. In all Ed's notes, there are no lines of poetry that are his. Evidently he could not express himself in anything resembling verse or structure. His ear was not for the language itself but for ideas that appealed to his sense of how things ought to be. Despite his remarkably acute ear for music he seemed strangely deaf to the nuances of language in poetry. Though his upbringing exposed him to recitations of the Book of Common Prayer, he may have had reservations about ritual and formal aspects of the poetry of language. In his copy of *Studs Lonigan*, at the bottom of the scene of the Christmas Mass, Ed wrote, "soothes not me, not me."

Still, as Ed well knew, poetry intends to mean all things to all readers. If part can be understood, the poet can be content, for the essence of it all is in what the writer committed to the poetic effort; and the meaning is a corollary to this essence. Was that what Shelley meant when he wrote "pinnacled deep in the intense inane" —or was he merely tired that afternoon and needed this phrase to complete a pattern? Had Ed seen such a book as Maud Bodkin's *Arche-*

typal Patterns in Poetry (first published in 1934), he could have approached these matters in a more enquiring spirit. Then he might have avoided regarding that rather tedious translation of *Black Marigolds* by E. Powys Mathers as "possibly the greatest love poem ever written."

Ed's attempt to define poetry provoked a long discussion with John Cage who was then teaching concepts of music in the San Francisco Bay area. The following exchange occurred as they drove to Monterey one evening:

[John Cage] and I had a very pleasant trip back. We worked out an understanding, almost a statement of our differences of viewpoint. It involves, as I suspected, a real honest to god fundamental, a right or left turn up the steep mountain, and surely involves in culture that same primitive cleavage apparent now in government: as an individual or a communal point of departure. And he represents the probably oncoming thing. Divine inspired geometry is a good term. A square or a black line is more nearly the same for all people—therefore a great leveller—than a folksong or a picture of a cow or a Shakespeare sonnet, or more even than the tones or words etc. of which they're composed. But all my tendencies are toward "meaning," while his are toward "organization" as such. I regard content as primary, he form. It's more than the old controversy, it represents actually a fundamental divergence (altho I still think its the mountain that's of deepest importance). And his is unquestionably the purest thing. He regards all sound (but especially sound devoid of previous (traditional) meaning) as the subject matter for organization in that discipline which is music; whereas the former tendency has been surely (but in music less probably than the other arts) to regard meaning, what the artist had to say, as the prime mover. The way he said it also was important, and a matter of discipline, but the important thing was that he had "something to say." The newer idea, of "inspired geometry" concerns itself with pure form, with pure building blocks themselves originally devoid of meaning. The meaning essentially attaches to the new form as an incidental but probably essentially sequential, by-product. But the thing is pure in itself "let the chips fall where they may." "It's what it is." Pure. And that's the point of contact I was interested in—since the pureness of a thing is what I like also, and therefore a common ground. His type of "word of god made man" works out thru form, a meaning attaches thru association for whatever it is, wherever it goes. My type (and the more conventional types from which it stems), derives thru what it has to say, and then—technic secondary and a result (altho an essential one and one that improves with work)—laboriously takes the form most suited to it, or the form in which I am most competent. It finally boils down to a matter of emphasis. And it is, after all, a vitally fundamental difference, but it's a difference of way, or of "Tao" whereas the thing of central significance—you just can't say it, it's so pure and refined—involves the central tao. It's the mountain that's important, rather than the way up it, which is also however important as being part of the mountain. (EFR to TJ, Dec., 1940).

While there is often a haunting suggestion of "the thing in itself" in Ed's writings, the philosopher of Königsberg was not among his favorite authors. He preferred the elusive mysticism of Jakob Boehme's *Signature of All Things*. At heart Ed was a mystic, seeking to fuse symbol with experience. He would probably have thought Hermann Hesse's characterization too severe, perhaps not "apropos," more art than nature:

> Mystics are, to express it briefly and somewhat crudely, thinkers who cannot detach themselves from images, therefore not thinkers at all. They are secret artists: poets without verse, painters without brushes, musicians without sound. There are highly gifted, noble minds among them, but they are all without exception unhappy men.[1]

To accept the world as it is and, at the same time, to seek to break out of it into some all-encompassing experience is as valid an approach to the *summum bonum* as any other. As later entries in his journal suggest, Ed had not stopped thinking and was beginning to wonder about the energy bases for the living system, and how such concepts fitted into the whole. As with many others, but especially with a person like Ed, these written remains are the cleaned and somewhat scattered bones of what was very much alive when they were part of a living person and his conversation.

And so, at least with Ed, it was all part of the same picture, as he so often said: and he wanted to bring together within himself all the different things and ideas which interested him to produce his own personal synthesis. "He hoped. . .to arrange and sum up all the knowledge of his time, symmetrically and synoptically, around a central idea. That is precisely what the *Glass Bead Game* does."[2]

Again from Hesse, the contrast between Narcissus and Goldmund suggests a comparable situation in Ricketts' life. In the latter case, Ricketts, a sensual lover of women, was reflective and contemplative while his friend Steinbeck, a creative artist, appeared austere and cool. As measured by his inclinations, Ed Ricketts had more in common with Hermann Hesse than with John Steinbeck. Ed responded to many of the same signals as Hesse: Jakob Boehme, Novalis, Lao Tzu, Zen, Goethe and Jung. Ricketts wanted to keep his mind in flux, constantly inquiring and re-arranging ideas. "Breaking through" was as much avoidance of stagnation and crystallization as it was attainment of a mystical state beyond daily liv-

---

[1] Hermann Hesse, *Narcissus and Goldmund*, Bantam Ed., p. 277.

As for Jakob Boehme, unfortunately I have not seen Ed's annotated copy of *The Signature of All Things*, which might explain what Ed made of this strangely turgid symbolism. The Everyman edition (which Ed had) has been reproduced in fascimile by James Clarke & Co., Cambridge and London, 1969. Those interested in coming to closer grips with the mystic shoemaker should consult John Joseph Stoudt's *Jakob Boehme, His Life and Thought*, Seabury Press, 317 pp., 1968 (Originally *Sunrise to Eternity*, Univ. Pennsylvania Press 1957).

[2] ". . .er hoffe in einem enzyklopadischen Werk alles Wissen seiner Zeit symmetrisch und synoptisch auf einem Zentrum hin zu ordnen und zusammenzufassen. Das ist nichts andres, als was das Glasperlenspiel auch tut."
Hesse, *The Glass Bead Game*. Holt Rinehart & Winston Ed., p. 166.

ing or the symbolic death of Joseph Knecht in the icy lake. Of course the break through was that too, as so clearly stated in Hesse's *Steppenwolf:*

> As I reflected, passages of Mozart's *Cessations*, of Bach's *Well-Tempered Clavier* came to my mind and it seemed to me that all through this music there was the radiance of this cool starry brightness and the quivering of this coolness of ether. Yes, it was there. In this music, there was a feeling as of time frozen into space, and above it there quivered a never-ending and superhuman serenity, an eternal, divine laughter.

The quiet beyond the tumoil is the essence of Zen also, and R.H. Blyth in his interesting book *Zen in English Literature and Oriental Classics* (Tokyo: Hokuseido Press, 1942) uses a passage from Bach's Organ Passacaglia as an example of the resolution of the paradox of theme and variation. " . . . and behold, the intangible is grasped, the unsayable is said." (p. 183.)

Despite the similarity of their thoughts, Ed seems never to have read Hesse. His conscious ideal was Goethe who sought to live in all his many talents while expressing fully his sexuality. Ed however, was short on many of the talents he most admired: the writing of poetry, ability to perform music, or draw. He was an admirer of such talents and their synthesizer in his efforts to bring all he knew together into some unified construction of his mind.

He thought of this as "the real unified field hypothesis," the true "deep thing:"

> It's that deep thot that Korzybski is chasing in language & thot
> that I pursued in non-teleol. thinking
> that lack of which (personal impurity) Jeffers regrets
> the breaking thru into which that Jeffers & Miller & occasionally Jn
>   [Steinbeck] extol.
> It's the central experience of chinese philosophy, the great Tao
> It's the thing Lao Tzu has in mind when he says "The tao that can be
>   tao'd is not the ultimate tao."
> The chasing of it vainly (in "wrong" words, wrong thoughts etc.) the
>   *Upanishads* have in mind when they make Death say "again &
> again he comes under my sway."
>
> (Journal entry, May-June, 1947).

And of course there was the idea that once attained, you "broke through" into another dimension of thought and feeling. In his essay "On the Philosophy of Breaking Through" there is a strangely prophetic paragraph indicating that Ed Ricketts at least would not have been surprised by the beatniks, hippies, the counter culture of our troubled times:

> These ideas use words only as a vehicle. But however unsuited to word expression, such a thing objectively seems to exist, even collectively, and it characterizes, is influenced by and influences or at least indexes a trend reflected philosophically in holism—that the whole is more than the sum of its parts; that the integration or relation of the parts is other than the

separate sum of the parts. Recently, I have been inclining toward the belief that the conscious recognition of this "breaking through" quality may be an essential of modern soul movements, and that the degree of its recognition comprises an earmark of whatever abiding quality modern (particularly non-abstract) art may possess: not dirt for dirt's sake, or grief merely for the sake of grief, but dirt and grief wholly accepted if necessary as struggle vehicles of an emergent joy—achieving things which are not transient by means of things which are.

However earnestly he strained to be a profound philosopher, Ed's best talents were his wit, his capacity to see the humor of situations and his ability to converse and participate with people. Often such participation meant putting himself in the other fellow's place. These are ephemeral graces that leave little record but show themselves best in the journal accounts of his expedition with Steinbeck to the Gulf of California and in the account of his travels to British Columbia. Both of these journal transcripts were prepared from his notebooks for John Steinbeck's use. The first, of course, became the backbone of *Sea of Cortez*. The essay on non-teleological thinking was a dimension beyond the travel notes that Steinbeck subjected to a sea change. Ed anticipated a similar enhancement of his old notes from the earlier trip to Alaska. The Alaskan material was scientific rather than philosophical and evidently Ed hoped for more of the science to be retained in the new joint effort. This is suggested in Steinbeck's remarks about Masset Inlet on p. lxiv of "About Ed Ricketts" but when he said "the light has gone out of it for me" he was too close to his loss to appreciate the value of what Ed had written for him. Ed's perceptions were decades ahead of his time. Now there is the added evocation of nostalgia in the best Rickettsian sense, not merely that these writings have remained so long unavailable but that now is added the seasoning of timelessness to Ed's concern for people, ideas and the life of the seashore.

IIC. The Tide

1. Excerpts from: The tide as an environmental factor chiefly with
reference to ecological zonation on the California coast. (1934).

At least the most obvious regulatory factor in the vertical distribution of
littoral life is the tide. By substituting the uniform oceanic environment obtaining at flood, for the varying temperatures, salinity, desiccation, wave
shock and light conditions obtainable during intervals of ebb, the alternating
tide effects all littoral organisms. Zonation on rocky shores is very noticeable,
and frequently has been recorded and described, usually with the assumption
that the tide was causative. But except for the accounts noted below, there
have been no serious attempts to evaluate or analyze this factor, despite the
fact that tides are particularly susceptible to rigid analysis, and that the new
science of oceanography is intimately concerned with the consideration of
environmental factors in their biological significance. There have been
elaborate studies of salinity, of dissolved nutrients, and of the penetration of
light; but of the most significant distribution factor for the shore forms with
which at some time or another every biologist concerns himself, there has been
little careful consideration.

This study was originally the outcome of primitive attempts some years ago
on the part of the writer to determine the shape of the tidal wave with
reference to fixed heights on the shore, and later to discover the correlation
between zonation and intertidal exposure. Observably, littoral organisms are
grouped into distinct and non-merging levels, but the presence or absence of
sudden breaks or new tendencies in the several published duration graphs (in
which total hours of exposure are plotted against heights on the shore) accounted only in part for these discrete quanta. My question finally came to
read: "To what determinable conditions directly referable to the tide would a
sessile animal attached at any given shore level be subjected?" These conditions, it developed, are grouped around at least three primary phases, which
until now have been considerably neglected, especially on the Pacific: the total
duration of exposure over long periods of time, the average and the extreme
intervals of emergence, and their frequency.

The tide as an environmental factor in the remote past, while the main evolutionary trends were developing, merits biological consideration. An important
theory of cosmogony, developed by G. H. Darwin, son of the biologist, postulates that tides were powerful earth-forming factors. In reviewing this
hypothesis, now apparently pretty well entrenched, (H. A. Marmer *The Tide,*
Appleton, 1926, Chap. XIX) indicates that the 24 hour day is being lengthened
one minute (about 1-1/2/10ths of 1%) every six million years by tidal friction
acting as a brake on the earth's rotation. The lunar month is becoming longer
and the moon's distance from the earth is increasing, resulting (since tide
generating forces vary as the cube of the distance) in decreased tides. So tides
in the past are supposed to have been immeasureably greater, since the rate of
increase also increases backward. "...The efficiency of tidal friction in
increasing the length of the day and the distance between moon and earth
therefore varies inversely as the *sixth* power of that distance. So that when the
moon was half her present distance from the earth the effects of tidal friction
were at a rate of $2^6=64$ times as great as now." (H. A. Marmer 1930, The Sea,
D. Appleton, NY, p. 299.). Even a slight decrease in the distance from moon to
earth would result in a considerable increase in tides; a decrease so great as

50% in the one would make the other 8x as intense.

According to this hypothesis, interesting in itself but only of incidental import here, it is mathematically predictable that the day was once 4 hours long, the moon almost touched the earth, and tides in both bodies were prodigious and mutually stimulating to the point of resonance. All matter, which is thought to have been comparatively archaic, was of course involved. This was certainly before the formation of the ocean, before even a solid crust had been formed. But the most reliable time estimates (p 7-8, The Age of the Earth, Bull. 80, Natl. Res. Council, Washington, 1931) place the age of the oldest rocks at the still considerable figure of 1852 million years. 910 million years are similarly assumed to have elapsed since the Cambrian, and at that time the main evolutionary lines had been formulated and all the phyla with the possible exception of the chordates were well established.

Since even now the tide establishes a measureable tho minute weight differential (according to Marmer, The Tide, p 26, the steamship Majestic loses 15 pounds of its weight under the full moon), in Pre-Cambrian times, more than a thousand million years ago, it must have been dominantly the most important single environmental factor for littoral animals. Displacement and body weight then must certainly have varied considerably with the rotation and phases of the moon (especially if the orbit was at that time elliptic, the sun's reinforcement having been probably slighter relatively). The varying specific gravities of the different organs and body fluids, varying surface tensions, and membranes of varying toughness furthermore would have established differentials within themselves and between each other powerfully influenced by even a slight decrease in pressure. Consider especially its influence on gonads turgid with eggs or sperm, already almost bursting and awaiting only some "last straw." Note also the dehiscense of ova thru the body wall of the polychaete worms of ancient lineage, dating back almost unchanged to the Cambrian. If we admit for a moment the potentiality of this differential, and the considerable effect of tides (even in post-Cambrian times) on gradually sloping shores, we have only to envision the concept of the collective pattern associationally involved in instinct, to get an inkling of the force behind the lunar ryhthm so deeply rooted, and so obviously and often present in marine animals and even in higher mammals and man. It should be noted also that even today the effect of the tide or tide-making forces on natural processes is more valid and more widespread than would casually be supposed, as indicated by the report (in Science Supplement, 80, (2069), p 7, August 24, 1934) from Labrador that radio reception is synchronized with the rise and fall of local tides. Witness the possible relation between fluctuations in the speed of light and the tidal rhythm near Santa Ana, California (Science, 81 (2091, p 101, January 25, 1935). One could safely predict that all physiological processes correspondingly might be shown to be influenced by the tide, could we but read delicately enough the indices.

It appears that the physical evidence for this theory of Darwin's is more or less hypothetical, not in fact, but in interpretation, and that critical reasoning could conceivably throw overboard the whole hypothesis—and with it incidentally the biological connotations—because of possible unknown links and factors. Possibly it should read the other way around: the animals themselves would seem to offer striking confirmation to the tidal theory of cosmogony; one almost is forced to postulate some such theory if he would account causally for this primitive impress. While not inconceivable (for instance through some "homeopathic" factor, or something analagous to allergic reaction), it is nevertheless far-fetched to attribute the lunar rhythm status actually observable in

65

breeding animals of the tide controlled breeding habits of the California grunion, of the Polynesian palolo worm, of Nereis, of Amphineura, etc., wherein whole collections of animals act as one individual responding to a natural phenomenon, to the present fairly weak tidal forces only, or to coincidence. There is tied up to the most primitive and powerful social (collective) instinct, a rhythm "memory" which affects everything, and which in the past was probably far more potent than it is now. It would at least be more plausible to attribute these profound effects to devastating and instinct-searing tidal influences active during the formulative (and hence impressionable) times of the early race history of organisms. And whether or not any mechanism has been discovered, or is discoverable, to carry on this imprint through the germ plasm, the fact is that the imprint (legitimately referable to instinct—although that only begs the question, there is equally no mechanism for transmitting instinct) is definitely there.

Conclusions and derived discussions.

The rather obvious conclusion is reached that the tide must be even now a profound important regulatory factor for littoral organisms. There are a dozen or more minor, and three or four primary ways wherein it establishes differentials significant to the populations involved. And there are hypothetical reasons for believing that in the past it may have been decidedly the predominant factor for shore animals, possibly for all organisms intimately connected as it must have been with the rupture of turgid sacs of sexual products. In the remote past the lunar cycle (especially if the orbit involved elliptics) may very possibly have been the calendar to which all life coordinated.

A comparison of the environmental effects of Atlantic and Pacific tides develops several differences, chiefly that due to the marked diurnal inequality of Pacific ebbs, the associations of the lowest littoral are exposed here only half as frequently and long as those on the Atlantic. The central California coast, with its dawn or sunset lows often coinciding with fog, is thought to provide especially favorable terrestrial conditions to these associations during their short and infrequent exposures.

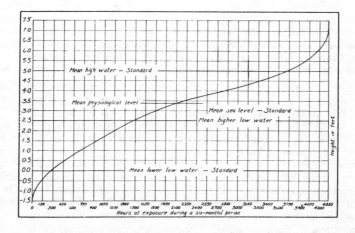

Exposure curve for six months period at San Francisco, 1931. (One of Rickett's original graphs for his paper on tides, as reproduced in Between Pacific Tides, 1st ed., 1939).

66

New information derives chiefly from analysis of the exposure-submergence curves based on actual tidal records for a period of slightly more than half a lunar year at San Francisco, where the extreme amplitude is slightly under 9.0', the mean range is 3.9', the diurnal range 5.7' and the spring range 4.6. Hypothetically, on the basis of this strictly physical evidence, there are at least three critical horizons for the local littoral organisms. These occur at mean lower low water, 0' (the datum for Pacific coast tide tables), at plus 3.5' and at plus 5'. Mean sea level is about 3.0' above mean lower low water at San Francisco; these horizons therefore read—3.0', plus 0.5', and plus 2.0' on the mean sea level scale. Two are based on sudden breaks, at mean lower low water and at plus 5.0', in the six months graph of the exposure-duration factor. Two (one coinciding with the 5.0' level established already) are indexed by breaks in the graphs of average and extreme emergence intervals, at plus 3.5' and at the above mentioned plus 5.0' level. These tidal readings, possibly with some others not yet appreciated or evaluated, are thought to exercise profound regulatory effects on shore zonation. Cursory (i.e. not quantitatively recorded or analyzed) observations on the part of the writer over a period of ten years roughly seem to confirm these zones, altho many animals seem to break off at plus 2.5' instead of at plus 3.5'—a situation thought by Mestre to be due possibly to the influence of overhanging seaweeds centered around the higher level.

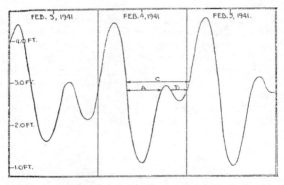

Graph showing the tidal curve during the three day period February 3 to February 5, 1941. On February 4, the lowest of the lower high waters for the year reached an elevation of only 2.9 feet. (From unpublished Master's thesis by B.J. Roberts, 1941.)

These critical horizons would divide the ideal California shore into four fairly limited zones, everything else being equal and granting at the same time that such widely divergent factors as physical and biological environmental factors cannot possibly be equal, wave shock, type of bottom, internecine and interracial competition for food, attachment, shelter, etc. being what they are. The index of vertical distribution may lie very possibly not in the sum total of these analyzable factors, but in their integration, since even a slight change in one factor may have considerable balance repercussions on the others by changing their mutual relations. So a sudden and abiding vertical shift of .1' in the tidal mean may be relatively unimportant—altho it involves supposedly the most important single factor, or it may affect the whole very profoundly thru upset equilibrium, especially if it impinges some critical threshhold. As in the hawk-ptarmigan relation mentioned by Elton (Ency. Brit. XIV Ed., Vol. 7, p. 916) there is no possible way of evaluating this situation a priori, each separate occasion being unique due to the multitudinous and interrelated factors involved, and the situation properly ought to be examined as a whole, as indeed must inevitably be done by the field man.

The chiefly sublittoral life occurring in the lowest habitat is thought to be limited in its upper range by the sudden increase in exposure total duration at 0.0', conditions from below the littoral to about this point being almost the same. As a matter of fact, from -1.9' to 0.0' the exposure conditions are almost identical, organisms stationed here being exposed to air only occasionally, more or less accidentally, and then for short periods, with long intervals of submergence before and after. This zone has literally the whole ocean to draw from, animals need not in any particular way be highly specialized in order to do well here, and it cannot seem surprising that this zone supports a number of species greater than anywhere else—altho the number of individuals per species need not be high.

Sessile organisms above 0.0' start suddenly to be exposed to greater total amounts of air, still in small doses, but occurring more frequently. Both frequency and size of dosage increase in the higher reaches of this zone, where it would be safe to anticipate further divisions into narrow belts. The upper limit at 3.5' is probably indexed by the suddenly increasing interval lengths, especially in the extreme intervals, and to some extent by gradually increasing total exposure duration. In order to persist here, the animals and plants must be to some degree specialized.

Above 3.5', the populations are suddenly subjected to larger doses of air and terrestrial conditions, at first very frequently, then with fewer immersions and with longer dry periods between, altho at this point the total amount of exposure isn't increasing much more rapidly than it has been in the past few vertical feet. Here additional narrow belts could be predicted confidently, since the changes, tho uniform, are very rapid. The upper limit at 5.0' is thought to be regulated, or at least indexed, by the rapidly increasing amount of total duration and by the sudden jump in interval, along with the gradual frequency decrease. Animals in this zone must be highly specialized with respect to the tidal rhythm factor, and those few which have solved the problem can be expected to occur in great abundance (vide barnacles, littorines and limpets) because of the lessened inter-racial competition. The struggle here isn't so much against other species, of which there are only a few, as between the tremendous numbers of the same species.

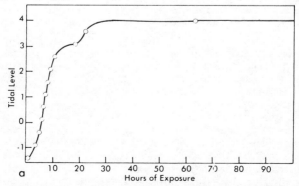

The discontinuities of tidal exposure on the California coast; apparently based on a lost diagram by Ricketts. From an unpublished Master's thesis by B.J. Roberts, 1941.

Above this point any persisting communities must be pretty well adapted to terrestrial life, since the conditions even at 5.0' are only 16% marine. From thence to the line marking 100% exposure at about 7.0' to 7.5' (surf for the moment not considered; this is a highly variable factor) animals are wetted only occasionally, and then for periods increasingly brief. The paucity of animals in this zone emphasizes again the fact that with littoral associations we are dealing with marine animals pushing up toward land, rather than with land animals colonizing downward. Some of the plants however (the tropical mangroves, and seed plants of local salt marshes) suggest that some at least of the land forms are migrating seaward, as well as vice versa.

In these concepts may lie one explanation of the confirmable fact that hosts of different animals inhabit the lowest zone with few individuals per species, while higher up there are more individuals of fewer species. The lowest zone has the whole ocean to draw from, and within this belt great numbers of animals unspecialized as to tidal rhythm may be competing. But in order to succeed higher up, animals must be specialized with regard to this factor, adaptations to other factors must be subordinated to this all-important one. They must be able to tolerate semi-terrestrial conditions, in this one thing at least having come a long way evolutionarily from the generalized situation. There cannot be nearly as many species that have succeeded in this adaptation as there are truly marine species, and what few there are can, and do exist in tremendous numbers. Applying similar ideas to plant distribution, we should expect to find vertical distribution a function of sunlight needs times adaptation to the tidal rhythm. Realizing that the dispersal point for marine-plants, which are at best comparatively few in species, cannot be below the shallow shore or upper pelagic zone—due to photosynthesis requirements— one would expect to see a balance struck in the mid-tidal, where actually the greatest plant production occurs, at least on this coast.

IID. The Philosophy of "Breaking Through"[1]

A personal interpretation of some modern tendencies, approached from an inductive standpoint.

> *Taking all hints to use them, but swiftly leaping beyond them.*
> Whitman: Out of the cradle endlessly rocking.

> *This is the stone which was set at nought of you builders, which is become the head of the corner.*
> Acts of the Apostles, 4:11

I

I remember it first when we children were living in a squalid district in Chicago. One winter night, the combined home and saloon of some Bohemian neighbors caught fire and burned to the ground quickly before much could be saved. I guess we knew them only slightly. Father bought beer there every night (this was referred to as "composition" in our presence; I used to notice how remarkably it smelt like beer), but they traded almost not at all at our grocery. On the whole, an observer would have seen that they were beneath us. I have no doubt but that my parents knew them as people; but a feeling of kinship with these foreigners—saloon-keepers, furthermore, and whose children were even allowed to draw beer for customers—wasn't in any way communicated to us. We probably scorned the Huska kids. I remember the boys were very bow-legged. This was presumably due to the fact that as babies they had been allowed to walk too soon, a preventable situation, and another indication of the family's inferiority. And of our superiority, since all of us were straight-legged. The father, Steve, was said to be fond of children, and I frequently saw him dandling the baby. It must have seemed quite impossible to me, if I had stopped to consider: how could such people exhibit traits like ours, really human traits! Obviously we were snooty people; we children were, at least: in the slums, but to our notions not of them. Any intimate mixings into our surroundings, furthermore, must have been frowned upon by our parents.

Anyway, on this occasion, something happened. The fire flared up suddenly. Suddenly we were all out in the street, watching our first close fire. But not only as observers. The Huska kids were probably crying, scared, not understanding their so-well-known father now strangely numbed at seeing his frugally-built security vanishing. All at once I, of our remote family probably the most remote and cold, found myself suggesting, and intensely meaning it, that Father should make sure Stefan Huska and his family had a place to stay. I, of all people, was asking him to bring these dirty (presumably; foreign anyway) bow-legged children, stocky, sturdy, in all ways the opposite of delicate—us, to our house. More surprisingly, I seemed to express a notion we all felt, flowing through us with a supra-personal beauty for which we were only vehicles. We must give, something, anything. And what we had to give, the sanctuary and former superiority of our home, seemed suddenly not enough. Nothing could be enough; there wasn't such a thing as enough. There could be no expression adequate to that glowing feeling of kinship with all things and all people. For the first time, and in the glow of that supposedly destructive fire, we children had become more than ourselves. For those few minutes, we

[1]"Revised July 1940, Mexico City."

were really living, we were "beyond," things had a new meaning, so that the former values must have seemed dwarfed and strange if we had stopped to think of them.

There were many lesser things of that sort. Years later, in the woods at Pacific Grove, our old landlord fell off the roof he was repairing, knocked unconscious with a fractured skull so that we thought he was dying. His wife was grand; not hysterical. Supposing also he had to die, she accepted it not as a frenzy. She kept saying "dear boy." Suddenly I found myself living the whole picture. I was seeing her in a flood of feelings that must have been as inundating as surf, recalling the early values of their relation, the old days—maybe not thought of for years—their struggles and good times together, related to their youth, and as charged as Conrad's "Youth." She may have led the sexually frustrated life we associate with English people of Victorian heritage; all that became instantly of little importance. She kept stroking his head and saying "dear boy." To herself, I suppose, because he could neither hear nor feel. Anyway, the physical manifestations were in themselves important only as something the churched [sic] used to call the outward and visible signs of an inward and spiritual grace—vehicles on which something beyond was integrally riding. Of the larger picture, they were no more than surface stirrings. I thought of myself (and was otherwise somewhat scandalized at the sacrilege) as beating time to music that was part of the scene and which was flowing also through me. There is a similar picture in Steinbeck's "Pastures of Heaven"; the woman who comforted her husband after the loss of his financial-illusion; and again in Marie's last (as it turns out) goodbye to her murderer husband in Hemingway's "To Have and to Have Not."

It was the same when I first heard "Madame Butterfly," my first opera; like the fantasy of an opera seven stories down and on a toy-like stage far out in front, suddenly more real than anything in life. There was the same quiet realization that no sacrifice (a poor word: privilege is nearer) would be great enough if one could only share that girl's sorrow. There was no mistaking, the thing was sounded quietly and convincingly. As "the mind knows, grown adult," recognition was sure.[1]

I had a flash of the same thing in considering the time my wife left, distraught, to go to San Francisco. Finally, all that hectic time of trouble and doubt seemed beside the point. There was a time when the sudden changes and fits of temper seemed consumingly important; the change from companionable glow to nothing or worse: hatred, and the remark that all the rest had been acting. Then I realized fleetingly the actual unimportance of all that diversion. It was away from a more essential reality. Even whether or not there was any love between us seemed not immediately significant. But it was important for us to realize that it's the tenderness that counts, however little or infrequent, that one walks along with one's wife, quiet above the hatred that often consumes both. Then, after clearly realizing that, whether or not one is physically bereaved is seen not to be vitally important.

Another example occurs to me, whether imagined, dreamed, or reported as an actuality I don't recall. There was a mine disaster. Some of the men were entombed by a cave-in; one already dead, others wounded. But one, unhurt, had access to a mine telephone whereby he could talk throughout the night while rescue work went on feverishly, with his wife, who had stayed at the mouth of the shaft since the first report of the accident. Now, some person—a relative, say—could come and stay there from a sense of duty; or a nurse, so as

[1]Jeffers "Sea Fog."

to be ready for contingencies; or a mine official, because he belonged. But I imagine this woman was there because she horribly wanted to be. When the rescue finally was effected, and her shocked and emaciated husband was hauled out of the shaft, dirty, unkempt and unshaven, she broke through into illumination. For years she had been repelled by his untidiness. She had blunted herself and him by nagging reform. Now, suddenly, all that seemed not very important. The fault was still there. If she paused to look, she could realize it now more clearly than ever before. She was actually less blind than at the time in her life, only now she saw things in their relation to a far larger picture, a more deeply significant whole. She genuinely liked him, she realized now, neither in spite of nor because of it; it was sufficient simply to face the fact that that trait was his whom she loved. She had accepted fully and without evasion the burden of anxiety, and something new was born again out of the ashes of struggle. His grime now became a symbol of her glory, associationally therefore she loved it and him more; not because of, but through it, all hate and recriminations washed away. That new thing, the Christ-child, was *deeper magic* than anything she could have anticipated, as a child, from a fairy godmother.

II

It's all part of one pattern, the burned saloon, the broken head, the departing wife, and the entombed miner; Cio-Cio-San, singing her grief and the world moving with it. I suspect now that the pattern is universal, that we fail to see the transcending simplicity of it only because of obstacles on our inward horizons. If it weren't for self-imposed or racially erected defenses, it would flow in on us from everywhere, we would be it and it we. In "Natural Music," Jeffers says:

> "So I believe if we were strong enough to listen without
> Divisions of desire and terror
> To the storm of the sick nations, the rage of the
> hunger-smitten cities,
> These voices also would be found
> Clean as a child's: . . ."

No doubt some few wise people know this merely through living. But many of us can achieve at least a clearer and more easily conveyed conscious expression of it through the spiritual motifs underlying literature, especially in poetry. In determining how clearly this un-named quality might be expressed in modern writings, I have been going over in my mind the teachers and authors, not all recent, whom I personally class as moderns: Keats (Ode to a Nightingale,) Emerson (Compensation, The Oversoul), Walt Whitman, surely, and in many poems, Francis Thompson (Hound of Heaven), even some of Stevenson (Will o' the Mill, A Lodging for the Night), Nietzsche; later, Reymont; now Jung, Hemingway, Faulkner (Ad Astra), Krishnamurti, Steinbeck (To a God Unknown). Sensing it dimly in Conrad's "Youth," I had also the feeling that in "Heart of Darkness" some great thing nearly broke through the surface. In Kipling's "Without Benefit of Clergy," they knew that glory above the commonplace, although probably not conscious of the knowledge. Pegeen found for her own "The Playboy of the Western World" and then bitterly lost that "vision that fools him out of his limits," but both must remember all their lives what Emerson calls the "depth in those brief moments which constrains us to ascribe more reality to them than to all other experiences." The son and the daughter, possibly even the mother, in "Riders to the Sea" were integral with that thing. Lacking deep consciousness and adequate articulateness, they couldn't know it, although they *were* it. Even Synge himself may not have realized it consciously; nevertheless, he has them speaking out of it.

But in some of Jeffer's poems, the thing is stated clearly, with full conscious recognition, and with that exact economy of words which we associate with scientific statements:

> "Humanity is the mold to break away from, the crust to break through, the
>   coal to break into fire, . . .
> The atom to be split.
> Tragedy that breaks a man's face and a white
>   fire flies out of it; vision that fools him
> Out of his limits, desire that fools him out of his limits,
> . . . .
> These break, these pierce, these deify . . . ."

(from "Roan Stallion")

and again:

> " . . . discovery's
> The way to walk in. Only remains to invent a language to tell it.
> Match ends of burnt experience
> Human enough to be understood, . . .
>   . . . feed on peace
> While the crust holds: to each of you at length a little
> Desolation; a pinch of lust or a drop of terror:
> Then the lions hunt in the brains of the dying: storm is good, storm is good,
>   good creature,
> Kind violence, throbbing throat aches with pity."

(Prelude to "The Woman at Point Sur")

No one before, to my knowledge, at least no Westerner other than some such mystic as Blake, ever announced that particular theme so boldly, or entered into the use of that motif with such full consciousness. With reference to this trait, it is as though in the others, Emerson and Whitman and Nietzsche, we have been hearing the build-up as of a Brahm's First, and now suddenly, as in the Third Movement, here it is—announced simply, but with no screen of subtlety or reticence. All along, we have been hearing that coming echo. The memory of the music bears its clarifying expression as a natural sequence. And as a result of the explicit statement in Jeffer's early poems, I have come to call this thing "breaking through," and to regard the cognitive considerations of it as "the philosophy of breaking through."

These ideas use words only as a vehicle. But however unsuited to word expression, such a thing objectively seems to exist, even collectively, and it characterizes, is influenced by and influences or at least indexes a trend reflected philosophically in holism—that the whole is more than the sum of its parts; that the integration or relation of the parts is other than the separate sum of the parts. Recently, I have been inclining toward the belief that the conscious recognition of this "breaking through" quality may be an essential of modern soul movements, and that the degree of its recognition comprises an earmark of whatever abiding quality modern (particularly non-abstract) art may possess: not dirt for dirt's sake, or grief merely for the sake of grief, but dirt and grief wholly accepted if necessary as struggle vehicles of an emergent joy—achieving things which are not transient by means of things which are.

III

I have been reviewing this situation also with reference to world movements in labor and in the class struggle, in economics, in science, as well as in personality problems—subjects as charged now with life as a religion used to be. Consider, for instance, the wisdom of a point blank refusal to arbitrate for the sake of arbitration in labor difficulties, insofar as arbitration represents a "milk and water" attitude, which it often does. Depending of course somewhat on motive, the refusal symbolizes wholeness, unity, the strong man unafraid in action; the other, humanism in its selectic and necessarily divided aspects, with the inevitable concessions. Then consider the meeting of honest representatives of both sides, neither willing to sell out, neither willing to concede, but both open-mindedly honest. Both will get to know each other; they will surely respect each other for those qualities, at least. They will learn new things, especially inwardly where strength and origins lie; to some degree at least, they will achieve the light of appreciating each other's problems, no small step in itself. So proceeding, they *may* automatically break through into a new whole, not composed of concessions, but built in a rooty sense on a deep and sympathetic understanding of both sides. Starting only with honesty and a determination to avoid concession and compromise, the deep understanding may come over them "as the wind bloweth," as the miner's wife achieved the new thing, as the boy in Chicago slums got a glimpse of the all-love that makes distant things kin, as the good wife and husband together work miracles greater than the sum of their separate wisdoms and possibilities. There may have been originally not even the intention of settlement—that would amount to bias. They may have had only the feeling that here was something worth fighting for, and that the battle was noble and just. But so long as there was equally no biased intent *against* settlement, the new thing might arise. The steps would be something like this:

(a) The agony of an intolerable situation;   . . . trouble

(b) A brave and non-conceding attitude on   . . . discussion,
both sides in facing, even embracing   rather than the
it, and in honestly presenting the   angry argumentation
main theses, however controversial;   which indicates bias

(c) The new situation, accompanied by   . . . the possible
joy, or at least by the release of   solution
energy formerly tied up;

Struggle, especially, seems to be a necessary prerequisite of the beyond quality and the greater the struggle, the greater the possible breaking through. That phase, at least, was recognized in early times: Socrates (Plato: Theaetetus) speaks of the labor pains of his midwifery. These pains, moreover, may be so patently devastating that the average observer in his natural concern with the more obvious aspects may overlook the emergent issue entirely, especially if, once the *Sturm und Drang* has passed, it should be announced without fanfare. So the indictments: "There's only horror and degradation in so-and-so's works," "nothing but coldness and destruction," or, at best, "I sense dimly something beyond the obvious evil picture." This was said of Nietzsche and Wagner, in the past, later of D. H. Lawrence, then of Stravinsky and T. E. Lawrence, now of Hemingway, Farrell, Steinbeck, Javlensky, George Grosz. And, in this light, Jeffers is seen to emerge as quite other than severe and difficult, pessimistic in thought and treatment, as often portrayed still, although less now than formerly. But of his many readers, even today, how few glimpse the "white fire" through and beyond the tragedy with which they are chiefly engrossed! In justice, that grief should be recognized as merely a vehicle (however necessary), incident to the rare breakings through. Or to the more frequent regressions in those who fall by the wayside, tested beyond their strength: "many are called but few are chosen."

Although it will be granted that intense struggle is one of the commonest concommitants to a great emergent, the presence of the former is no invariable index of the latter. Where there is refusal to accept the hazards of grief and tragedy, as occurs more frequently than not, I should expect to see the struggle belittle, rather than deify, since whatever *is* has to be taken and accepted in order for development to proceed. Discrimination and will provide means of determining whether a thing is inevitable or not, and of accepting it if it is; but once it has been determined to be inevitable, only evasion would tend to project it vicariously, thus refusing to face it. Projected grief or trouble obviously isn't accepted, and certainly isn't embraced, and the issue not clearly defined and faced cannot ever give over to the vigor of living growth. It exists then merely as a block on the horizon, an unresolved problem that contaminates what it touches.

The struggle is between opposing forces, each honest in its own right and without evasion, but limited in scope or vision. Obviously, any conflict is evidence of error on both sides because, due to the catholic nature of truth, there can be no conflict if either achieves this illumination, the illumination itself being the "answer." Between error and error, there is conflict; between truth and error, none—plenty of work in ironing things out and lining them up in the new light, but no real conflict. All-embracing truth includes all apropos reality, and an error stated, even believed in, is a relatively real thing. Thus, in conflicts, the least speck of truth comprises the start of the new thing, the emergent. Honestly pursued and developed, it may resolve into one flowing line all former conflict with reference to that particular set of relations. The happy mother, for instance, doesn't dislike to change her baby's diapers, because "they're his, and he's sweet," although the same woman may object strongly to cleaning up the cat's mess, which is objectively no worse. The intuitive understanding implied in her reason exists on a level above any conflict into which the less happy or less wise parent may get involved.

The common conflicts are between individual and society, persona and anima. Such challenges, honestly met, may give over into the new thing. Confused, not recognized honestly, or pushed aside, they result invariably in stalemate. Recognized and accomplished, the result is symbolized by the loving tolerance of the parent for his child's foibles (sometimes the other way around: our children may be lovingly tolerant of us, they aren't fooled!); by the gentleness of some doctors who understand their parents far more deeply than in a merely physical sense; best of all by the dear insight through which the good wife understands the shortcomings of her husband. She doesn't blind herself to them or refuse to face them, no one knows them more clearly than she and, because of that clear knowledge, none can help and love more than she.

Examples of this duality and trinity are many and traditional. A concommitant of haphazard growth without conscious consideration for other possibly conflicting growths, the duality is literally everywhere. Less frequent, the unexpected or at least previously unknown solution through the new thing completes the trinity. The new whole is built on the old opposites, without concession, through "magic" growth; the third person partakes of the others only in a rooty sense—obviously a function of conscious and disciplined work, which is less common than happenstance.

Possibly the most obvious example is embodied in a trite and somewhat sentimental poem of Kipling's which I dislike quoting here, but which is, after all, an excellent example of what has been discussed. Observer A remarks: "Well, you know I always say, with Kipling, who certainly knew, about these hybrid marriages, 'East is east and west is west and never the twain shall meet'." Mr. B., who is less superficial, corrects him: "There is more to it than that, a larger view which almost contradicts your statement, and it is said further along in the same poem by the very man you quote: 'But there is *neither* east nor west, border, breed *nor* birth, when two strong men stand face to face, though they come from the ends of the earth'." The statement "there is neither"—there isn't such a thing, there is none—implies that there *is* however something "beyond," which he neither names nor specifies. To digress a moment, that idea sums up very well the negation aspects ("night," "death," "quiet") which in mysticism are so often considered quietistic by laymen. Those symbols are merely ways of indicating the deep thing, the path of no path (*vide* Lao Tsu, Tao Te Ching, No. 14) which is and must be nameless. It cannot be said. It can be hinted, conveyed, symbolized, but never explicitized, else it ceases to be itself and you have to go on from that new step, seeking it again. See also Jeffer's "Night," Novalis' "Hymns to the Night," Whitman's figure of death in "Out of the Cradle" and "When lilacs last in the dooryard bloom'd," and Francis Thompson's "Their sound is but their stir, they speak in silences."

The traditional religious concept of father, son and holy ghost is another example of this trinity, but one which is no longer living and which is therefore rarely understood. The following, although possibly a trifle obscure, are more apropos to these times:

(1) environment and times (2) a leader: the cause
(1) water (2) waves: the sea
In literature: (1) tradition (2) desire: The Roan Stallion
In medicine and in human relations:
(1) hyperthyroidism (2) neurosis: irritability
(1) tenderness (2) technique: sexual relations in marriage
In modern physics of light:
(1) particle (2) wave: The Fitzgerald contraction to zero dimension in the direction of travel and the expansion to infinite mass at the speed of light, as in the photo-electric effect

The solution doesn't always come—statistically, its appearance is actually rare; the struggle may be so intense as to result in failure and regression. But it never comes without birth struggle, and its most common vehicle is something with which we have association of fear or evil. Less commonly, it may derive through the embracing of joy, as in love affairs, works of art, but even these involve a struggle, the severity of which is directly proportional to the intensity and newness of joy. So there is the familiar legend of the distressed medieval woman who, forced to embrace a dragon, finds it changed to an attractive young knight. And so Shelley significantly remarks: "welcome joy and welcome sorrow." Thus relative to this quality, there is not only the necessity for struggle, but an equal necessity for accepting it when, but only when, it arises inevitably in the natural flow of events. The successful person [1] welcomes the struggle as a vehicle. The foetus wins through to birth. The child plays at being a man, finally achieves manhood actually after many struggles, and despite regressive tendencies so common as to be universal, such as the wish to remain a child (a temptation strong enough to cause stasis however only in psychopathic conditions). Greater struggles are met with increased growth, up to the greatest test possible in this physical life, the one from which in due course no successful person shrinks. And Bach sings "Komm süsser Tod" so that my daughter used to say "Daddy, that doesn't sound to me like death." Nor to me. More like "Tod und Verklärung," I think.

And there is further not only the necessity for struggle and for eager acceptance, but there is deep wisdom in not seeking the test, actually in avoiding it except where inevitable. Grief or love aren't to be brought on, they're to be taken when they come. No one can make the wind blow; the wise person will realize it must blow sooner or later of its own accord, and will be correspondingly prepared. It will come inevitably in its time, "feed on peace while the crust holds." Maeterlinck remarks somewhat flowerily (Wisdom and Destiny): "Let us wait till the hour of sacrifice sounds; till then, each man to his work. The hour will sound at last; but let us not waste all our time seeking it on the dial of life," following apropos preceding considerations. I am reminded also of Hemingway's remarks (Esquire, April 1936) on the eventual certainty of danger at sea in offshore fishing, and on the wisdom of attempts on the part of even the most adventurous sportsmen toward avoiding rather than rushing into it deliberately. Sacrifice or emergency inspire one almost magically, in fact they are lucky who are so exposed—it's the deadly desultory which makes demands of courage—but deliberately to seek unnecessary struggle is another subtle evasion, cutting into the living body of time. As a hypothetical example, suppose a very intellectual but unbalanced youth, who had led a cloistered life, were to determine by scrupulous observation that maturity and charactral integration followed only in the path of pain and struggle, were to say, "Well, what I need is pain," and were to put his hand deliberately into a flame. The unlikely maturity achieved that way would be ridiculously roundabout, might easily defeat its own purpose. The time must come inevitably, and frequently to people who live amply, when the great gift of sacrifice cannot honestly be withheld, and parallelically, when the struggle must be met, at which time the resources of strength and growth which may have been developed during the more quiet times of acquiring or enjoying can be drawn upon.

Note in this connection also the often-mentioned correlation between physical insecurity and the flowering of painting before and during the Renaissance. Plague during that time was no respecter of persons, whole populations might be suddenly decimated by it. Machiavellism and wholesale graft such as I doubt if the world knows even in these times, also meant danger to non-expedient truth-seekers such as artists, scientists and thinkers. Yet Giotto, da Vinci, Michelangelo and Galileo, whose very lives must have been insecure to a degree we can scarcely conceive, tower as giants clear to this day.

From these and from other equally obvious considerations, it would seem that an insecurity, either outer or inner, may be actually an important motiva-

---

[1]The growing person; success as often used implies compromise to the point of smugness or stultification, mistaking the earmarks of success for success itself, as with material wealth, fame, or acquisitions in general. [E.F.R. note]

ting force for the significant-truth-seeker in any field, and that having accepted this insecurity to the point of achieving a "breaking through" even a few times, he is cast forever beyond continuous peace and rest as we ordinarily conceive the term. He cannot ever, except at recurrent necessary periods (comparable to sleep and repair in the physical realm) honestly enjoy any peace other than the active joy of effort, which is not only the antithesis of quietism but also the opposite of what we usually think of as rest and peace. That insecurity well may be only a symbol of the eternal struggle to which he is irrevocably pledged—pledged until he starts crystallizing or diminishing as a result of failing or evading one of the tests. [1]

Until then, he cannot ever know any peace other than that; he will always be working toward a clearer and larger merging with it.

IV

A

In the inward growth of an individual, it will be granted that integrity is the most important thing in the world. But there are levels and emergents even of integrity. There are, conceivably, individuals so integrated and great that they are willing to contribute that most priceless gift of all—integrity—to something "beyond." If their really-honest destiny lies that way, they must follow that star, however perilous, making sure only that that *is* in fact the only way. And the determination as to whether or not their destiny lies that way is a matter for their own deep and personal scrutiny, fraught more than is anything else in the world with the hazards of evasion, since there is the great difficulty of making sure that the very adventurousness or difficulties of martyrdom of that way isn't itself an evasion by which a personal neurosis is conciliated, rather than faced. The hairline is difficult. That "beyond" is nameless. No classifications mark or constrict it, nor can they do so, else it ceases to be itself. "The Tao that can be tao-ed can not be the ultimate Tao." (Goddard translation of Lao Tsu, p. 27).   Its most common vehicle is love, love of a cause, of people, of a person. And whether or not the greater integrity lies in saving or in giving up integrity or, in some remoteness not even glimpsed by the masses, depends on the "way" of the involved individual. This is free ground, beyond any rule, as the Lao Tsu statement emphasizes. And hence derives the correctness of the notion that no valid a priori ultimate-evaluation can be put on anything. It can only be said that, at a given time, this or that evaluation is "comparatively more ultimate" than others—a contradiction in terms—and that the human mind has a sense of truth which, although varying with the individual, seems to be cultivatable through vision and effort and honesty [2]—"the high and fine intuition of the wise"—and so can wisely be heeded in borderline cases. Suicide and masturbation are 99% evasion, but on some remote occasions, conceivably, they may be the very vehicles of salva-

---

[1]The logarithmic immanence of these tests is expressed by a drawing I recall—it may have been a mural or the reproduction of a mural in a life insurance lobby—wherein death shoots with increasing accuracy at people of increasing age. At the youth, he aims clumsily with a bow and arrow; the young man is only slightly threatened with an old-fashioned blunderbuss; the mature man with a shotgun. The elderly man must run the considerable hazard of being fired upon by a high-powered rifle. Finally, those who have come to senescence unscathed are slain unerringly with a machine gun. [E.F.R.]

[2]This word circled in typescript.

tion under a given set of circumstances hard to imagine, just as life and normal sexual relations may occasionally be "bad" as representing evasions.

Granting the validity of these considerations, it would appear that anyone who very honestly and fervently espouses *anything,* however erroneous, up to the limit of his ability and discrimination at the time, must live a life more full and more aware than the average. Even such a man as Clarence True Wilson, if as single-minded, if as willing as he seems to have been to do anything, even to sacrificing personal honor, to his supra-personal objective—the Anti Saloon League, must have had a singularly luminous life. He will have had the not inconsiderable joy of being "Dr. Wilson-right," although he may not have had the joy of being also "world-right" by being more nearly in line with the "absolute" truth.

If there is a growing antipathy toward humanism, as witnessed by the increase in totalitarian states, it may easily be accounted for. On the present majority level, the bland humanists have had their day, the time of eclecticism is past. We embrace now wholly, without reservation, and the belief that something else may be just as "good," or the suspicion that some part elsewhere may be even "better" is thought now, holistically, to amount only to bias, an inhibition that prevents the full light from entering.

B

In speaking of acquaintances, my wife and I once evolved a classification which seems to be widely valid. Children and probably peasants, maybe old-fashioned farmers and laborers also, are unawakened, unconscious, live unknowingly in the flow of life; *naive.* The much larger conscious group includes a huge *sophisticated* majority either seeking, puzzled, bitter, or resigned; and a small *mellow* minority who, usually later in life, are luminously adjusted to their lot, whatever it may be. Although development may stop anyway, these three growth stages provide a normal progression. In occasional naturally wise people (these are rare), the mellow seems to proceed directly from the naive. Usually, however, there is a time of intervening struggle, with search, bitterness or bewilderment. The path to home is difficult. Once away in the first place (and the adolescent must have the experience of leaving home), the way back is long and uncertain, but the journey deeply enriches the recovered home to those who achieve it. This applies not only to the large pattern of lives, but to separate specific problems, such for instance as the brotherhood of man, now to some extent re-living in the hearts of occasional sincere communists. And in the religious belief situation, the pattern is similar. There is the original naive, child-like or savage belief in a personal diety. This is ordinarily followed, soon after the function of intellectual cognition develops and is put honestly to work on the problem, by a period of loss, bitterness, and atheistic insistence: the sophisticated stage. Then, by breaking through as a result of acceptance of struggle with its challenge of work in attempting a deeper understanding, some feeling for the symbolism of religion, knowledge of the "deep thing beyond the name," of "magic" and of the "dog within," ultimately may illuminate the whole scene. The attempt toward conscious understanding of what formerly was accepted naively and as a matter of traditional course, apparently imposes a struggle from which only the breakers-through emerge into the mellow group.

C

I am recalling how interestingly all this is tied up with the religious ideas of the trinity, with the old sturdy ideas of Hegel, and with the new ideas of holism and of the ecologists and the Jungians and the mathematical physicists: the issue of the union of two struggling opposites, each honest in its own right but in scope limited, as a "new thing" which completely transcends the old, which is part of it in a rooty sense only; which uses the old forms of duality —form and function, matter and energy, material and spiritual—only as emergence vehicles toward an integrated growth. Beyond the naive man, Adam in the garden; beyond the sophisticated one, the apple eaten, by strife driven from the Garden; there is the yet greater possible heaven of gain or probable hell of loss. —The crust broken through, the mellow man, Krishnamurti's awareness, Neitzsche's superman, Jung's individuation. —None entirely possible on this earth, where perfection exists only symbolically in man's mind, but is often glimpsed hearteningly. As though there were a forced tropism toward a decision which, in terms of religious symbology, either achieves the grace, not of the father, not of the son, but of the holy ghost, or else descends into utter oblivion.

IIE. A Spiritual Morphology of Poetry[1]

I

This near contradiction in terms is as close as I have been able to come in working toward the one-phrase abstract which all good titles comprise.

Considered evaluations of the *spirit* of poetry are, so far as I know, entirely lacking—at least rare—although there have been many analyses of *form*. These terms may be contrasted as follows:

"spirit" is the difficult-to-define essence or breath, used in this case largely as a phase of content, and as opposed to the more physical aspects of "form." Verse form, style of presentation (ponderous, tender, facetious, etc.), diction, even the separate words themselves, are thought of merely as vehicles or as a vehicle, however lovely, of content. *What* is conveyed, relates to content: *how* it is conveyed, to form. Spirit content is similarly considered as something which motivates or enlightens a given work, or as the motivating aspect of that which is poured into a given vehicle. A related picture is suggested by the archaic Latin origins of the word "spirit," literally "a breath," so a form receives or is acted upon by a breath of life, the spirit.

Although *how* is commonly considered at the expense of *what*, poetic content as the expression of a metaphysical (more frequently implied than stated explicitly), seems to me one of the fine features of fine poetry. Content which is conceptually significant, or which transcends concept, may be unlovely in architecture and diction—although the converse is far more likely to be true. But usually, great rates great, and thought, moving "as the wind bloweth," more frequently is clothed well and carefully, even inspiredly. In any case, most of the examples chosen seem to me world-great both in form and spirit, and they usually, furthermore, either hint toward, or actually work out, definite symbolic or concrete thought patterns.

II

A

Since the emphasis is on content, *form*, as comprising the following, will be considered only in outline:

A. Architecture—the structural pattern by which the work is built. In any consideration of work as a whole, the architectural plan necessarily is intricately interwoven with content also, as the purpose for which the building is intended, for instance, but ideas relating to style, and words such as "sonnet," "epic," "lyric," etc., suggest a superficial architecture of form.

B. Diction—the choice of words and the manner of putting them together.

C. Beat—conventional rhythm where present (many studies of poetry are devoted exclusively to this), or the subtle beat of Whitman.

D. Rhyme, if present.

E. Alliteration, if present—the sound alliteration of Poe, etc. Alliteration of Hebrew poetry is partly at least one of content.

Non-western poetry may have additional qualities, such as the Chinese tonal

[1]This draft typed July 1939.

Ed's library at the lab.

patterns (see p. 223, Vol. 6, Ency. Britt., XIII Ed., for scansion diagram which can be intoned wordlessly with no knowledge of Chinese), their probably automatic and half-conscious analysis of the pictograph origins of the written characters, even when the poem is read aloud, and their alliterative pattern whereby corresponding words in consecutive lines have related meanings, as in the following modification of an example quoted by Giles (op. cit., p. 222):

> Bright sun completes-course behind mountains
> Yellow river flows-away into sea

The remote but compelling qualities of *content* can be considered analytically most easily by reference to architecture. Consider, for instance, the inward crescendos and climaxes experienced by the sensitive reader in poems such as Francis Thomson's "Hound of Heaven," with the climax-thunder of such lines as "That Voice is round me like a bursting sea."

There are inner coherences both of feeling and of thought content which lead the reader quickly into deep participation, although this is more apt to occur in connection with sudden vignettes such as the wen-han-ch'u example quoted further along. Not easy to indicate here, I find Chinese poetry full of such subtle frameworks. The poem at first may seem to consist only of disconnected scenes, however gemlike, but, with deeper familiarity, it falls suddenly into coherence, "flowing as water, blowing as on the wind" (p. 20, Ayscough, Tu Fu, Houghton-Mifflin, n.d.), the integrating wind of spirit comparable, in tying together these apparently unrelated pictures, to the flow of water in a varying stream bed, with sand, weeds, riffles and fallen leaves all streaming away in conformity to the current, or to the wind that patterns a blustery day. The following probably inadequate translation from Book of Odes compiled 2500 years ago by Confucius from poems then already old, achieves a holistic tenderness sounded inevitably by that striking last line:

> "The morning glory climbs above my head,
> Pale flowers of white and purple, blue and red.
> I am disquieted.
>
> Down in the withered grasses something stirred;
> I thought it was his footfall that I heard.
> Then a grasshopper chirred.
>
> I climbed the hill just as the new moon showed.
> I saw him coming on the southern road.
> My heart lays down its load."

> (Helen Waddell)

Reading this, I feel tenderly related to some un-named, half-articulated girl back in the remote past, glad that she felt finally at home that night so long ago, and happy that her resolved loneliness should be inspiring still unimpededly through all these years; all physical traces gone even of the town she lived in, only that memory of beauty remaining. That deep thing, nameless, is near immortality, it passes outside of time, into another culture, race and language.

The best example I can recall immediately of a picture that induces participation is from a Tu Fu poem (literal translation by Ayscough, op. cit., p. 74-5) of which she says: "The three characters in line eleven -*wen*, to hear; *han*, cold; *ch'u*, a baton—which in translation I have been obliged to expand—are often used in conjunction and convey, to the Chinese reader, a perfectly definite autumnal picture: the picture of women by a stream, in their hands batons rather like those our policemen use, and folded on stones before them, thick cotton clothing, which, in preparation for winter use, they beat and rinse, rinse and beat again." In order to render even partially this content, and to carry the picture, Ayscough transposes the position of *han* and *ch'u*, and translates the three characters:

wen (hear)   *ch'u* (baton)   *han* (cold)
Hear   pounding   of cold weather garments beaten and rinsed.

Now imagine the wealth conveyed in this poem (all of which should be read in this connection), by those three monosyllabic characters. Sensitive Chinese natives reading this anywhere anytime would be led at once into deep participation in this picture: two good friends, waiting for audience in the courtyard of the official who is to decide their separation-destiny, hearing from the near stream a sound that for generations has meant the coming of winter and the corresponding cessation of travel by which separated friends might communicate by visits or even by letters.

There are other occasional or almost inscrutable qualities, possibly more imagined than real, such as the quality which I have been thinking of as an "echo," which follows certain lines. In reading the next to the last stanza of Keats' "Ode to a Nightingale," I fancy it can be heard in the pause which, for this purpose, should follow:

"... when, sick for home,
she stood in tears amid the alien corn."

The next lines, read too quickly, shatter this "spiritual echo." There are other examples: in the last stanza of Whitman's "Song of the Open Road." To my ear, this sounds still more strongly at the end of "Once I pass'd through a populous city," and I was interested later to discover in this connection (Halloway, Whitman, Knopf, 1926, p. 66) that the poem originally included two additional terminal lines since deleted by the author, which to some extent carry the music which I fancied could be heard echoing. But perhaps most obviously of all, it may be heard throughout, and especially after the last line, of Shelley's "Music when soft voices die," which exactly describes the situation in so many words.

There may be still another, the most subtle of all content-phrases, which I cannot be sure is real; it may be subjective projection. In occasional mediocre or even inadequate poems, I have sometimes supposed that I was sensing or hearing the movement which the author tried unsuccessfully to reveal. I feel it surging up in memory, and needing such expression as one gets by reading over haunting lines. But when I look up the verses to which the feeling apparently relates, they seem not satisfying; it just isn't said right. I have wondered if it may not be that I was feeling the very *Anlage* which the poet sensed but expressed inadequately, and which of course I, however reactivated I may be by it, cannot express at all except through reading lines which fail to carry it other than hintedly.

III

However, most of the significant qualities which come under content are related to what I have been considering as a *spiritual morphology,* thought to embrace four possible *growth stages.*

A

The first step is expressed by *naive* poets, and in its most primitive phase extols pastoral beauty. Their poetry involves a simple and fresh statement of the joy of existence, in the love of landscape, God, home, wife, country, friend; extols some quality such as courage; praises or supplicates for help in inward crisis, some loved object. Figuratively, they derive through the Garden of Eden before consciousness wells up over the threshold in the guise of eating the apple. Their only philosophy is the unconscious one embodied in expressions of joy; their only consciousness is in the joy of singing. These poets unreasoningly know that this thing or that thing is "right," the "good" is right. There's no question, no thought of doubt; the separateness of "right" and "wrong" is axiomatic.

Most western poetry falls in this group, all the pastorals, prayers, hymns, love songs, songs of patriotism or heroism, drinking songs, most of the ballads and simple tales. The following poems seem to me to be good examples. They are incidentally superb poems, whoever reads them again will be repaid amply, however worn they seem at first thought; I have just re-read them with the original moving beauty enhanced by my own intervening years; as a propos subject matter, I wish they could be included in full:

Marlowe: "The Passionate Shepherd." Pastoral, love.
Shakespeare: "Shall I compare thee to a summer's day." Love.
Johnson: "Drink to me only with thine eyes." Chivalry, love.
Blake: "To spring." Pastoral.
Wordsworth: "Earth has not anything to show more fair." Pastoral.
Keats: "St. Agnes."
Shelley: "Tonight." Nostalgic pastoral.
Cardinal Newman: "Lead, kindly light." Prayer.
Yeats: "The lake isle of Innisfree." Nostalgic pastoral.
Stephens: "Deirdre." Nostalgia for another time.

and many poems quoted elsewhere in this consideration: even the beauty *of* sorrow (not the beauty *through* sorrow) is treated poignantly in Lamb's "The old familiar faces," and *of* (not *through*) brave acceptance, in Douglas Hyde's translation of "I am Raferty."

Beyond simple eulogy, and above the more descriptive statement of joy, many of the quoted examples furthermore achieve an *emergent*[1] of thought or feeling quite different from the lessons which the less significant poets are always drawing from their subject matter. In this connection, compare the slightly inane moral of the elsewhere moving "To a waterfowl" of Bryant, with the truly emergent last lines of Keats' "Ode on a Grecian urn." Milton's sonnet "On his blindness" transcends in such a way its significance deriving not through complaint, but from an acceptance of facts as they are. And Tennyson's "Ulysses," possibly his best lyric, ascends toward something "not unbecoming men who strove with gods."

To the typical poet of this category, all loved things are beautiful (but uncritically so), even the sadness of nostalgia; he has no need of offering anything in the way of remedy or suggestion, his honest expression is to extol. He doesn't know about clay feet; the bitterness of grief isn't a subject for his poetry—the beauty *of* grief, possibly, but not ever the beauty *through* grief.

[1]Joe [Campbell] suggests "discuss emergent. This is an important element in your thesis, and the reader should not be left to work out the meaning for himself." [E.F.R.]

The more *sophisticated* poets—Matthew Arnold, Swinburne, Baudelaire, etc.—are on the contrary conscious particularly of the clay feet, and each reacts characteristically with honest expressions of regret, resignation, repudiation or substitution. Sensitive men of wide perceptive and intellectual ability, they can see only grief, failure, or evasion, in all situations to which they apply their best functions. Lacking the dogmatic clarity of the naive person who can accept unthinkingly the tradition to which he is born and for whom, therefore, the difficulty doesn't exist, they are much confused by the problem of right and wrong. In their experience, unmitigated joy is possible only to souls unconscious. But *they* have eaten the apple, and the flaming sword has driven them out—so recently that they can consider nothing beyond the lost pleasures of the garden.

Examples of this are common among the more searching poetic intellects of Victorian times, but Keats, many years before, complains magnificently in the "Ode to a nightingale". Arnold, despite occasional suggested palliatives, examines and finds wanting incident after incident:

> "And they see, for a moment,
> Stretching out like the desert
> In its weary and unprofitable length,
> Their faded ignoble lives."

(Youth of Man)

reacting often with the calm and lovely submission of a really great character faced with inevitable tragedy, but sometimes with world [sorrow] and not ignoble repudiation as in "Dover Beach." Heine is filled with a gentle feeling of failure, expressed over and over again in his short lyrics. Baudelaire and Poe often embrace the very terriblenesses they protest. Another group insists on the substitution of a romantic and untried pattern: the fairy realm of Yeats' "Land of Heart's Desire" and to some extent of Tennyson's "Idylls of the King"; Swinburne's mythology and anti-Christianity; Arnold's classicism. But all are united in realizing and bewailing the ubiquitous clay feet.

B

These poets are minutely conscious in an individual sense, they are however still not conscious of the blinding beauty of possible succeeding stages, although they catch glimpses. Swinburne alone occasionally comes through this test of fire, as will be considered later. Even stricken Arnold, in the rather spotty "Youth of Man," hints that:

> ". . . fruit
> Grows from sorrow such as theirs."

But on the whole, their only apperception of anything beyond what the naive poets see is in a negative sense. The naive understandings are their postulates —the things that "set them off" on their journey of frustration.

The scarcity of fine poets in this stage may be attributed to its crucial and transitory character. Most of the truly great men who achieve the need for critical introspection either cannot pass the test, and so are destroyed by it without having created any lasting expression, or go through it to come out on the other side with Whitman and to some extent Jeffers—since the assimilation of all experience, however bitter, bears fruit which expresses every significant trait of the sufferer, now illuminated.

In any case, these poets know only that "it's all wrong," although they have nothing to offer beyond romantic substitutions which seem to me fundamentally evasive. Nevertheless, as honest and articulate artists needing expression, they must state their convictions in the form of honest regrets or complaints.

C

Through *specific vehicles* of pain and tragedy, a comparatively few *mellow* poets, also banished from the garden, but by now acclimated to their lot, catch glimpses of a new promised land, a heaven far greater than the Eden which is all its inhabitants can know.

In their heightened consciousness, the realization of a "beyond" quality has arisen particularly through the assimilation of the very clay feet of bitter grief, war, and death, which the sophisticated poets excoriated or morbidly embraced. Their "right" derives chiefly through what is conventionally "wrong"; they have gone through the "right-wrong" confusion of the sophisticated level and have come to accept as holy the very traits rejected by tradition—the stone which the builders refuse thus has become in such a way the cornerstone of the new structure. As indicated in a previous essay, it seems to be easier for individuals to achieve toward "The Tower beyond Tragedy" under the sting of grief, than in the ordinary placid course of life. Primitive people know this out of unconscious knowledge and accept freely whatever "is"; folklore has its proverbs referring to the essentiality of the test of fire.

Poets in this group are led (sometimes falling over themselves awkwardly, in the zeal of their discovery) to extol the traditionally terrible "come sweet death" vehicle, as in Whitman's "Out of the cradle endlessly rocking," and "When lilacs last in the dooryard bloom'd." Jeffers pays homage symbolically to silence and darkness in "Night," and entirely relinquishes human life at its oridinary level, in his explicit statement starting "What is humanity in this cosmos" (Roan Stallion), but in favor of a very real although undefinable "beyond" quality, as contrasted to the romantic substitutions of the sophisticated group. Swinburne, although rarely belonging here, seems to get through pretty definitely in Hertha, and comes very close in the "Hymn to Proserpine." I suspect Baudelaire of having occasionally glimpsed this place, but he makes few entirely conscious statements, and one can only infer it from such lines as:

"...Always, behind the tedium
Of finite semblances, beyond the accustomed zone
Of time and space, I see distinctly another world—"

(p. 71, Dillon-Millay transl.)

"Thou who upon the scaffold dost give that calm and proud
Demeanour to the felon, which condemns the crowd,"

(p. 117, do)

"... Harlots and
Hunted have pleasures of their own to give,
The vulgar herd can never understand."

(Epilogue, transl. Arthur Symons)

Most Chinese poetry speaks from this plane—the enforced separation of friends being the common vehicle (Li Po, Tu Fu, and some of the older poets in translations of Waley, Lowell-Ayscough, Hart, Obata, Ezra Pound and Powys Mather). The theme of a most deep sexual love, heightened by separation and imminent death, of the Sanskrit "Black Marigolds," is a fine example not well known, actually one of the greatest poetic expressions, even in translation, that I have ever encountered. But, most consciously of all, Jeffers expresses it again and again in the "humanity is the start of the race" theme of "Roan Stallion" and "The Women at Point Sur," and as symbolized in the flight of the eagle in "Cawdor."

The typical poet of this group extols ugliness, tragedy, even the clay feet, not for themselves, but because they are vehicles of that beyond quality, the significance of which they have come to realize, but which Jeffers alone specifically mentions as such. These poets "know it's wrong," but they *have* something to offer and, although they may be unable to state what it is, even at their best (maybe no one can express this conceptually or articulately), it's just "beyond."

D

The *all-vehicle mellow* poet, not yet emerged at least in this culture, would be in, and speaking out of, the heaven glimpsed by his predecessors, the heaven-beyond-the-world-beyond-the-garden. No great poetic mind has yet spoken from this plane, partly because of the elimination barriers ("Many are called but few are chosen"), which weed out great percentages at each progress step, and chiefly at this greatest-of-all-steps, because of inherent difficulties. Because of the barriers which for instance no one, without being in it at the moment, could write, except inferentially and through recognition of which makes men leave what they have, to go searching on,—through tragedy or death, whatever vehicle it occupies for them— which may induce them to repudiate all life for what is beyond life, will be seen to be *equally everywhere*. That quality will sound in their quickened ears with "the quietness of thunder" from their starting point, the very place they left to start out on the search, at "the start of the race," as well as at the goal. "I am he whom thou seekest" (Francis Thompson). "When me they fly, I am the wings; I am the doubter and the doubt" (Emerson, Brahma). "Man, equal and one with me, man that is made of me, man that is I." (Swinburne).

As a side glance: repudiation actually hurts one's relation to the thing in favor of which the repudiation is made. "Thou dravest love from thee, who dravest me" (Thompson). Compare, for instance, these two attitudes: discovering the inadequacy and error of childish fancies and hence repudiating and discarding them with the feeling that one has been "taken in," as against making all that (lovely) childhood belief the foundation on which a still more sturdy structure is erected. As also: one loves war not as war, but as a concomitant of people and of one's self (as soiled diapers are concomitants of infants) and as a vehicle for breaking through if that may be; who hates war furthers its cause, since it works through individual hate as an expression of the collective hatred which characterizes all wars; if hatred isn't present or cannot be manufactured, there can be no war worthy of the name.

". . . the darkness of the cave itself turns into enlightenment when a torch of spiritual insight burns. It is not that a thing called darkness is first taken out and another thing known by the name of enlightenment is carried in later, but that enlightenment and darkness are substantially one and the same thing from the very beginning, the change from one to the other has taken place only inwardly or subjectively." (p. 13, Suzuki, Essays in Zen Buddhism, First Series). There is another concise statement from the same source: "Before a man studies Zen, to him mountains are mountains, and waters are waters; after he gets an insight into the truth of Zen through the instruction of a good master, mountains to him are not mountains and waters are not waters; but after this, when he attains to the abode of bliss, mountains are once more mountains and waters are waters." (ibid., p. 12).

Although no great poet has yet stated this clearly and consciously, there have been hints. Blake, rarely a great poet although frequently a great mystic, came near when he said, in "Visions of the Daughters of Albion," "All that lives is holy." He could have said, more deeply, "All that *is*, is holy." Whitman trembled on the brink when he said, "Taking *all* hints to use them, but swiftly leaping beyond them" ("Out of the Cradle"), and Whitman is a very great poet. But consider most of all Jeffer's "Signpost," the most conscious statement I know of yet from this emergent country:

> ". . . At length
> You will look back along the stars' rays and see that even
> The poor doll humanity has a place under heaven.
> . . . but now you are free, even to become human,
> But born of the rock and the air, not of a woman."

and compare with his previous "what is humanity in this cosmos" idea.

It can be said of the hypothetical poet in this class: he praises all things. These poets would know "it's right, it's alright": the "good," the "bad," whatever *is*. Whatever is necessary is *so*, so long only as it *is*, and that includes all things, even errors and illusions.

IV

Poetry is a discipline of sensitivity and articulateness, the necessary expression of which is a rhythmed diction. Since the fruits of deep participation are what we have come to expect of poets, inclusion in that society presupposes utter honesty in abandonment to their art in what they honestly sense. Poets of the type we have been considering are ready, and have the courage, to face with their utmost capacity whatever "is" (for *them*, and this of course includes any errors into which they may have been caught, until, if ever, they come clear). There can be no evasion, nothing can be held back. They must "go-along-with" whatever they discover, even if it leads through or to disappointment, despair, intellectual or emotional loneliness, social ostracism—unlikely contingencies, however, if they can achieve "world-rightness," the aim of all published work, while at the same time being true to themselves. And they must express whatever they find equally honestly, with whatever directness they can command.

Naive poets have only to work out their best possible statements of pure unconscious joy in extolling the particular vehicle—love, religious ecstacy, nostalgia, etc., which transported them over into their certainty of beauty. To them, there is no "tragedy", everything is "beauty", "right" is right. Those sophisticated have the sad task of expressing courageously the statement of regret, complaint, noble repudiation or submission which they consider necessary with reference to the clay feet they particularly find or espouse, sometimes suggesting a romantic substitution. To them, everything is "tragedy," there is no real beauty, "right" is surely wrong. But in these very clay feet, poets of the next emergent-plane find a vehicle to something "beyond."

They recognize and extol these often horrible things, but only as vehicles. But in doing so, they achieve a reputation for being gloomy or morbid psychopaths, muck rakers, evaders or quietists (which they are only insomuch as they fail in their work or in its expression), by readers who miss their deep message but who are open to their beauty of word and power of thought. To them, only "tragedy" is not tragedy, the only real beauty is in "tragedy," "wrong" is right. But to the fourth group, there is no "tragedy" at all; all is beauty, everything, including "wrong" and "right," is right. So that, finally, an idea not yet expressed in world-great poetry, the truly mellow ones must find that *all* things, "good" as well as "bad," are vehicles; coming back after long journeys, enriched and experienced, beyond Whitman's "All things please the soul, but these things please the soul well," past Blake's "All that lives is holy," to the "latter silences" of the second birth, all the former beauty still below, part of the rooty foundation on which they stand.

> "My robe is all worn out after so many year's usage,
> And parts of it in shreds loosely hanging have been
> blown away to the clouds."

IIF. Notes and Letters for an Essay on Nostalgia

Nostalgia—projection

(another example of the 5-year-old medieval boy looking at the castle)

When I remember a church cantata once I sung, as a child, I get a sense of haunting lovliness which it would be easy to tie up with the music. It was a good time in my life; I was very much ten-year-old in love with that good Ethel. The new snow was on the ground when I walked home with her; we dragged behind the others; doesn't matter what we said, perhaps nothing, maybe we just walked along silently in brilliance. But there aren't any words for what that was. It was a very *real* thing too. Now I tend to invest that thing in her, and more in the music. It was real enough, but it was *not* she, nor I. We only were cloaked with it (altho I know of course it came from us) but it was greater than we were, than we are even now. And particularly it wasn't the music. We merely invested the music with it. And I can bring that thing back faintly anytime, merely by remembering the tune. Actually the music was very second rate. In spite of the nostalgia I'm certain of that. And now I'm clear enough so that an outsider could belittle or even ridicule the music without bothering me. I know it's fit only for ridicule. But what we put in it was the real thing.

It's particularly fortunate for me that my wonderful glow got tied up with music so inconsequential. Think if that had been a Bach Cantata! I mightn't ever get clear. Now I have to face the fact that the important thing isn't the inconsequential music. What's important is what I projected into it.

Of course there's nothing wrong with the nostalgias themselves. They contribute richness and enjoyment. You can object only to the limitations related to them.

In the face of all this, you wonder how any new thing can arise at all. Some people have such a drive for truth, or such perfectionism, that they investigate new things in the face of nostalgia. These then, discovering a true thing in all their searchings, use that same drive to make it known. Then they shine so they attract disciples. Their sons anyway. And these are conditioned then so that their security and joy gets associated to the other thing, the new thing, and a cell is formed that spreads wherever they go, in turn associating other youngsters with the new thing.

To John Steinbeck
August 12, 1946

Dear Jn, I guess you'll have to bear with my tirade on use and nostalgia. A common word with you, one of the few who know its power.

But the turn of events of another sort got me to considering the relation of use and tradition. Only result being a sense of frustration. Allegedly, man is the only logical animal. His illogicality amazes me.

How could there be more illogicality. We can't buy bedsheets. Gradually we get used to sleeping on blankets. The manufacturer's strike is easy to understand. —But if it were a workers' strike that kept us sheetless, wouldn't the newspapers howl! —The amount of cotton needed for a two or three dollar sheet, dyed and designed and advertised as a swank woman's dress, brings $20 or $50 or $89.85. The people may not be served, but profits are!

But that's both understandable and logical actually. Right at the moment I'm frustrated by a pica which is both illogical and profit consuming. —A tribute to tradition only. Like our calendar, like our system of weights and measures.

I can't get forms printed up for accurate use with the typewriter. Along about the 5th or 6th inch, my typing comes halfway between the printed lines. The pica, the printer's unit, is just slightly less than 1/72nd of an inch, and hence incommeasurable with the inch which is the basis of typewriter line spacers. This has been going on officially since 1860, so long we've lost track of it. We don't even think of it anymore. We think of one in terms of another until we're brought up short by the incontrovertible fact, and I for one get a fine feeling of frustration out of it. The printer assures me that he'll adapt my printed form for use with the typewriter. Then he doesn't. He can't. Why didn't someone tell me this!

Why doesn't someone say to me right nowseehereeddiethis humanis prettysuch ofafoollogically. His profit system, eating itself, eventually deprives him of profits, even of the actual dollar profits. Power gets mixed into it. Or conservatism more often gets involved. And even profits aren't served!

The things that served our youth, our childhood, maybe even our infancy, are the really important things. Around these our most primitive nostalgic emotions get entangled. And so we want to preserve these things at any cost, not for the things themselves, but for the associated emotions. —Because in a certain day in the morning of my life everything was well with me. The straw roofed house and the castle in the distance and my flaxen haired mother throwing the slops out of the door get related to that wonderful feeling of security and well being we get when we're young. So when I grow up. I want my children to see that same castle on the hill. No one can talk me into any new fangled notion of hygiene. Or art. Or government. When I was seven years old, that sunny morning was so wonderful, that I will have it continue for my children and their children. And every change will be over my dead body. The noble says "These people don't want to change, they like to be serfs, and poor, and plague ridden and sometimes hungry." And he's quite right. With the blood of my daughter virgin no longer on his couch.

I can see that whole thing. A girl I know whose hair was so golden that she brought actually the outside sunlight into my alchemist's den when she brought in my lunch. She was laughing all the time. And I felt more confident than I've ever felt in this life. I was just on the verge of intellectual concepts. What I was doing with mercury and lead was only a fulcrum. But what made me confident was that I was skillful, I could swim and dance and use tools, make my own. And that girl laughing wonderfully. That was a long time ago. In a way it's a dream. It's as strong as the time Buxtehude came in here, an irascid old man, two hundred years and more out of his time, confused, irritable, fusty old clothes, everybody laughing at him, in all this stretch of mechanized canneries and impossible times, out of another language, and a German not even spoken any more recognizing only one thing. A phongr record of his chorale fantasy "how beautifully shines the morning star." Fabulous organ, he'd never heard such a thing, must be in the loud speaker. Stamping up and down. What a crazy business. I must have told you. Had me finally in a real sweat. I *had* to get that man to the Princeton University old-organ-replica. Right away. By plane. And I had to find not only some really proficient German scholar, but a scholar of 17th century German. I got to thinking of Blinks at HMS and then Van Niel. What a relief to run into Van Niel. Just from toying with the idea. Well you don't toy with an idea like that; it gets *you*.

Like where I got led by the idea of nostalgia. The world's most powerful motivation. It relates the thing not to its use, but to the powerful emotion, I guess of security, anyway of beauty, that goes with it. No one knows that. Well you know it. Thomas Wolfe certainly did. Power and profit and love and hate are the motivating forces. Who realizes the power of nostalgia. You can examine art, business as a system of power, government—especially government, religion. Science a hundred years from now. Right now its too vigorous, no one's powerful enough to hold it now to nostalgic dreaming. Or bureaucracy best of all. In any institution, socialist or profit making, no difference. At the base there's that great pyramid of the way things used to be. In the good days, the good old days. "These are the days of our youth, the days of our cominion. All the rest is a dream of death and a doubtful thing." And it's really true, that's the funny part of it. And I'm tied up to some curious vision of golden hair, though I don't like blonds particularly. Well what strong thing are you tied to mister j s beck, mister brook mister stone brook which I haven't seen for a long time.

Best thing I can do now is to go back to designing what can't be done; a printed form for the C Ids survey, a form accurately adapted to convenient use with the typewriter. You better wish me well because I sure as hell need it.

[The following pages were placed in a file with the foregoing letter, and were probably mailed to Steinbeck at or about the same time. Some of the writing is a reaction to the death of Ed's mother.]

Couple of things occur to me as interesting-amusing or both. The truck that people gather around them I suppose is their life in epitome. I was thinking about the confirmation and baptism certificates that mother carted around with her from Massachusetts to Wisconsin to Chicago to the Pacific Coast; the funny old greeting cards of 75 years ago. Mostly I got a fine nostalgia out of Frances report that at the bottom of mother's trunk there was the funny old fashioned voluminous dress, entirely hand made and so ruffled and hemstitched, in which I was baptized and I guess Frances and Thayer too. How terribly unfortunate that the generations are so discontinuous. That my children and Nancy Jane's (she's going to have a baby this month or next) couldn't be baptized in the same one. Like a Pope's mitre; how charged it becomes in time.

And another. Directly after mother was taken very sick, she wanted an Episcopal priest. Terribly unfortunate that a few months before this, the satyr in Rev. H. caught up with him again. He got to fooling around with little boys. The wicked old women, of the church that was founded by charitable Christ, turned on him viciously. As of course they would. The mothers would, understandably. But worse the old maids who had nothing to lose, but who were afraid of sex even in its normal expression. So out he went, an old and broken man without—now I suppose—even any money, and most of his Holland relatives dead or scattered. So that real friend of hers; as she still of his, wasn't there. Frances suggested Rev. Clay whom we all love and like. Mother was maybe a little out of her head then already. Or maybe more in it than she'd been ever before. So she said "But he has such a long face, I'd like someone more jolly. Can't we call someone who likes to kid." Already when they got someone she was out, but I suppose it did her as much or as little good one way as another. Consciousness isn't everything.

I really didn't have a bad time at all. I have enough training as a nurse—tho not complete and not very good—to have the MD's regard for a very sick per-

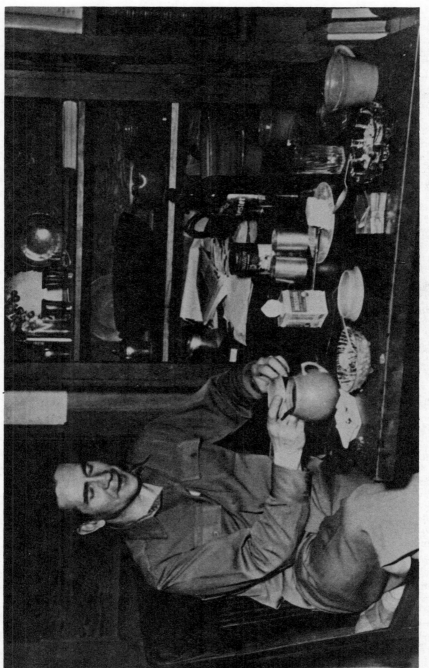

Ed at home.

son as someone to be worried on, like a specimen. Not at all lacking in love or consideration or even personal feeling, but just that notion of scientific doing-well-for. A deeply unconscious person is like an anaesthetized specimen. The things we know and like are mostly in abeyance.

Well, I never liked my parents too well. Now they're both gone I feel pretty much the same, but with regrets because I didn't. Not personal regrets. It's the pace we're moving at. The generations aren't connected and they can't be. But it's a pity. Both lose so much.

Frances sent over to me among other things an old writing desk that mother had ever since she was a child. Gosh how I lusted after it when I was 5 or 6; probably because she had so much affect charged into it. They certainly made things to last in those days. But now its only a vehicle for nostalgia. And to make me wonder what happened to all the potential of that undoubtedly potential woman. Probably beat out by reality on the middle level; now all tied up in that writing desk as mine is tied up in the ghosts of letters to Irene and Jean. That Ed is certainly a jazz specialist. Armstrong Mahogany Hall Stomp, Mezz Mezzrow, Jellyroll Morton, the Missourians, a fine bunch taken over long ago by Cab Calloway when he was good. Wonderful Duke Ellington still.

And a Chinese Idol I still like. But most of the folks things were gone, frittered away, broken, given away, thrown out by Frances when her different and then immature tastes took charge. Before they moved to the more fashionable apartment in Chgo, Frances had the junkman cart off—now in memory I bet she kicks herself—some commodes, tables, etc., of carved chestnut, marble tops, elaborately scrolled mirrors. Worth a lot now as antiques. I had the beautiful chest, I guess a highboy, that grandmother used as a curio cabinet. And I did too. Grandfather's sea chest; why I don't know; he never went to sea. I guess in those days it was a good thing to have a sea chest. All burnt. With so many things of my own, and with dagauretypes [sic] of both families. My mother was certainly good looking and feminine as a girl. I wonder what possibly could have happened to all those warm characters. Got beat out by her executiveness I suppose. By unrelaxed marriage. Probably all of us children were welcome, but I went my own solitary way not sensing it particularly and now I feel a little cutoff. Like Goethe in the Faust dedication all alone. Well of course that's it, isn't it, what you wrote about. That feeling of aloneness. Those feminine imprints are certainly put onto a person mighty young; no wonder I like gals with big eyes and thick lips. Everyone of course has to have a mother image to love. And if you don't particularly like your mother, poor woman what a fate for a woman, why then you're particularly lost. But I still wonder what happened to all that gorgeous potential. And because I think I can even work out in my own head and correctly what's wrong with the world, the how to cure it if I were God himself I wouldn't know, makes a person perhaps feel lonely too. What's wrong with the world is nostalgia conditioning that fears change, nationalism and its handmaid xenophobia and its father power-drive, the profit system and the propaganda and advertising of special interests that keep it in the saddle safe from change, the mechanical-ness, the engineeringness that rides us, plus the usual personal greed of black markets. Science is pure, but *unbalanced* by being engineer-driven. Unbalanced anyway. Religion is deadish or cultish or wishful. If science leads us where are we? And science leads us alright. That editorial of De Voto in the July 1946 Harper's Easy Chair is very very good. Maybe the best thing is to close the plant and go fishing. But I think perhaps that's been done too much by too many good people while the others build an empire on carelessness and uncitizenship and prejudice blown into intolerance. But who says what's wrong with the world is the avoided bringer of bad news. Bernard Shaw that ass to the contrary not withstanding. Still, he's an ass about only a few things. How he rides the antivaccination, anti-vivisection hobby horse. But also how he does look on the avoided minority side of almost every other question. Incidentally even you couldn't have done better with prejudice. First thing I know I'll be looking it up.

It's funny that your book will get into me though I don't know it; my nostalgia second hand into you. Norman Geschwind here has some good ideas, tho so mixed up as a person, such a curious sly arguer. Still he has a slight "ultimate reality" back in those ideas somewhere. And Jorgen Bering, for all his fascisms. So hard to talk to, so easy to fight with. People that give their life up to an idea that they're sure of. Is fine. And what's wrong with the world is of course what's wrong in epitome with every individual in it to some degree, mister "a" almost completely avoiding the pitfall which almost completely captures "b," and Lao Tse almost avoiding nearly every one of them. Ed Jr just came in here with an almost perfect negative of an isotherm chart that Hedgpeth drew for the (when?) new ed of BPT. I said "It's perfect" Ed said "Isn't it! But I'll get a better one!" Wotta guy.

To Toni Jackson
Feb. 4, 1948

Maybe a chance for that long letter I've been promising myself. And to answer in detail your several letters which I've replied to shortly.

Jn as always. He showed up here 4 PM Sunday after calling Saturday from LA in the expectation of getting here not until late the following evening. But there was an all night party, nite before, he was still a little high, we drank and talked until far into the night, and the following morning he waked up early and started to read. 5 hours sleep for two nights. And then the next night the same, and when I got up early to go to work who should be awake and coughing and smoking but that John. And the night following it was still later. Maybe in the long run I can keep up with him in drinking and unsleeping, but certainly not in any given short period. Now though he's slowing down to the business of seriously relaxing. . . . I have been out as much as possible because as soon as it got noised around that Jn was in town, working up for a movie etc., all the movie mad people of the region and all the celebrity hunters, not being able to find Jn, grabbed on to me. And I can stand just so much of that social extroversion. Jn himself for that matter can't. He poops out about the time I do. And Alice can stand less than any of us. So in spite of all the publicity we've managed a few completely quiet nights, and none with any strangers. Last night Jn came over alone for dinner, no one else showed up, we had a quiet evening of Jn reading, Alice playing the phonog and I working on ideas in my notebook. Of the very greatest things The Art of the Fugue, Don Giovanni, Goethe's Faust, the Beethoven quartette No. 16, and Finnegan's Wake. Now I know the Wake is the greatest book I've ever come in contact with, greater even than Faust & I got excited to the point of translating again the last few lines of the 2nd part.

And in that connection, do you have any recollections on my pretty German Faust—the one that Evelyn gave me. And on the MacI [MacIntyre] Faust—the one in English and German that I read you that pretty night so long ago? Been gone sometime. Has some of my own literal translatings in it. Last time I remember the MacI—or perhaps the both of them—was in connection with your talk in Carmel when that woman challenged you, and we dug out the MacI and some originals, worked out "calls a spade a spade" for the line "Wer darb das Kind beim rechten Namen nennen" and you wrote to the woman. Did you take the volumes to Crml, or perhaps leave them in a restaurant somewhere. Don't bother replying unless you recollect something. If no reply I'll assume there's no lead there.

So then anyway I considered those 5 great things, and several lesser. Don Giovanni, Contrapunctus XIX of Art of the Fugue, and the Beethoven late quartettes finally break, and go down into noble tragedy. The statue comes for Don Giovanni who fears for a moment, then recovers himself, carries on his magnificent evil, refuses to be saved by the prayers of Dona Elvira (is it?) and allows himself to be dragged down to hell. Contrapunctus XIX goes into that great thing which I think of as beyond life (and death), it speaks out of it, but no Bach could finish it, and he dies with it uncompleted on that magificent shrieking high note suddenly, as Biggs, bless his heart, plays it on the Harvard Baroque organ. The lesser Beethoven glimpses that beyond, he speaks out of it for a moment and dies. All of these show magnificent tragedy, but tragedy nevertheless. But then consider the affirmation of Goethe and the Wake. It's funny, of the two very greatest—for me the greatest in the world; one—the Fugue, is "negative," the other, Finnegan's Wake, is affirmation.

The last of Pt. I Faust is obvious, Mephistopheles saying of Margurite spelling "she is lost" and the chorus of angels saying: "she is redeemed." Literal translation of the last of Pt II "All passing-ness Is only a likeness The inadequate Here becomes actuality The indescribable Here is it done The eternal womanness Draws us up." Or actually: "All transient things are only symbols (likenesses, similarities, shadows) The potential here becomes fulfillment. The unthinkable is here achieved. The eternal principle of femininity leads us on." The original is deep and natural; translations are inadequate; the one best known is terrible.—"All of mere transient date, as symbol showeth. Here the inadequate to fullness groweth. Here the ineffable Wrought is in love. The ever-womanly draws us above" even tho it does preserve the meter of the original. The eternal principle of femininity could be expressed by Eros, the symbol for relation, relatedness, which implies an apperception of the whole, which is in turn related to a sense of proportion. But the Wake is best.

> "Coming. Far!
> End Here.
> Us Then.
> Finn, again.
> *Take.*
> Bussoftlhee, mememormee!
> Till thousendsthee.
> Lps.
> The keys to.
> *Given.*
> A way a lone a last a loved a long"

Sometimes when I read that even to myself it seems that humans aren't great enough to bear the visions they conceive. Softly. Thee. He. Memory. More me. Thou ends thee. thousands end. thousands end in theee. he. And that little lisping sound when current meets wave. the sound that scared Jn and me in the gulf, whistle wind on water that turned to hissing small waves on the shore. Take Finn again and again. Take the keys. And that magnificent fine final affirmation: Given.

Well I got so elevated, and on that yesterday I was so tired from no sleep, and I had the curious sadness of knowing then that you were off to Palestine, and allergy I hadn't had for a long time, that it all piled up to I guess the worst choking spell I ever had. A person's throat (which is a part of the person) closes us so it won't give him air; one part threatens suicide to the whole; even a happy whole. I got that sadness of things that aren't any more; as when I talk to Kay in the still same back room (I've had no time to change it around. Es war nicht gewesen sein. It was not to be. And of course: OK. Because everything can't be. All potential can't become reality. You've got to select. But it makes you sad.

III

THE SEA OF CORTEZ

III A. The View from the 1970's

This section includes first, Ed's transcribed notes of the trip to the Gulf of California on the *Western Flyer* that were part of the material used by John Steinbeck to prepare the narrative for the Sea of Cortez. These transcribed notes—or journal—included lists of species, notes on collecting, and notes from published sources which have been omitted because this material is available in the appendix of the original edition of *Sea of Cortez*. A number of people got the impression from John Steinbeck that there was an extensive amount of unprintable material in Ed's journal; this was simply not true according to Toni, who typed the final version, nor is it suggested by the contents of other notebooks. Ed did not write like Henry Miller.

Both Ed and John were at times vague about dates and places; accordingly the original log of the *Western Flyer* kept by the captain, Tony Berry is included here for reference. The third item in this section is the version of the long mulled over essay on "Non-Teleological Thinking" that was typed for John Steinbeck, and which he revised as the Easter Sunday chapter of *Sea of Cortez*. All of this resulted in the book whose structure was interpreted by Ed in his undated memorandum titled "Morphology of the Sea of Cortez."

After returning from the trip to Mexican waters, John, later followed by Ed, spent some time in Mexico City and environs on location for the documentary film *The Forgotten Village*. Ed and John disagreed in fundamental ways about the Mexicans and their way of life, and Ed prepared an "antiscript" to *The Forgotten Village* (as he knew it from the printed book by Steinbeck).

The central position of *Sea of Cortez* in John Steinbeck's writing career has been recognized by several critics, and has been examined in some detail, on the basis of the materials included here, by Richard Astro in his essay "Steinbeck and Ricketts: Escape or Commitment in the Sea of Cortez?"[1] The book was also part of Ed Ricketts' experience of their journey together—in some ways perhaps more so than Steinbeck's. For while John was midwife to Ed's cherished ideas and loaned his writing ability to the occasion, it was Ed who took care of so many of the tedious details, working himself to a state where he began to worry about his stomach, to say nothing of the proofs and the quality of the illustrations.

The changes anticipated for La Paz in the published version of *Sea*

---

[1]*Western American Literature*, Vol. VI number 2, pp. 109-121, 1972. The misprint "Sea of Cortex" on p. 116, if indeed it is a misprint, owes nothing to Sigmund Freud.

of Cortez (p. 118)[1] have come, but not perhaps as severely as feared. La Paz is still a pleasant place, even if it now has docks, small boat marinas, paved streets downtown, and here and there a stoplight. There is now an airport, with several flights daily from Los Angeles. In the season, the passengers are prosperous looking people bearing heavy fishing poles. They are whisked away in taxis or chartered cars for the Cape, where they seek bigger game, and leave La Paz pretty much alone. The enterprising little boy mentioned on pp. 112-113 is indeed a successful business man now, operator of a charter fishing boat service.

Completion of a paved road to La Paz has not resulted in the anticipated increase of traffic. The road is too narrow for trailers and heavy campers, and near the border the danger of thieves and toughs has discouraged travellers. After the first year, travel dropped off.

"Now, approaching Guaymas, we are approaching an end," so John Steinbeck wrote. He was tired and ready to go home and did not care very much for Guaymas (see p. 245). Ed was not quite so negative. He liked the town and would liked to have stayed a few days longer. The waterfront that he knew is gone now, for the most part. An expansive new plaza occupies the area by the stone quays, guarded by a large statue of El Pescador who faces the sea. His large hat is a choice perching place for sea gulls. The tourist activity has removed from the town itself, and is infesting the bays to the west and north of the city. There one may find motels to suit his choice, and a seaside villa development called "Miramar." The curio shops are now a mile from the center of Guaymas, in deference to tourists who will not stop for the bric a brac if they cannot find a place to park. One wonders, looking at the wares in these stores, if the invention of pulsating pigments has been good for popular art. Cortez glows in international orange on a background of black velvet with quivering chartreuse accents. The new Mexico is to be found in Guaymas in the large new building of the Escuela de Ciencias Maritimas y Tecnologia de Alimentos Guaymas, which can be seen on the hillside above the motels as one drives toward Miramar. But to reach the school one must drive off into unpaved roads that give no assurance of reaching the buildings—now lost from sight until the gate is indeed reached. The school, a branch of the Instituto Tecnologio y de Estudios Superiores de Monterrey, is supported by private assessments from the fishing industry. It is well equipped with many of the modern gadgets of science for the oceanography laboratories, and an expensive array of equipment, including a freeze-drying apparatus for pilot runs with various kinds of processed sea foods. It is a bright new shiny place with a student body of perhaps a hundred and a new building going up (1972). The view from the site is spec-

---

[1] All page numbers in this section refer to *Sea of Cortez*, or the Viking editions (both hard bound and paper back) of *The Log from the Sea of Cortez*; pagination is identical in all these editions. Type was reset, however, for the Bantam edition.

Isla del Carmen. Photo by Nick Carter.

tacular, reminiscent in its prospect of bays between steep hills of the view at Friday Harbor or Auke Bay. The students are encouraged to go north for higher degrees and obviously Mexico is taking very seriously the hope of more food from the sea. In addition to this school, there is also the Escuela Superior de Ciencias Marinas of the Universidad Autonomia de Baja California at Ensenada; although on the Pacific it is concerned also with marine and fishery affairs in the Gulf. One wonders where Mexico will find appropriate positions for all these hopeful young professionals.

The Bahia San Carlos near Guaymas—mentioned as site for a shore collecting trip on p. 239—was evidently undeveloped in 1940, as there is no reference to the beginnings of the present development of expensive motels, sea side villas and all, with the Guaymas International Yacht Club and an airstrip. In the words of a gaudy brochure from the tourist information offices: "San Carlos Bay, is a planned development. This is where you may discover your scape [sic] from Society's mounting problems."

In his typescript version, Ed did not mention the Seri, or very much about Tiburon Island and vicinity. The entry for April 3 in the *Sea of Cortez* (pages 230-237) has quite a bit to say about the Seri, all of it quoted from sources (obviously from one of Ed's notebooks on reading). The Seri are doing well. They have a thriving village about 15 miles north of new Bahia Kino. Old Bahia Kino is an unenterprising fishing village of the most impoverished sort; but northward along the beautiful bay in the lee of the odd shaped island called Alcatraz there is New Bahia Kino, a development of seaside villas (of which that belonging to the Governor of Sonora is the most elaborate) along two miles of shore, ending in an enormous trailer park for gringos from Arizona. (Most of the parked cars in the various villa driveways have Arizona and California license plates.) There is an air strip. Somewhere off to the north of the road that starts out for the air strip, one follows a well graded but unpaved and unmarked road (except for stacked rocks and sticks here and there) for 15 miles over wild country to the Seri Pueblo. When I visited in July, 1972, I found some very important business in progress involving a truck from the Fisheries Commission or whatever, several barrels of fuel and a detachment of the military armed with automatic weapons supervising the loading of a small boat that eventually departed for the sand bar a few hundred yards away where a bright blue pleasure craft was stranded by the tide. Beyond the bar was Tiburon, a high and barren island from the mainland prospect. I had ignored the Indians and they finally could not stand it any longer: some half a dozen enterprising squaws began to thrust ironwood carvings toward me or held up strings of seashells. But I had no money; this was no drawback however, for the proprieter of the one room shack that was the local soft drink bar and grocery eagerly converted my traveller's check to pesos (and at a better rate than the city motels and supermarkets would give). I understand I got a bargain with my sleek shark, and certainly the price of these carvings doubles in the fifteen miles between the village and the motel at the end of the pavement. But the Seri are selling so many carvings the ironwood is getting scarce. Their baskets (out of season in July) command high prices as well. There were several automobiles parked in the village among the hovels. As I was there a group of women and children climbed aboard a pickup truck, perhaps to go to town and spend the money they had just extracted from me. In any event, the Seri no longer have to eat people to make ends meet.

The boat culture is changing these pleasant backwaters everywhere. On the way to Hermosillo from Bahia Kino, I passed an enormous boat trailer being dragged by a car from Arizona; it must have come at least three hundred miles along the narrow, unbanked Mexican highways and had probably been dipped into the water for a day or two over the weekend and was on its way back. The development of fiberglass hulls has made this sort of thing possible and there are thousands of inland yachtsmen now, willing to put up with the strain of driving hundreds of miles along the hot sunblasted desert roads for brief interludes of aquatic diversion. No place that can be reached by pavement is immune from them. All that is needed is a place to park the car or truck and a ramp to the water.

Few people given to spending so much time and sustenance on expensive boats, elaborate trailer rigs and long drives buy much more than drink, provender and fishing tackle; but there are now elaborate guides to the Gulf of California for yachtsmen and a small but growing library of books for naturalists, "Baja buffs," and sedentary explorers. The log version of *Sea of Cortez* is available in two paperback editions, and the original book itself has been reproduced in facsimile (including the color plates) by Paul R. Appel (Mamaroneck, New York, 1972, $22.50) in an edition of 750 copies. It is a very good reproduction, and the binding is even better than the 1941 edition. The book did not become available to Spanish readers until 1968, when the translation by Teresa Gispert of the Log version (including About Ed Ricketts) was published as *Por el Mar de Cortes* (Luis de Caralt, Libro Documento Ediciones G.P.)[1]

Many of the books about Baja or the Gulf are embellished with quotations from *Sea of Cortez;* even that polished refugee from The Modern Temper and later desert naturalist Joseph Wood Krutch found a suitable quotation (from pp. 166-167) for his *The Forgotten Peninsula: A Naturalist in Baja California* (William Morrow & Co., 1961). Writing about Baja does seem to bring out the organ tones in people;Krutch let himself go a bit in the beautifully illustrated Sierra Club book, *Baja California and the Geography of Hope.* Except for the yachtsmen's guides, however, there has not been very much published about the Sea of Cortez and its life outside the specialist liter-

---

[1]Distributed by Plaza & Janes, S.A., Amazones 44, Mexico D.F.

Near Loreto. Photo by Nick Carter.

ature.[1] One of these, however, would have been hailed by Ed as a major event, as it certainly is. This is *Sea Shells of Tropical West America* by A. Myra Keen, now in its second and augmented edition (Stanford Press, 1971). The coverage is from Baja California to Peru incuding the Galapagos Islands. Its publication of course makes pages 478 to 560 of the Appendix of *Sea of Cortez* obsolete, and provides the visitor to Baja's shores with a guide to all the shallow water molluscs known, and every species is illustrated.

And at last we have a guidebook to the common invertebrate fauna of the area, primarily by Richard C. Brusca but with the assistance of his colleagues, most of them with first-hand acquaintance with the northern part of the Gulf of California: *A Handbook to the Common Intertidal Invertebrates of the Gulf of California* (University of Arizona Press, Tucson, 1972). This should make possible more serious studies of the region. The illustrations and descriptions are clear enough to make the book useful for the casual fisherman as well, especially those whose curiosity about what they see is strong enough to bring them to such a book in the first place. A new edition is now in press.

The best yachtsmen's guide is *The Sea of Cortez* by Ray Cannon (Sunset Books, Lane Magazine & Book Co., Menlo Park, Calif., 1966); it is excellently illustrated, with all sorts of information, including an illustrated guide to "Fishes of the Cortez." There is also a road guide for the highway to La Paz, which tells how to get to many of the places visited by Steinbeck and Ricketts, then accessible only by boat.[2]

[1] Some of the history of scientific expeditions and mollusk collecting trips to the Gulf of California is recounted in a voluminous paper on bottom assemblages associated with various kinds of sediment at various depths by Robert H. Parker ("Zoogeography and ecology of some macro-invertebrates particularly mollusks, in the Gulf of California and the Continental Slope off Mexico." Vidensk. Medd fra Dansk. naturh. Foren, vol. 126, pp. 1-178, 15 pls. 1963). The interpretation depends rather heavily on what the computer did with the data entrusted to its discerning intellect. There are some plates of various assemblages.

[2] Miller and Elmar Baxter, 1977, *The Baja Guide Book*. A complete new map guide to today's Baja California. Baja Trail Publications, Inc., Huntington Beach, Calif. 180 pp. illus.

Ed aboard ship.

IIIB. Rickett's Notes from the
Sea of Cortez

Gulf of California Trip
March-April 1940

11 Mch Monday: Tony Berry, Captain. Tex Travis, Engineer. Sparky Enea, Seaman and Cook. Tiny Colletto, Seaman. Purse Seiner, *Western Flyer*, 76', 25' beam, 165 horsepower Atlas Imperial Deisel Engine, direct reversible. 20' skiff, 10' skiff. John, Carol, Toby to San Diego only, myself. [John Steinbeck, Carol Steinbeck, Webster Street]

Out into fair weather but sufficiently pitchy and rolly so that Carol was sick until well into the night, and Tony was tired. John was OK and I miraculously stayed with it.

First night, a few porpoises. Many schools of fish off San Luis Obispo. A few sardines. But mostly bait fish, as proven by spotlight.

12 Mch Tuesday: Following AM smooth to the point of oiliness, running through Santa Barbara Channel. Many porpoises. Boys were very tired and ragged, only scanty and few hours sleep, especially Tony.

Last night, I was talking with Tony about how funny it was that waves off a headland were always higher than elsewhere, even though we might be several miles off. He said, "The point draws the waves." I thought it a good primitive statement of the relation between receiver and giver. The relation is through waves a - a - a - a, etc., each of which is connected by torsion to its inshore fellow and touches it enough, although it has gone before, to be effected by its torsion, and so on and on into shore, the last wave of all actually touching and breaking upon the shore.

I was thinking also that steering a boat is an objectification of what I have waveringly and at last come to know of ways of living.

Steering a boat by compass in heavy seas is for me difficult, exacting and, at first anyway, uncertain work. But the choice involves only two alternatives; that is, when you try to keep the needle steady, it swinging in a variable arc from 2 to 10°, and when you forget which way to turn the wheel in order to make the compass card swing back where you want it, you can push the wheel only two ways, either left or right.[1] The fact that there is a lag, and the boat may be swinging so rapidly in one direction that no matter how rapidly you push the wheel correctingly, the needle still continues to swing the wrong way, complicates things when you're tired. I remember only, doggedly, that (going S) no matter how the boat and the compass card may be swinging, you push the wheel to the left to make the numbers decrease E, and to the right to increase them W. Old hands at that work, or people who learn rapidly, soon get a feeling for the relation between compass and steering so it's natural and easy for them, but those things come to me slowly and through hard work and thinking and acting through thought.

Also, in considering the wake, which is a posteriori [sic]—a finished path: if you steer well and carefully, the wake can be a straight line. But even if it may have been a true straight line immediately upon completion, currents and winds (of public opinion and understanding, I suppose), may swing it

[1]There are only *2* alternatives, yet you can get mixed up even there, or rather I can! [EFR]

around so that it becomes actually wavering. There is a unified field hypothesis probably available in navigation as in all things. The internal factors are the boat, the controls, and the crew, but chiefly the will and intent of the master, who must be more or less a navigator. The external factors are the sea and the land, the current, the waves, the wind, and chiefly their effect in modifying the influence of the rudder in this or that position against the varying tensions of water.

If you steer *toward an objective,* you cannot, exactly and perfectly and indefinitely, steer directly at it. You must steer to one side, else you will run it down. But there is one thing you can steer *exactly* by: a compass course; that doesn't change, objects achieved are merely its fulfillment. In going toward a headland by direct vision steering, for instance, you can in the distance steer directly toward it, changing your course gradually and by degrees almost imperceptible, so as to pass outside it the necessary mile or miles, avoiding the shallow water about it or the rocks which comprise the actual point. The correct and efficient way to achieve this result is by steering a compass course. Knowing something about such things, and having a chart available, you plot a compass course in a straight line (or in a great circle line if the distance is great), from where you are to just outside your next objective (well outside, if you want to save fellow voyagers from sea sickness, because the point "draws the waves"), before changing course for the next compass path.

Small boat navigation along the coast of California and Lower California is comparatively simple. From well outside Pt. Pinos, for instance, you set a compass course for offshore Pt. Sur (this is worked out in degrees on the C. and G. Survey Charts and the course is already lined out), or you head toward it at first by direct vision, keeping well offshore as you round it. Then you veer slightly to set another straight-line course for Piedras Blancas Light. Then a long course for Arguello, and another for Pt. Fermin, by-passing just outside Pt. Vicente. If you try to stay too close to land, as the tyro sailor might tend to do, uninstructed, you not only expend fuel and time unnecessarily, you may jeopardize the boat on shoals.

The working out of the ideal into the real, a constant process, and the relationship between inward and outward, or microcosm and macrocosm, are all here, as they are everywhere; the compass representing the ideal, the headland the real.

The navigator, however, has to set the course, and it is he who changes it; any experienced helmsman can steer.

Object is to feel steering quickly the new tendency (which effects the rudder), so as to respond quickly and so not to have to turn the wheel too far or too suddenly, because in the latter case you have to turn it back just as far, else the boat gets to oscillating without full forward progress.

This eventually becomes automatic, I suppose, but when I'm tired I have to repeat a formula, and I think it was the same on Jack's boat when Joe and I stood wheel watch: to decrease the numbers on the compass cards, push the wheel left.[1] Only, sometimes, to fulfill an oncoming rhythm, you do the reverse. Sometimes I have been able to get the "feeling" of the boat in its relations to the sea that way, avoiding seasickness.

I may be able to understand, in a moment of enlightenment, and to formulate, a unified field hypothesis, but to fulfill it is another thing. And to fulfill

---

[1] A reference to the 1932 boat trip with Jack and Sasha Calvin and Joseph Campbell in Southeastern Alaska.

The Western Flyer. Courtesy Salinas Public Library.

it constantly is an impossibility; that would be the perfect Tao that leads to or that is Nirvanah. Or for anyone else to use that formula is difficult, although it may be correct for me, and objectively correct, too. A child may not be able to use an algebraic theorem despite its objective correctness.

In the development of navigation in the minds of men and in the mind of any learning man, think how often they or he must have wished for some constant point on the horizon to steer by. If the course, for instance, were 170°, how simple it would be if there were a star in that exact position just above the horizon. Well, very often there is, on a clear night. And in the early misty development of navigation, how many people, uninstructed, must have been fooled by that. The first lesson is that the stars swing from east to west. Think how happy mankind must have been in discovering Stella Polaris. But it shifts too, very minutely in an arc, and its position is constant only relatively. And in the centuries it will have shifted and will shift again. It just happens that its position relative to the earth is subtended by a line drawn through the earth's spinning axis—in other words, over the North Pole—and so to anyone in the northern hemisphere who observes such things, Stella Polaris has become the symbol of constancy.

What you want is something on the horizon or just above it that doesn't change. Except for something dead ahead, which you'll run down if you steer into it directly, everything that you steer for (as a headland or lightship for instance) must be sheered off from to the R or the L as you approach. That's the reality, the time constant. But one thing doesn't shift as you approach, because there's no real approaching: the compass-point 170°; the abstract, Schiller's and Goethe's "Ideal, ee-day-ol", to be worked out in terms of reality. So Beethoven writes a 9th Symphony to Schiller's Ode to Joy.

Someone said of the tidepool area: "The world under a rock". So it could be said of navigation: "The world within the horizon".

Of steering: the external influences to be compensated for are in the nature of oscillations—seiches. They are of short or of long period or both, of regular or irregular (currents, wind, rain) nature or of both. The mean levels of the extreme ups and down of these oscillations symbolize opposites in a Hegelian sense. No wonder that in physics i, the symbol of oscillation, the square root of minus one, is fundamental and primitive and ubiquitous, turning up in every equation!

When, on dead center, a R bearing external influence (for instance) swings the boat off course and the compass card spins counter-clockwise (all this applies to sailing S), you compensate by swinging the wheel left of dead center, holding it there until the compass card swings back clockwise to the course. But it doesn't stop there, it tends to swing equally far to the left. Having experienced this often enough to get the feeling of it, you start to counter-swing before the recovery has gone too far, and so anticipate the over-recovery tendency. Thank heavens, the compass doesn't have a periodicity of its own to complicate things!

to 15 Mch Friday: Into San Diego through beautifully quiet water. Saw the Mexican Consul, got necessary papers, complimentary visa, cleared, signed on ourselves and the boys to articles, talked to a gang of reporters, succeeded in getting by without having pictures taken, got nets, a few supplies, saw Herb Klein and...Ford, had a good steak dinner with cocktails and brandy, after having got rid of some relatives of John's or Carol's, who were most persistent (Herb really put the skids on them). I tried to get "No Star is Lost" for Marge Lloyd, who may be able to understand—she certainly tries hard enough, kindly and willingly, and "Zaca Venture" to take along for ourselves, both without success. Papers from Mexican Department of Marine having been mislaid, I was delegated to go back to the Consul and try to get new set; hated to do it, but by the time the taxi had gotten there I was all pepped up, smiling and relaxed and feeling genuinely good and friendly and could probably have done it, but in the meantime they had been found and someone from the boat had phoned the Mexican Consul to that effect. So we all parted best of friends, the Consul satisfied with having done his part wisely and competently, and we also. Toby and Herb both left us.

Off Pt. Baja, Lower California. Water is brilliantly ultra-marine blue, what the boys call "Tuna Water." John saw two sea turtles. This is the Region of the Sea Turtle and the Flying Fish. An essay on life at sea would consider navigation, food, and living aboard small boats; all are special techniques.

16 Mch Saturday: In oily quiet water, 2 PM, in slight fog, over 50 fm bank N of Magdalena Bay. Tiny speared a sea turtle about 2½' long. Probably *Eretmochelys imbricata,* tortoise-shell turtle. There were a couple of barnacle bases on the shell, and many hydroids which were preserved in 2 vials. There were 2 *Planes minutus,* pelagic crabs related to the Pacific Grove *Pachygrapsus,* male and female, together back of the tail under the flipper. We examined the intestinal tract for tapeworms. None obvious. From gullet to anus, the digestive tract was filled with a small lobster-like shrimp almost identical to the Monterey Bay and Puget Sound Minida, rock lobster (*Pleuroncodes planipes* Stimp.), of which a few near the gullet were whole enough to preserve. The gullet was lined with hard and sharp pointed spikes which apparently ground the shells of the lobsters. Fine adaptation to food supply by structure, or vice versa. So, in a half an hour, we got to know in reality more about sea turtles than the average person hears in a lifetime. John saved the shell to cure for a playroom trophy.

Planes minutes, the Turtle Crab. Drawing by Joel W. Hedgpeth (after Rathbun).

Group of new kind of porpoises (we have seen none since leaving Central California), gray where the others were brownish, slimmer, and with paddle-shaped proboscces. Very fast, in great group, jumping in and out of the water the way porpoises characteristically do. Look like Tuna. This discontinuous distribution is another indication of the possible correctness of Cabrera's law of ecological incompatibility. [Steinbeck did not pick this up. A pity. J.W.H.]

They swim entirely by vertical movement of the laterally compressed tail. Blowhole opening and closing. Actually small whales.

The abundance of life here gives me a sense of exuberance. I can't get a full sense of enjoyment from the high Sierra because they're so barren. But here the surface is teeming with life, sea turtles, flying fish, pelagic rock lobsters, bonita, now these porpoises. And the ocean bed underneath is likely equally rich. And microscopically the water itself will be teeming with plankton. Tuna water.

The completeness of the turtle—*Planes minutus*—hydroid—barnacle—*Pleuroncodes*(which is what the pelagic "rock lobster" turned out to be; the Mexicans called them "langustina") association is very pleasing. There was the whole thing laid out before us. The tremendous hordes of very hard-shelled little lobsters. The turtles with their gullets ideally adapted to using that type of food; grinding gullet starting a digestive tract filled clear to the anus; they must be storing food in the form of fat—excess energy—for a barren season. And the hydroids and barnacles perching on the nearest attachment site, which happened (at the time the floating larvae were being liberated) to be that turtle shell.

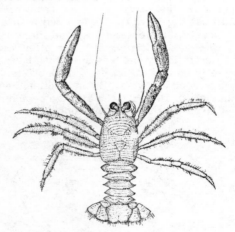

Pleuroncodes planipes. **From an article by Carl M. Boyd in** *Pacific Science.* **Vol. XXI, No. 3, July 1967.**

5 PM above: About 70 miles No of Pt. Lazaro, hosts of brilliantly red (shrimp pink) *Pleuroncodes planipes* Stimpson (p. 163 Schmitt 1921), looking very beautiful against the ultramarine of Tuna water. In March, 1859, it was thrown ashore in considerable numbers at Monterey, California (Stimpson). One of those queer years, probably, when ocean currents transported a lot of typically southern forms far northward.[1]

17 Mch Sunday: 2 AM passed Pt. San Lazaro on the 1 to 4 shift which Tony and I had; 2nd lighthouse apparently never did show up. Another of the bad coastwise points where you change course. Like Cedros Island

[1]It reappeared at Monterey in 1960, a hundred and one years later.

passage, where it's always bad, even in good weather (or like Cape Horn), and when it's bad it's horrid.

5:30 AM awakened by motor idling; John was catching a great bunch of *Pleuroncodes planipes* again. Several female ovig. Said he started to see them as soon as it was light.

2 small dolphins, *Coryphaena equisetis* Linn, of the most startling beautiful, and rapidly changing colors. Smaller was 3¼ hands long. This is another of the everywhere-appearing forms described many years back in Sweden by Linnaeus, father of modern zoology, Darwin's godfather intellectually.[1] Described some still-valid species of *Lepas* (goose barnacle) and (as I recall) *Balanus* (acorn barnacle) and some other ubiquitous forms that are known by zoologists everywhere.

Arrived San Lucas Cove a little after midnight—that competent Tony, landing us at night in such a difficult-to-find spot, all the headlands and coves looked alike to me in the dark!—after putting in what seemed to me dangerously close to a sand-bank shore before reversing engines. The light station was amusing here; the pilot book said, "A light is shown on the end of the cannery wharf", but we found none. In the morning, when the cannery started up and the generators were started for the cannery power plant, then the light went on!

18 Mch Monday: Cape San Lucas. Rocks. S of the tuna cannery. Tide 12:07 PM San Diego time. 0.0' .

Uppermost rocks with Sally Lightfoots, but almost uncapturable, with white Littorines. Below that, barnacles and *Purpura*, crabs, limpets. Below that, serpulid worms. Below that, inshore, the multi-rayed starfish *Heliaster kubiniji* of Xanthus (who was tidal observer here for the United States Government in the 50s or 60s, and a very active man he was, in more ways than one).[2] A few urchins. Outside, many urchins and rock oysters (*Chama?*), with limpet species No. 2. Lowest, inshore: Gorgonians. Lowest, surf-swept: a gorgeous fauna of bryozoa, brachiopods, polyclad worms, flat crabs, large *Cucumaria*-type of holothurian, some anemones, many sponges of 3 types (a smooth encrusting purple, an erect white calcareous, and a slime sponge), many snails, including cones and Murex, 2 or 3 species of limpets, a nudibranch or shell-less tectibranch, hydroids, a few annelid worms, a red pentagonal starfish (probably *Oreaster occidental*, illustrated in the Bingham Report), which we were subsequently to know as the third most common starfish of the region. 3 most common starfish of the whole Gulf to date, April 4, are: the multi-rayed *Heliaster kubinjii*, the slim 5-rayed gray or purple *Phataria unifascialis,* and the red pentagonal Oreas. Thatched barnacles about which Cornwall[3] will be glad, and miscellaneous small crabs, including abundant brilliantly red hermits. Strangely enough, no chitons were apparent, although I should have imagined the region to be ideally adapted to them.

A fantastic region of violent rocks.

[1] Linnaeus was *not* the father of modern zoology. As for Darwin, who needs a godfather with a real, albeit incredible grandfather like Erasmus?

[2] See: Henry Miller Madden, *Xantus, Hungarian Naturalist in the Pioneer West* (Palo Alto: Books of the West, 321 pp. ills. 1949); Chapter IV, pp. 97-151 concerns Xantus at Cape San Lucas. Madden remarks (p. 126) upon the enthusiasm for natural history Xantus "was able to inspire in female society" and gives the names of seven ladies who collected birds nests, seashells and insects for their Hungarian friend.

[3] I.E. Cornwall (now deceased) a Canadian specialist in barnacles.

Cape San Lucas, in the days of Xanthus. Copy courtesy R. Brusca.

It seemed to me that life here is very fierce. The starfish and urchins here are more strongly attached to the rock even than those at Pacific Grove, Pt. Lobos, etc. But of course the surf must be fairly high here at times, even within this shelter, and outside the cove, just over the fringing rocks, it's tremendous even now with a quiet sea. Lowe, who visited here in 1930 or 1931 spring, notes a most powerful surf outside.[1] The big brilliantly-colored Sally Lightfoots, which are almost literally everywhere, are so nimble as to be safe from capture. We got only 2 or 3. They are fast, alert, and they see well. They dodge magnificently, faster than a human being can grab.

In the late afternoon and evening, we drove a mile or so through a fantastic and lovely landscape of cacti and shrubs to a funny primitive little cantina at the town of San Lucas. No ice, no lights other than gasoline lanterns. Lots of insects. (And lots of cockroaches in the little shack houses around the cannery, a population of some 200 cannery workers was last

[1]Herbert N. Lowe, a conchologist who published on his collecting trips in Mexican waters.

winter washed out of its housing by tropical storm and flood water, some drowned; Chris says the people were wet and cold, the children crying for something to eat and there was no food and no way of cooking it even if there were). English-speaking and very pleasant Chris, superintendent of the cannery, was most hospitable.

Grapsus grapsus, the Sally Lightfoot. Drawing by Lynn Rudy.

The Governor was to be here tonight to consider housing problem. Sr. Ruiz, who is Port Captain (fees were $19.81), went with us. Got 2 cases Carta Blanca beer; we all got big hats, the sun is just plain poison and we all needed a portable shelter to keep heads out of it. Apparently only one car here, that of Sr. Ruiz. Chris says Damiana is aphrodisiac and it really works, but so do many other foods and drinks, someone should turn up an anaphrodisiac.[1] Incident of the light over the grave of the guy who died on Monday. The Bluebird record was D-3-216, "A Mia Nomas."

A large hemispherical snail with domed surface camouflaged with corallines and other algae so that it looked like a boulder or a knob on the reef.

A dugout canoe came up with two men and a woman (she bundled up—malaria? and covering her face—from evil breath of white people?) with a few perlitas. Wanted to trade for cigarettes. Valued their pearls at $1.00 U.S. John gave them carton of cigarettes, although not wanting pearls. Sorry I didn't get more dope from them on native names of marine animals.

Anchored for the night near Pescadero Point,[2] preparatory to running into SE end of Espiritu Santo Island for tomorrow's tide.

Previously, the boys caught a skipjack, with stomach full of langustinas; we saw two giant rays.

[1]As for the alleged beneficial properties of Damiana discussed on p. 67; there is nothing to the story, or the recipe has been changed since 1940; I got my bottle across the border without trouble and tested it liberally with negative results.

[2]Coyote Point, near S. approach to San Lorenzo Channel.

20 Mch Wednesday: Left night anchorage at Pescadero Point shortly after 5 AM PST, which is 7 AM Mexican time (at the Cape San Lucas tuna cannery, Chris keeps astronomical time, which is still 1 hour different, in between).

Collected on bouldery reef S of Lobos Point, SE side of Espiritu Santo Island.

A good, kind Indian who adopted us was given a pair of pants by Tiny and he gave him a note for the man who would accompany the pilot and the Port Captain when they boarded us at Point Prieta quarantine. This Indian, who was all smiles and good nature, came aboard with a pal who, however, stayed in his own canoe at the rail. Gave them wine. They talked, or rather the affable Indian talked until late. Had fun. Told us lots about the region. Barefoot, using spear. Incredibly poor, clothes patched and mended; asked us for empty cans whenever we started to throw one overboard.

"Almazan muy fuerte", with gesticulations and gestures. That became a by-word with the boys, then Alberta adopted it, and last I heard, her sister and brother were using it, by then highly modified.[1]

21 Mch Thursday: Entered La Paz, a beautiful town, lush, palm trees, white buildings with contrasting roofs, houses with inside gardens, kids everywhere to guide you—and you need a guide to get around that scattered maze. No wharf, discharge of freight is by lighters, of passengers by curious water taxis—dugout canoes from Nayarit. Carta Blanca beer put aboard the first thing.

Collecting on a rocky flat being drowned in sand, ½ to 1 mile E of La Paz. It was said that there was fine collecting at the first point between La Paz and the Lighthouse, but, since the outboard motor was tempermental (de Lawd bless Mistah Johnson), we didn't attempt such a distance. Tide said to be *a las quatros,* Mexican time.

A type of mud-living mussel, occurring in clusters half-buried. *Callianassa* or *Upogebia* in shrimp pink color, called "langusta" locally, and snagged out of their holes by innumerable small boys for 15 centavos each. By hard work and cleverness, the boys search out populated burrows (the animals dig down quite a way in rock-strewn flats), get their small harpoon (every child has one here, as city kids have hoops and sticks) below them, and snake out the animals, in some cases alive and unhurt. If it weren't for the kids, we shouldn't have been successful in securing a single animal, lacking the patience, experience and street Arab cleverness of these children.

The profile was easy to get: holes with langusta; clusters of old coral with *Eurythoe,* anemones, brittle stars, sponges, small crabs, and beautiful purple polyclad flatworms in the interstices, and often an encrusting purple tunicate.

22 Mch, Friday: La Paz. Sand to muddy sand to sandy mud at El Mogete, 1 mile N of La Paz. The important items were: *Cerianthus, Dentalium,* big sinpunculid and new cucumbers.

When we returned, 40,000 kids were on the boat awaiting us with [all sorts of animals.]

Four things today:

Church, Good Friday—*Viernas Santo*—11 to 12, women in black widow's clothing, smell of people and of perfume, some blondes, fine earnest priest,

[1]Acquaintances Ed made in Los Angeles at the end of the voyage.

Tidepools near Coyote Point. Photo by W.M. Shepherd.

black eyes blazing, good voice, old Spanish chants like madrigals with quarter-tone wails, chorus of children's voices singing loud and out of tune on the notes they know, coming in pretty strongly on some of the obvious or tuneful phrases.

Then good completely protected sand flat collecting.

Then talking to earnest good customs man aboard (at La Paz, a customs man is stationed aboard day and night, as a guard?), male counterpart of woman I drove last year from Tijuana to Ensenada.

Then into town during the evening, and a little, fierce-eyed black boy (not the two or three regular guides who adopted us), maybe terribly scared, waiting a long time at the door of the saloon, then following us doggedly, not saying a word, then, at the last minute, as we were disembarking (we brought in our own boat to save a peso per person toll from the water taxi men, and miraculously the boat wasn't this time brought back to the big boat tied up), desperately asking for *cinco centavos*. Poor, good, funny frightened child; I gave him twenty *centavos*. And such a feeling of relief and kindness from him then! When he had the money, and no service required! We felt good, and happy and thankful; he tried to untie our boat and he was too small or too unskilled. So I helped him and I said, *"Buenos noches"*, and he went home—I hope and suspect—with a warm heart. So I say, "Bless him."

The Mexican fleas are quite fierce, and they like me as well as do the California fleas. The name of the aphrodisiacal cordial that Chris told us about is Damiano (cream de Damiano), available in La Paz at Casa Gomez. The English speaking boy who worked at collecting so hard and well with us: Raul Velez (or Avelas).

The one little boy (he said 13, I think, but surely he's not so old) who was so kind, but not so efficient as the cold and business-like one, I loved very much. I gave him two pesos, more money, I imagine, than he had in a long time. The fat boy was very efficient. They carried our packages and guided us, tried to be the very most efficient personal servants, secretaries, and major domos, tried to anticipate our wishes and were fairly successful at it. Tremendously good-natured and tremendously loyal. La Paz has many poor people, kind and loving, but with no work and simply frantic for money, like shadows for money, but not thieves, not menacing, and never unkind. By being a little careless with tips, we have supported several families for several weeks by our two or three-day stay here.

The system of yacht brokerage is very efficient and very fine, a little expensive (not much, tho; our port fees, pilotage, cost of customs guards, etc., came only to some $23; the agent apparently charged no fee whatsoever; he devoted much time to us and squired Carol around town one whole afternoon), but absolutely necessary if reputation of Mexican officialdom is true.

The peso is 5½ or 6 to 1 here. I bought swank-looking huaraches for one dollar and one peso (7 pesos), and a fine iguana belt for 2.50 pesos; Epsom Salts at a clothing store, Casa Gomez, one peso per kilo. I liked the blonde daughter. The girl in the pharmacy, I found entirely charming. The people are wonderful here. Ice is cinco centavos per kilo; not very good ice, tho. ¼ liter of Carta Blanca beer is 30 centavos per bottle, about 10 pesos per case, with 2.50 peso bottle return. I got 3 cigars from Sr. Gomez from his personal stock for 60 centavos, twisted—not wonderful, but satisfactory—Vera Cruz tobacco.

23 Mch Saturday: Fine wilderness anchorage along the west shore of San

Jose Island at Amortajada Bay, about 1 mile N of fantastic small islet with an inadvisable channel beyond. Collecting on a barren-looking (and it was barren!) reef or islet, apparently Cayo Islet.

Iron rings in cliff; we got some old chain. Evidence of fires, shells of clams and conches and turtle cooking on an island that has neither the firewood, the water, nor the animals. What would anyone want here?

The animals didn't like the rocks. Everything is wrong. We got there maybe 4:30 or 5, after outboard motor wouldn't run and we had to row. There wasn't much of any tide, and what there was was already running in, although the tide tables reported San Lorenzo channel tides as 6:30 PM and -0.8'. Little biting insects—Jijenes?—very bad. Also, I have a couple of pretty bad La Paz fleas. Now at midnight, while I'm writing up these notes, the boys are good-naturedly, even humorously, complaining about being unable to sleep; all bitten up. I sleep and awake bitten, but that's better than not sleeping and being bitten.

Gorgeous and fantastic region, high barren hills, vivid colors.

The tidelands on Cayo Islet are "burned." Barnacles, a few limpets, many anemones, some cucumbers, a few small *Heliaster*, some green things, maybe minute sea rabbits, or shell-less limpets.

Many many Sally Lightfeet, 1 only taken, 1 small sipunculid—looks like *Physcosoma. Aletes and* serpulid worms, 2 or 3 types of snails, a few isopods and amphipods. Fine and abundant anemones.

24 Mch Easter Sunday: From about 10 or 10:30 until 11:30 or 12, Tiny and I walked along the ridge between Amortajada Bay and the lagoon beyond. On the lagoon side of the ridge, there were thousands of burrows, presumably of a big land crab (since we saw what I took to be one, which, however, scuttled into his burrow in a hurry). Hopeless to dig out, lacking time, shovel, and man power. The shore of the lagoon were teeming with fiddler crabs and estuarine snails, of which we took representatives. Mangroves (the flowers may have caused the fine, fragrant, tropical hay-ey smell we noticed while coming into Cape San Lucas that midnight). A Salicornia-like shore plant. From where we were wading around in the lagoon, there was a fine picture of still water, with the green fringing trees against the burnt red-brown of the distant mountains, like something out of Conrad, or like some fantastic Dore engraving of heaven.

When we were pulling out, we saw quite an extensive ranch, the only one maybe for miles around. Several houses, a scow, and seven boats.

Easter Sunday, another time to be with your own family, not with your parents or your children's family; I was alone except inwardly, and there all day I had a sense of presence. Gregorian chants; "spirit ditties of no tune."

24 Mch Monday: Collected on the afternoon tide on a southerly pile of boulders, a central reef, and a northerly pile of boulders just S of Narcial Point which marks the southerly limit of Agua Verde Bay. The afternoon tide now is getting bad, or else I am hitting it wrong; should still be good according to tide book. Only a few polyclads (which here are high on the rocks), 2 large and many small chitons—the only place so far we have found them—or is it that we have not heretofore been forced to collect so high in the intertidal? Urchins abundant on the reef, but too far down. Larval shrimps in swarms. 10 PM at anchorage by light; pelagic isopods and mysids.

25 Mch Tuesday: Same place, same day—or rather, early following morning, got up at 4:05 AM by kitchen clock, left about 4:15 arrived ashore maybe 4:30, back on boat 6 AM. We just about hit the tide which was pretty fair, and which was starting to come in fairly well when we left.

One of the highly-colored spiny lobsters (apparently not *Panulirus interruptus*). We spotted him in a crevice on the reef by flashlight. I made careful preparations, then grabbed him suddenly, expecting the furor that spiny lobsters set up when detained forcibly. Not a kick, not a murmur. Many club-tentacled and sharp-spined urchins, in addition to the usual *Strongylocentrotus*-like forms. *Aglaophenia.* A few sea fans. 2 *Phataria.* 1 apparently new starfish. Several *Heliaster kubinjii.* One flat holothuria-like cucumber. 3 interesting things: (1) time of lower low tide established; (2) we saw brittle stars and puffer fish "out" and actively feeding during these dark hours; (3) we took lobster, sea fans, and desirable urchins.

In the afternoon, John and the boys went collecting in the mangrove reef a little outside the entrance (and gulfward) to Puerto Escondido, then a fisherman helped to get stuff (he was very good, brought in stuff for two days); then Carol and Tiny went out the following morning, when John and I were up on the mountain.

In the mangrove cove, there was truly magnificent collecting, characterized by the craziest gigantic worms like a tubeless *Chaetopterus,* or maybe an apodous holothurian, that I've ever seen. Two new starfish. Gorgeous material in general. Many *Cerianthus.*

The fisherman brought in what he called "abalon," but which was really a gigantic fixed scallop, not an abalone at all; good for food; a pearl oyster, a small hacha; several giant conches; and much other stuff.

26 Mch Tuesday: John and I went up into the mountains on an overnight trip with the customs man and the school teacher from Loreto, two Indians, and the owner of a local ranch. The ranch had 3 good deep wells with irrigating pumps worked by mules and made in Guadalajara, several houses, mules, horses, a few cows, many goats, etc. Ranch started 1½ years ago. People very proudly looking forward to completion of road to Loreto (trail only, now) so "cars" can come through. Indians wore barefoot sandals, old guy who was guiding us could and did outwalk and outclimb horses and mules. We walked ahead the entire trip, tiring out the animals. We six rode until too steep, then led horses to flat, maybe 1500' up, near 300-400' drop waterfall. Little water, but good pools. And such an oasis around it; known probably and loved for hundreds of years. Fresh and cool. green; the shadow of a rock in a weary land. Or, rather, in a fantastic land, since the plains and hills over which we came were rich with xerophytic plants, cacti, mimosa, brush and small trees with thorns. Branches you musn't touch and afterward rub your eyes.

The little waterfall canyon up in the mountains was steep, unapproachable from below because of cliffs; we got in from a side canyon above. It had palms (date palms—*Datil silvestre*), some tree with edible fruit—we couldn't make out what it was and they couldn't tell us (no one spoke English except the customs man, and he slightly, was learning by a correspondence course). And maidenhair fern (infusion used on women after childbirth), bracken, lichens. Tree frogs about pool, tadpoles, water striders and horsehair worms within. Doves.

The two Indians went after *boregas*—mountain sheep. None. Apparently left for Gigantas. The men looked after us kindly, fed us well, gave John a

Ring on cliff at Cayo Island. Photo courtesy W.M. Shepherd.

blanket (he had none), fixed up pillows for both of us. Good friends! I thought we should leave a gift, but customs man said none. He is a good fellow.

In the meantime, the mices was playing, as John says. A little scurrilous drinking got done, and bread crumbs instead of Epsom Salts got put in anaesthetizing tray of cucumbers, but they had been previously pretty well started and some came out alright.

This is one of the really good places. The good places to date are: Cape San Lucas, Pulmo Reef, La Paz area, and Puerto Escondido.

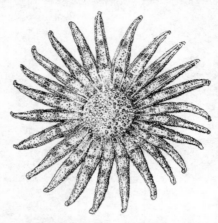

Heliaster kubinjii. **Drawing by Lynn Rudy.**

The outstanding ubiquitous animals so far are:

Heliaster kubinjii—practically everywhere, the sunstar. *Cucumaria* sp, possibly the Puget Sound and Monterey Bay *lubrica,* green or yellow underneath, dark or purple above, nearly everywhere, providing there are rocks for it to get under or crevices for it to crawl into.

Eurythoe, the stinging worm. Wherever there are loosely imbedded rocks, coral clusters, etc.

A purple urchin, much like the Pacific Grove *Strongy franciscanus* (red urchin) wherever there is rock or reef exposed to wave shock or strong scouring currents [*Echinometra vanbrunti*]. The usual barnacles and limpets on suitable bare rocks high up.

Anemones quite like the small bunodid forms at Pacific Grove.

Several small crabs; a porcelain crab and a *Panopeus.*

A red-legged hermit crab.

Our visit to Puerto Escondido was quite possibly an event in the life of a barefooted Indian fisherman (who spoke good Spanish) and his son. They have seen yachts before, probably many times, and some outside purse seiners, may even have been on them, but I imagine they may never before have been treated with living and considered kindness by Americans. They may never before have been offered a cup of coffee by an American host before he helped himself, and with a polite bow, and addressed as Senor, and all perfectly real and heartfelt. Although he may have been a pest, no doubt was, to the different time sense of Tony particularly—all Indians are that way—he was nevertheless a good man, and I respected and like him for that and for his abilities, and he no doubt knew it.

26 Mch Tuesday: Puerto Escondido. John noticed the son, thinking himself unobserved, examining a pocket knife lying on deck, doubtless being utterly charmed, wanting but not taking it. But if a person is going to spend more than a day or so with such people, he has to realize that, for all their naivete and real nobility, they (like the boys around the lab), have avarice, may have manners that seem boorish to us, and in any case can take up more time than most impatient Westerners have to spare.

I am wondering what curious factor in distribution results in "burned" reefs. (I saw the term used elsewhere also, possibly in Yonge's *Years on the Great Barrier Reef*).[1] There is no specific distinction that I can lay my hands on, yet I can as a rule determine when I first glimpse a given region, whether or not it will be rich, so there must be some differential apparent, perhaps subconsciously.

27 Mch Wednesday: I have been thinking that the anaesthetization of cucumbers, even the cursory way I've been doing, might have little value. But today, after having collected 15 of the big flat holothurians at Puerto Escondido on early tide, I put them directly in formalin and saw very quickly that even the sloppiest narcosis is more than a gesture.

John and I got out before 5:30 AM Mexican time, encircled Puerto Escondido entirely, mostly by flashlight. Fine tide. The E shore was dominated by the big flat brown *Holothuria*, with the mussel-like clam with hard and thick wavy shell, and a fair under-rock fauna. There were no sand flats until we got around west; there, there was some of the knobbed green coral. *Cerianthus* in both locations wherever the substratum was suitable. Spicy smell of the mangrove flowers. Mangroves occur here on both rocky and (apparently) sandy shores. We saw one of the gigantic worm-like synaptids walking around before dawn. At the entrance, and thence outside, was a fine fauna with the red and green cushion star, very plentiful, one other cushion star, a most remarkable colonial-solitary soft coral in great knobs and heads in one restricted location on the rocks. A large pelagic anemone ?? caught in the rocks by the current ?? that stung me quite severely. Really very severely. Like several bee stings. But practically over in a few hours. A giant *Spheciospongia* or similar is an important feature of the tidal scape. Giant sea hare. Clams. One small hacha.

There are many poisonous and stinging forms in these waters: urchins, sting rays, morays, *Eurythoe,* stinging anemone, botete.

Loreto: Stopped at Loreto about 11:30 AM, Mexican Standard Time, to mail letters, to buy beer, and to see Loreto Mission.

Main part was pretty much in ruins with part of the roof tumbled down by earthquake, but some fine woodwork and hinges still standing. One section was in present use and I was very moved by the altar decoration from Easter. The virgin was a vision of loveliness; I should think that very naive people would be rather overwhelmed by the rather gaudy loveliness. She was

[1]C.M. Yonge. *A Year on the Great Barrier Reef.* London and New York, Putnam, 246 pp., 1930.

I am unable to locate any reference to the term "burned"; perhaps Ricketts had in mind the discussion of coral death from high temperatures at low tide on p. 78. It is of incidental interest to note that the Crown of Thorns sea star *(Acanthaster planci)* is not even mentioned by Yonge; destruction of corals by this predator was not observed in those days. Another species of coral eating star, *Acanthaster ellisi* occurs in the Gulf of California and is occasionally collected intertidally near La Paz. Steinbeck & Ricketts collected a few specimens at Puerto Escondido in 1940 *(Sea of Cortez,* p. 376, entry K-117).

The church at Loreto. Photo by Nick Carter.

so lovely, I don't like even to use the word *gaudy*. For most people, it must be a great privilege to be able to pray to such a lovely lady. The virgin is all men's secret and unconscious mistress; to all women she is a symbol of the thing deepest to womanhood—maternity. Also, one of the paintings, second from the right as you face the altar (I looked at it from the locked grillwork) was very El Greco-ish.

Postmaster spoke a little English. People very fine. Not forward; apparently not looking for tips. The boy who attached himself to me was kind and straight-forward, apparently his only expediency was genuine interest in the stranger, and he asked only for cigarros. Only begging was from a small-boy portador who helped haul beer. He groaned at the weight and complained how poor he and his family were. Only High Life Beer, from brewery at Hermosillo, was available.

Ed and John collecting on NE shore of long westerly-extending point of Coronado Island, cursing outboard motor. Barren region, almost burned, but many cucumbers, some anemones, one starfish. I found what might have turned out to be a *Tanais,* but it failed to show up in the catch. Best of all, we found solitary corals in clustered heads. A yellow hemispherical sponge strikingly similar to the Monterey Bay *Tethya* or *Geodia* is a characteristic feature of the Coronados intertidal.

28 Mch Thursday: Good sleep. Didn't go collecting this morning; it seemed not worthwhile to expend good morale in a bad place, and we needed sleep badly.

Started 9 AM for Conception Bay, expect to arrive 6 or 7 PM; boat rolling a little for the first time in the gulf.

I was amused at Tiny, theoretically the hardest-boiled one in the bunch, finally, after lots of grief and dopiness and some actual sickness, keeping his head covered and keeping it covered religiously to the point of draping a handkerchief behind his hat so as to cover his neck a la Legionnaire. He is quite kind to the Mexicans and Indians, too, going along, rather than trying to buck their different time sense, and their half-starvedness, both for food and for human contact, whereas even a guy like Tony tends to be a little intolerant and stand-offish. Average Nordic, especially average Englishman, certainly doesn't get along very well with anyone but another Nordic; no participation. Getting along with the Indian or with the local ranchers—if a person wants to—involves lots of coffee, cigarettes, canned fruit, cold beer and patience; ability to go about the necessary work with them hanging around, like kids grown up, only they sit quietly, don't ask so many questions. Visits aboard whatever boats tolerate them must be rich experiences, horizon-enlarging experiences which no doubt furnish subjects for much future conversation and speculation. Like the Indians up north, these come to visit and sit quietly for hours, maybe days.

Thinking of that reminds me of the barefooted Indian fisherman and his boy at Puerto Escondido, the one that Tony said had been hanging around all the time—couldn't get rid of him. When the Loreto schoolteacher and the customs man and that group came aboard, he was there and shared in the canned fruit.

When they went away with indications on both sides of real affection, he said simply in Spanish, "Good friends." I thought what a true thing that was, and what a commentary on the whole non-western character which emphasizes the spiritual values of European-American insistence on material values. Not many American people have as many or as true friendships as those people up on the mountain near Loreto had for each other; not many Americans put as much into their friendships nor know so much about them; they are busy with another set of values, not necessarily better but not necessarily worse, either, just different. To recognize that difference might mean to have better respect for another race; to participate in it is to experience richness.

5:30 to 7: PM. Tide seems to be stationary at what I judge to be high, about 15 miles S in Concepcion Bay along the E shore (the W shore of the little peninsula that forms one boundary of the bay).

In 2½ to 4' of water on the sand shore (foreshore covered with pebbles), there were hundreds, probably thousands of two species of sand dollars, both pierced; *Encope grandis* and possible *Mellita*. In the same association, brilliant red sponge arborescences on occasional rocks (great clusters—some of these were dried). They are important horizon markers and ought if possible to be determined. Also, on other occasional rocks imbedded in the sand, clams with tunicates and the usual small ophiurans and crabs. Closer inshore, many brilliant large snails. One of the masked rock clams had on it a group of solitary corals.

A few rods inland along the shore, there were some pools of bitterly salt water with a gang of fiddler crabs on their banks and one only greater crab.

One only sea serpent-like moray taken at night by light. Also, Sparky took a flying fish. Also taken thus pelagically at anchorage were several small swimming crabs, other morays seen, *Penaeus*, bright green flying fish, many hetero-nereis and other free swimming annelids, some fish (probably larval flying fish), and some almost entirely transparent ribbon fish visible chiefly by shadow.

Animals brought up in crab nets, etc., from 4 fathoms anchorage sandy bottom in Concepcion Bay, about the middle of the peninsula (E) shore. Large voracious snails (probably *Phyllonotus*) eating dead fish bait in crab nets, new starfish. Everything gets eaten here in a hurry. Several hermit

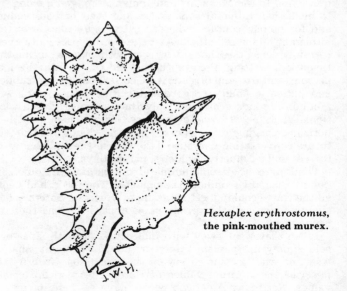

Hexaplex erythrostomus,
the pink-mouthed murex.

crabs on the half shell. Very large, very active sea urchins with long vicious spines. The *Phyllonotus* is probably *bicolor*.[1]

One of the finest eating fish I have had in many a long day is the Mexican Sierra.

29 Mch Friday: E side of Concepcion Bay, L. 26° 35' N. John and I went ashore about 7:30 AM, Mexican time. The tide, still running out, was already way below last night's stage. When we were ready to return at 9 AM, it was considerably below the position of the stake with the handkerchief which we had adjusted to the water level at 7:30 when we came ashore. And at 10 AM, the water level may have come up a little (as per examination from boat with binoculars), but not much. I should say that ebb water was about 9 AM.

The place in which we collected was something like this:

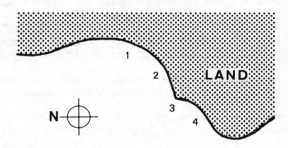

The two species of cake urchins, apparently co-mingled, were at Position 1, in from ½' to 1½' of water at low tide, which was maybe 3' or so below high tide. The ordinary cake urchin here, with holes, is probably *Encope californica* Verrill. The grotesque keyhole dollar is *Encope grandis* Agassiz. The large regular sand dollar, of which only 3 specimens were taken, more or less without our knowing we had them, may be *Clypeaster testudinarius* Gray.

A little deeper, at Position 2, were another (new to us) species of Holothuria, fairly flat and sand-encrusted. The giant heart urchins, probably *Meoma grandis*, which in some places were so abundant that we could have gotten almost any number, started between Positions 2 and 3 and reached their maximum at Position 3. They were all under 2½ or 3' below water level.

The shore here is much like Puget Sound. In the high littoral is a foreshore of gravel to pebbles to small rocks, sandy in the low, and sand with occasional rocks well below the tideline. In this zone, with a maximum at Position 4, there were growths of some algae, presumably Sargassum, lush and tall and extending to the surface. Again exactly like Puget Sound, except that we had no eel grass. Giant conch with eyes, same flat holothur-

---

[1]*Hexaplex erythrostomus.* Evidently the Gulf of California species were never formally assigned to *Phyllonotus*, which Myra Keen in her *Sea Shells of Tropical West America* (p. 517) regards as primarily an Atlantic genus. The species has at times been referred to as *Murex bicolor*; under whatever name it is the most abundant "murex" of the Gulf of California. It may be taken by the bushel in trawl hauls as far north as Puerto Peñasco.

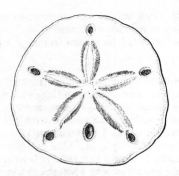

Encope micropora, the "ordinary cake urchin" (*E. californica* in the text).
Drawing by Lynn Rudy.

ians as at Escondido, *Cerianthus,* and sloppy guts, the anemone. At Position 1 at 9:30 AM, we found a few hachas, and at 10:30 Sparky got several fine big ones by wading and diving.

The surfaces were encrusted with sponge and tunicates, under which were crabs and snapping shrimps. Great scalloped limpets were attached also to the shells.

While we were walking along shore in this region, which was to me ecstatically beautiful, a great group of porpoises went by, quite slowly and blowing loudly. We heard again the lovely doves up in the hills, one of the prettiest sounds I have heard ever anywhere, except as Shelley should have said it, "And so they voice when thou art gone," or "Now at thy soft recalling voice I rise." The sound of the doves was like a soft two-toned yodel. In the distance especially, it was mellow. They answered each other like echoes. The green of the tall giant cacti is lovely against the burnt color of the mountains. Walking through them as I did last night was like going into a peaceful green valley. If I had time, I should have liked to walk all the way up into the hills—not far—just to be alive and to hear the doves calling at evening and again in the morning. I have never heard so many; they put a mark on the place. Reminded me faintly of when I was a child in Dakota; on a hot day in the cool creek draw, hearing the mourning doves.

After we had returned to the boat, Carol and Sparky went inshore again, coming back about 11:30 with another big load of sand dollars (it was in this load that the three specimens of the third different species turned up). Also, many hachas, many of which had a large shrimp, apparently a commensal Thallasinid.

San Lucas Cove: Arrived 5 PM outside San Lucas Cove. Sand bar and salt water lagoon. At 6 or 6:30 PM, the tide was still flowing into the cove; yet I'm practically certain we'll find ebb at 9:30 AM or so.

A few hermits, a few snails of 4 different species and several individuals of a very high tide small clam were picked up.

30 Mch Saturday: San Lucas Cove. Started about 8:30 AM, returned to boat about 11:30 AM. Collecting inside the lagoon (which I should have called a slough): San Lucas Cove, S of Santa Rosalia. The tide seemed to be starting back in about 11:00. I would put the ebb at about 10 or 10:30 AM. Wasn't very low. I don't think the *Cerianthus* were ever exposed; the ones I got were in 4 to 8" of water.

Cerianthus very very plentiful, and I collected maybe 20 or 30. John took some *Chione;* someone got a small smooth Venus-like clam; I took one razor clam. Carol got a large male *Uca* and several fleshy tubes which are apparently Enteropneusta. John dug up some small and not very active *Amphioxus.* We picked up a few snails. Saw 1 Emerita, several hermits and quite a few swimming crabs like *Callinectes*—of which we took 5. John searched long and intently for pea crabs, as he was extracting the anemones and the probably commensal sipunculids, but without success.

San Carlos Bay: Arrived 6 PM and went ashore immediately, returning about 7:30. The tide was slightly low but still coming in strongly, presumably from the mid-day low. Such tides!

I picked up a few beach hoppers under high shore masses of decaying seaweed. Had a great scramble for them. The animals down here certainly know how to take care of themselves by either running or stinging.

9-10 PM by light hung over side: another squid, a larval *Squilla*(?), a great run of transparent fish, including a new type; the usual heteronereis and crustacea.

31 Mch Sunday: The tide, which was very poor (about 2½ or 3' below the uppermost line of barnacles) ebbed slowly for a long time and started slowly to flow about 12:30 PM. John and the others started out about 10 AM; I got over there about 11:30. Before I got there, the wind was up, which made collecting very difficult.

However, partly because we were entirely unable to get into the low littoral—where I'm pefectly sure the lobsters and other finds would have been located—I was able to make quite a fine survey of the upper regions.

One fact increasingly emerges: the green and black cucumber (*C. lubrica*?)[1] is the most ubiquitous Gulf of California shore animal, and *Heliaster* runs it a close second.

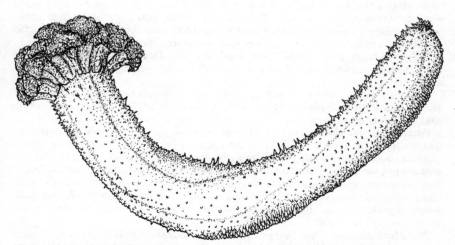

Selenkothuria lubrica, the common sea cucumber of the Gulf.
Drawing by Lynn Rudy.

[1]*Holothuria lubrica,* a.k.a. *Selenkothuria lubrica.*

San Francisquito Bay: Made anchor about 6 PM. Bad wind. Water was very very cold. We went ashore at once and set up a tide stake at 6 PM; the water was then 2 or 2½' below the highest line of barnacles.

Below that level were 3 types of crabs. One was a porcelain crab under rocks, one was *Pachygrapsus crassipes,* so far as I could see, one was maybe *P. transversus.* On the sides were barnacles and great limpets, two species of small (Tegula and something like a small *Purpura*), anemones as before. A few and very large smooth brown chitons, 2 or 3 of the bristle chitons.

Further down under the rocks were great masses of *Filograna,* some tunicates (one very large, flat, brown), *Astrometis,* cucumbers and *Heliaster* as usual, a few hermits. I saw one flat worm and Tiny took one octopus.

Tiny took the freshly cleaned (by isopods or amphipods) skeleton of *Panulirus,* apparently *interruptus.*

On the sand beach, I took, out of multitudes, a few *Emerita*-like forms.

About 10 PM, Carol took by hook and line 1 only *Gyropleuodus francisci* (Girard), the horned shark of the Family Heterodontidae, which I preserved, and 2 *Mustelus californicus* Gill (apparently), one about 3½' long, which we used for bait. Half-dozen scorpaenids in red, 1 black.

1 Apr Monday; San Francisquito Bay. When John got up, 8 AM, the stake on shore was high and dry, about 6"vertically maybe. When I got out, half-hour later, the gap of sand beach between the water and the stake was smaller, and when we got under way about 9:15 or 9:30, the stake was slightly submerged. So the tide was coming in fairly rapidly.

Got out big camera and started working out its operation again. Got every thing doped out except how to put shutter curtain back to larger aperature without making exposure. One way is to put in slide and snap the shutter back to correct speed, but there must be some more instantaneous way.

Angeles Bay: Went ashore at Angeles Bay about 3:30 PM. The tide was running out rapidly. A boy and a man ashore (there is little community here, and unscheduled, uncharted! Rum runners! John said possibly gun runner, because plane landed here, with sportsmen who said they were from Hattie Hamilton Ranch in their own plane) said low water was *mas tarde.*

Collected from 3:30 to 4:30, on a bouldery flat. Granite on coarse sand. A few hundred yards to the S of the big new adobe building with glass windows.

The high rocks had anemones, cucumbers, "sea cockroaches," a few (very scarce) small porcellanids. But no Sally Lightfoots and no large crabs whatsoever. A few *Heliaster.*

Further down, the dominant animal was easily the shell-less limpet or tectibranch, which occurred by the thousand in fairly large individuals. Some chitons, both the smooth brown and the fuzzy kind. Great clusters of Filograna were very very plentiful. Bryozoa, flatworms. 2 octopi, one quite large. Both seemed to be *Polypus bimaculatus.* Further down and entirely submerged were yellow Goodia on the undersides of rocks, and magnificent pink erect globular or hollow-vase-like (where largest) sponge masses, some several feet in diameter.

The algal zonation was very apparent. A sargassum-like form was submerged about 2 to 2½' at ebb, above this there were no algae, the rocks were completely bare. Below this narrow belt (like the narrow zone of shallow eel grass up north) was a great zone of the flat frond-like algae. On the few occasions when the wind died down sufficiently so we could look into this zone, it seems sterile except for the lush growth of algae.

About 5 PM, we took the outboard motor boat over to some fine sandy mud flats (compact, not mucky, with more sand than mud, but fairly fine grained) on the N shore of the bay.

Most of the biological accounts of expeditions have featured and illustrated only the rare forms. This is understandable; the more common animals have been described and possibly illustrated years ago, often, however, in publications now difficult of access. But it seems to me that the purposes of travellers and even of zoologists can be served best by accounts and illustrations of the common forms, particularly the ubiquitous forms, or the horizon markers. When I go into a new region, I am only secondarily curious about the occasional animals, unless they represent spectacular or curious types. But I do want to know something about the common, the obvious, the ubiquitous, and the economically important forms. Sometimes it's a job just to satisfy that simple requirement.

2 Apr Tuesday: Puerto Refugio, Angel de la Guardia Island. Arrived about 2:30 or 3 PM. John, Carol, Tiny and Sparky started collecting at once. I wrote up notes and didn't start collecting until about 7:30 or so. At that time, the tide was at its greatest ebb, quite low, possibly 7 to 10', on the point, below the highest line of barnacles.

The point was jagged volcanic rock, very hard and washed clear. Toward the E, there was a flat with fairly smooth (and terribly slippery) boulders on a flat of coarse sand. Not on the whole a very rich region, but surprisingly productive, nevertheless.

3 Apr Wednesday: En route to Tiburon Island, we ran by a great group of jellyfish. Apparently Ctenophores, 6 to 10" long, Zeppelin-like. Or possibly siphonophores. Caught one with a very slight way on the boat, but it went to pieces and passed right through the net, so we made no other attempts.

SE of Red Bluff Point on SW corner of Tiburon Island, we had good anchorage.

Collecting inshore 6 to 7:45 PM was very good. Reef was SW, a few boulders SE.

Reef had *Heliaster,* cucumbers and anemones, as usual. A giant snail was enormously abundant; I suppose we could have collected 500. High up, there were great clusters of a Tegula-like snail such as we found at Cape San Lucas. No shell-less limpet-like tectibranchs (except one that Tiny took in the boulders). Limpets and keyhole limpets. Geodia. Clusters of coral-like anemone. *Pachygrapsus.* John got one Sally Lightfoot, 2 solitary corals, some *Plumularian* hydroids. Barnacles. Many Phataria, Linckia, some *Strongylocentrotus*-like urchins, many club-tentacled urchins, some brittle stars. John located a most remarkably attenuated spider crab which, fortunately, we were able to catch. Sponges. Tunicates. Male and female stingrays found copulating and captured. Hydrocorals, very very plentiful.

On the more bouldery shore, Tiny took a few small crabs, searched long and unsuccessfully for a furry crab that had a hole in the sandy mud of a pool, several sand-living cucumbers. Took 3 Sally Lightfoots.

In the evening, John speared 4 or 5 barracuda-like fish with the harpoon from the big boat. The bats were very very plentiful and Sparky finally got one with a spear. Several of them seemed then to drive right at him and he broke and ran for the galley in some fright. Then every bat disappeared from the region, as though by command. It was some time before any of them came back, and they never came back in quantity.

4 Apr Thursday: Left for Guaymas environs about 8:30 Mexican time. Two Mexican Sierras taken en route by trolling jib. At Port San Carlos, outside Guaymas Bay, 6:30 PM. Completely land-locked harbor. Another pretty fair collecting place. I went ashore at once with Carol, Sparky and Tiny. John followed later on. Some new snails, a couple of Echiuroids under rocks, usual anemones, *Heliasters* and cucumbers. The water was soupy with shrimps and after quite a little work, I went back to the boat (partly at Carol's instigation; she'd seen several swimming crabs) and got the dip nets. Then I got quite a few of the shrimps. John picked up some of the swimming crabs which had lovely ultra-marine claws. A few chitons. Some under-rock crabs (porcelain and *Cancer*-like).

10 PM. Great flock of little fish about. Boys terribly excited. They tried netting them with bait seine, but no good, too fast. Tiny and Sparky, however, were finally able to work out a technique with the dip nets, and soon the nets full of little fish were being handed in through the galley window, literally into the frying pan and, almost literally, they wriggled into our mouths. Very rich. Pelagic stuff taken that night included shrimps, swimming crabs and transparent fish.

7 Apr Guaymas: We have been here since Friday noon. First to agent's office; very good, business-like man with German or Hungarian name— Hunaus. Then to American Consul, who is usually stationed at Juarez. Lots of mail for John. Two letters for me, one from lab forwarded from La Paz postmaster, one from Frank Lloyd, concerned with bawling out from Ritch [Lovejoy]. Then, agent having asked Captain Corona, the shrimp man and a port official, to contact us, we went to Carta Blanca saloon on the waterfront where he joined us. Captain Diego Ramirez Corona; speaks and thinks both in English and Spanish, is interested philologically, and is somewhat of a philosopher. Highly-developed consciousness. He told us lots about the shrimp industry, now pretty much in the hands of Japanese, was very humorous and kind and interested-ing. The Japanese big boats are 10,000 tons, the smallest feeder boats 100 tons and over; now they trawl for shrimp here (where they formerly used tide nets) as they do in San Francisco Bay and Puget Sound. Captain Corona himself runs three boats. He sent some shrimp aboard and returned subsequently Saturday for visiting.

Then we went to Mitla, a restaurant, had beer (but only High Life) and started drinking Hennessey VSOP. With the second bottle, a couple of English-speaking Mexicans joined us. One, a local druggist, very good man, United States educated, who with brother runs a drogueria and botica, the largest one here. And a half-Italian, half-Mexican dry goods salesman who is very good man. When we left, a couple of the waitresses, Soccoro and Virginia, very nice and jolly, said they'd like to go along. Someone sent ashore for a guitar-player and for more liquor. I got sick and went to bed, waking up subsequently, vomiting, sick drunk from too much brandy and too much cigar. In the meantime, all the crew had come back from town half drunk and joined the party; they all got stinko and many of them, to judge by the deck in the following morning, got puking drunk. I was sufficiently out so that I heard only occasional echoes, but the reports in the morning from John, who was very post-alcohol depressed, were that the Mexican girls got very drunk, and Socorro especially dissolved in pools of vomit until they, with Antonio, were poured aboard a water taxi. The rest I heard from Antonio, whom I met in the morning when, first thing, John took me ashore to get the cold beer which is my picker-up. He said Virginia was able to walk home, but Socorro was drunk and crazy and crying and hollering, in no fit condition to go home. Policeman finally nearly arrested the lot, but Antonio succeeded in getting Socorro into a hotel where he had to bribe the night clerk to take them in. According to his report, he then wanted to go and leave her as a vomiting mess, but she insisted he stay until they got ousted, and she went home when the night clerk went off duty at 6 AM.

I got up several times during the night to find everything awry. I couldn't find the bronionol, and the pheno-barbital disappeared completely and is still gone. I couldn't find the sea-water bucket or my flashlights, but finally took a nembutal, my stomach feeling still squeamish, and went back to bed after cleaning up around my porthole. Didn't get well back to sleep however, despite nembutal, and got up around 9 AM. Got cleaned up and went to town for beer; felt fine after about five bottles. John took me in with outboard, himself staying with boat; I brought back case of Carta Blanca, cold, and we stopped en route back at the Velero II for a couple of bottles with Captain and Chief. Coming back, found Carol had cleaned up the boat a little. Tony still in bed very sick. Tex didn't show up at all this morning, having stayed ashore where we thought he might be in jail. Sparky in swimming; then Carol jumped in with her clothes on, starting a rumor inshore (so it was reported) that she fell overboard.

Back in town, saw Socorro in Mitla, looking fine, but I'll bet not feeling so good. Wouldn't touch a drop, and Virginia failed to show up for her later shift, so Socorro had to work right through. Antonio very kindly took us in hand, he refusing anything to drink. I was unable to eat more than soup and oyster cocktail, but drank the fine Bordeaux wine that the druggist bought. Went shopping in the market where I was much moved at seeing little Indian girls, 4, 5, 6 or 7 years old, sitting at stalls:

> ". . . patient and cautious,
> . . . A flight of pelicans
> Is nothing lovelier to look at;
> The flight of the planets is nothing nobler; all the arts lose virtue
> Against the essential reality
> Of creatures going about their business among the equally
> Earnest elements of nature."
>
> (Jeffers, "Boats in a Fog")

It was the essential reality of these (inwardly, to me) unbelievably beautiful children that affected me so deeply.

> ". . . Beautiful beyond belief
> The heights glimmer in the sliding cloud, the great bronze gorge-cut sides
> of the mountains tower up invincibly,
> Not the least hurt by this ribbon of road carved on their sea-foot."
>
> (Jeffers, "The Coast Road.")[1]

The three or four deep things for me about this trip to date: the Good Friday service at La Paz; the still-used wing of the Mission at Loreto; the little Indian girls at the Guaymas market. Oh, yes, and the sad, fierce Indian boy who attached himself to us last and frenziedly at La Paz. And going ashore on the seaward peninsula at Concepcion, with the abundant straight

[1]*The Selected Poetry of Robinson Jeffers*, Random House, New York, 1931.

cacti so green against the barren hills, and the pigeons calling.

And so back to the boat for a much needed couple of hours rest, and into town again for evening prizefight, where Tiny was to be knocked out. Socorro said she'd like to go with us but, when I called for her, she said the other girl was too sick to work and she had to pinch-hit for her.

Fine evening with three or four good Mexican people. Captain Corona and the druggist and Antonio being pleasantly with us by preference, and accepting us quietly. One American was very unpleasant, drunk, raucous and insulting. And the gallery of Mexicans, being razzed by him viciously, razzing back amusedly.

With our different outlook as to time and mechanistics, probably it's not surprising that we should find inscrutable (except during temporary enlightenments), the genial and slow-paced social kindness of the Mexicans. Against our furious pace and impatience. When I think of Corona, of Antonio, of the drugstore man, of the drunks we saw Sunday at the waterfront bar, of the friendly people at Mitla, of the boy who hired the orchestra Sunday night, it seems impossible that so many people can be so kind in a non-expedient sense. I keep wondering if I should not interpret their actions in terms of temporal expediency, but I think that in many cases that expression is inadequate, and in some cases it doesn't apply at all. Many people here have done things for us, even casually, that have no reference to material remuneration or to social, political, or financial advancement for them. In other words, that whole field of human activity that you would call "physical," i.e., material, scientific, cause-effect, temporal, conceptual in an intellectual sense, they haven't been working in. The only repayment their actions could have reference to is a payment in kind, or in spiritual things. (Like the army officer in the Tolstoy play who says, when criticized for his wildness in chasing around with tramps, that his gypsy girl friend carries him to heaven by her singing, and all she wants is a little insignificant, common and mundane thing: money. That's an example in reverse.) But some of the things offered, the spiritual or the friendship things, I have a feeling, are offered out of the "deep thing" which underlies both spiritual and physical; in other words, they are given for what they are themselves, without either physical or spiritual expediency. Whenever I accept those things, so freely and even joyfully offered, I have a sense within myself of accepting an obligation in kind also. But in some cases, that's not the point; maybe some small percentage of such things are offered not with the unconscious hope of reciprocity, in which case they're pure and free. You can't easily tell, because the words and actions are identical for the superficial or expedient thing, and for the deep thing. The only discriminating quality I've ever heard of is what the Upanishads call "the high and fine intuition of the wise." Now, most Anglo-saxons, most Germanic people, won't do those physically non-expedient things (leaving out for the moment whether or not they're spiritually expedient). I do, and usually without much, maybe not any sense of establishing an obligation. But when I'm accepting such things, it's usually with a full heart that makes me hope they will show up in California, so I can do likewise, not necessarily so I can discharge the obligation, altho that feeling is sometimes present, too. I have thought that about Indians who have been good to me up north. But suppose that fine old Indian at Cape Flattery would sometime show up at the lab, he having almost literally given over his soul and (if I'd wanted) many of his poorenough worldly possessions when I was his guest. I had a feeling that he had a feeling (as I had first when the Bohemian neighbor's saloon burned down)

Brown Pelicans in the Sea of Cortez. Photo by Nick Carter.

that what he had to offer he found not enough, couldn't be enough, and that the only nobility was in the giving, not in what was given. Yet, if that Indian would show up, he'd simply sit down for maybe a couple of days in one place, and he'd smell up the lab, and all my other friends would hate him (soon) or be embarrassed after their original interest or condescension had worn off. A person can go from race to race all right; it's the coming back that involves violation. Yet I know that that old uncivilized Indian was greater, in the way I rate greatness, than the younger, less naive men on the reservation, who are familiar enough with our customs so as to fit in better.

I think, increasingly, that the tie-up of a different culture, with increased interest in temporal and material things ("civilization") is through good roads and high tension power transmission. I used to think that, in Mexico, increased interest in such temporal and material things as education, public health, housing improvements, etc., was through such political vehicles as national socialism, communism, etc., but now I believe it's chiefly a matter of good roads and power hook-ups, or through the influence of people who have been affected by their virus. La Paz and Loreto were "local" towns, although Loreto had the bug for progress ("progress" is a starry-eyed term for people like the young customs guard at La Paz, the custom official at Loreto, maybe, or certainly for the Ensenada woman with whom I had such a long talk last year). Ensenada is tending toward cosmopolitanism, and that whole northern district of Lower California is starry-eyed with hopes for woman suffrage, for the trade high schools that are thought to be fitting the children for a more abundant life, for irrigation, for General Rodriguez' model canneries and company houses and farms; or upset with disappointment when they find that the vehicles into which they put their hopes have clay feet. I thought all this was related to the renascence of Mexico, but it's more likely a zeitgeist, infection by the virus of civilization, the most obvious indices of which are good roads and power hook-ups and maybe canned foods. A 110 volt d.c. local power line and a windy dirt road doesn't change a community very rapidly or drastically, but a high voltage a.c. transmission line, operating day and night and supplying all the power that can possibly be used (since the infinity of all the power produced in western United States is behind it) and a cement road will do the trick in a hurry, whether the locality is conservative England, modern United States, Asiatic Russia, or Indian Mexico. That zeitgeist operates anywhere.

Interesting prize fights, not much science or training, but lots of intent and vigor and good health. Tiny, who had been training on the bottle, even the afternoon of the fight, took a bad beating from an unskilled, but longer-armed and more sober Mexican who was in good training.

Toilets here are bad and few, as in the smelly Juarez bars in the old days. And as at Ensenada; but I haven't recently had much experience with them on account of camping out. Here in Guaymas, as at La Paz, they are very bad and very public. The kind of places you have to chase the chickens and the kids out of first, if you're modest. The kind of toilets where the kids would play toy boat, if Mexican kids were given to playing toy boat, which they're not. The Indian-Latin combination results in much more openness in matters of sex and excretion than with us. Funny. And in much more real democracy, too, as in the Mexican middle-class families, who seem to be glad to have their girls screwed by American sailors who stay all night right in the girls' homes.

7 Apr Sunday: Tony, Sparky and Texas went in to church, were too late, and had a bang-up dinner as guests of Jugoslavian, who was affiliated with the fishing industry here, and with several Japanese and the Chief of Police. From Sparky, I got a picture of trade unionism as expedient as in the United States, but far more obvious, intense and widespread. And with no checks, since there the CIO isn't fighting the AF of L with opposing ideologies. They pictured a trade union situation that was far more of an out-and-out racket even than it is here. They had a fine time, were well-received and treated wonderfully and hospitably. The "ins" can always be genial.

I wanted to see more of Guaymas, which seemed a delightful city. John was in a deep post-alcohol depression, feeling very low, not wanting to go in town and not wanting ever again to see even beer, so that he shivered when I mentioned it. But Carol wanted to go in. And so did Tiny, who felt depressed about his defeat, the first in his life. John was concerned also, because there had been a note about him in local paper, but I couldn't see it had any effect on most of the people we met who had never heard of Steinbeck and who didn't care if they had; didn't mean anything to anyone but some American tourists who took me for John and asked for autographs. So we three went in, the inevitable small boy looking after our boat, and Carol, Tiny and I discussing the salutary disciplinary effect of defeat. Seemed to me that if Tiny hadn't known defeat before, which is a common concommittant of life, it was high time he was meeting it.

Went to Mitla, where the druggist joined us in a bottle of wine. Later, Antonio. Had a pleasant quiet time—too quiet for Tiny who, I imagine, wouldn't have tolerated it half an hour if he hadn't been suffering from depression on account of his licking—listening to jam session of orchestra, tuning up, as we supposed, for the dance which was scheduled for 10 that night (but which never came off). Orchestra played Carol's "Mi Partita" several times, skipper of the *Velero II* joined us; he and Antonio started "remembering when" about the *correctos*, which bored us, and which bored Carol particularly. So we three took a pleasant walk along the waterfront to oyster shucking place (fisherman co-op) and back through the whore-house Yankee-town section. A few girls with the universal earmarks of prostitution. Not attractive, I thought. District lacked the usual severe segregation of prostitution. There were children all about; in most red light districts, there's curious hush and I've associated it with the lack of children, as though the region were "burned." We met the boy who beat up Tiny, and he came out to greet us open-armed. Shook hands with a genuine democracy most charming, was really glad to see us and expressed it freely. A thoroughly nice boy. We asked another passer-by about a great building, if it was the *juzgado*. He said, "no, preeson." And went along with us a while, there again without any expediency except that he wanted to, as an expression of apparently genuine courtliness and hospitality.

Then in saloon next to Mitla, we had a few, not-so-good High Life beers and were joined by Sparky. No dance. Some other Americans came in for a while. One of them, thinking I was John, asked for autograph. Carol obliged. I asked if he wouldn't join us in a beer; he said they were going over to stag at California Cabaret, presumably after side-tracking their women. Tiny got date for himself and Sparky with Socorro and Virginia. They wanted to be taken to California Cabaret, which Sparky couldn't figure out, since that's sort of a whorehouse where you dance with a girl and take her to a room and pay her 2 to 5 pesos, she presumably squaring with the management for the room rent. (But Tex, ashore the other night without any money, got taken care of all night free.)

Carol wanted orchestra to play "Mi Partita" for her as they did that afternoon and Tiny sent over 2 pesos as before. But a group of young men who had rented the orchestra for the night returned the money, which for awhile made Tiny a little sore. But then the orchestra played the piece complimentarily, the young men being very courtly and kind (no women in the party). Subsequently, the guy who was throwing the party came to our table and asked what we would like to have played. Then we asked him to join us. A friend of his sat in for awhile also. They wouldn't let us buy any more liquor, and invited us to dinner and to the municipal dance from midnight to 4 AM. A pansy made a play for Tiny. A nuisance. Finally stopped by one of the water taximen, who simply told him not to annoy the Americanos. The 30-year-old boy who was giving the party was very genuinely kind; said he wanted to talk English but just was too dumb to be able to learn.   Carol understands pretty well. I, poorly.

Went then to Municipal Dance, which was well-filled. Antonio and the *Velero II* skipper were there. Antonio got Tiny a dance right away with a not very attractive but exceedingly good person. Mexican gal who took him home to sleep with her at her family's house. And her sister wanted some friend, too, but there was none. I ought to have stayed on, if Carol shouldn't have been put back aboard ship *and* if my bladder hadn't been so ungodly full; Antonio had warned me against urinating in the street (which I found, subsequently, was perfectly OK).

So we went to find water taxi. Impossible at that time, Sunday night. Sparky, who had previously announced he had all night date, had been sitting there for an hour or more, disconsolately trying to get back to boat. He and the *Velero II* captain borrowed a canoe, picked up the *Velero* launch, and took us aboard for a drink and some pickled oysters before he took us back to *Western Flyer* about 2:30 or 3 AM, where John and Tex had been waiting up, John very low.

8 Apr Monday: Captain Corona was aboard and invited us to lunch. We saw American Consul and agent, arranged for groceries, beer and ice, got leatherware and other curios for presents, and had long, fine, and gracious lunch with Captain Corona. Carta Blanca beer, Santa Tomas white wine, Habanero. Fine, funny old adobe house with courtyard with bougainvillea. No English, in honor of Mrs. Corona, but the captain and his wife spoke so slowly that even I was able to follow some of it. An amusing thing happened while we were there. The phone rang several times and we got to talking about telephones, of which there are several hundred in the states of Sonora, Sinoloa, and Nyarit. When Corona picked up the phone, he would ask for Senor So-and-So's store, and the house of So-and-So. Although numbers were listed in the book. He said that at one time the phone company insisted that the subscribers should use numbers. But, he said, "We were able to get along for a few days without using the telephone very much, so then the phone company didn't mind so much if we didn't use numbers."

Off at 4 PM, piloted out by Captain Corona, who gave us 2 giant shrimps, one mounted crab, 2 dried sea horses, and gave John some very hot chile rellenos, etc. The shrimps turned out to be *Penaeus stylirostris* Stimpson. The sea horses were male and female; the male carried the young in a "zipper" pouch. The captain stopped some of his shrimp boats, poor, funny little miserable craft like the smallest Puget Sound shrimpers, and took us over there in the pilot launch to see what they had. They had gotten only 1600 pounds shrimp, merely showing the big Japanese boats (as Corona said) where the shrimps were located. Then they come over with their big fine equipment and clean out the beds, so that Corona said it scarcely paid the Mexican boats to operate. But from what I saw of Japanese efficiency later, I should be inclined to believe that the Japanese boats were perfectly capable of finding their own shrimp.

Anchored for the night right outside Guaymas Harbor, opposite Pajaro Island light, where John promptly caught a bunch of fish that looked, acted and felt like catfish, and the boys went ashore to dig a bucket of clams that looked like *Venerupis staminea*. [*Protothaca grata*].

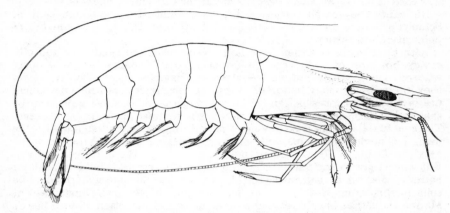

Penaeus californiensis, **the brown shrimp. Courtesy Richard Brusca, by permission from** *A Handbook to the Common Intertidal Invertebrates of the Gulf of California*, **Richard C. Brusca, Tucson, University of Arizona Press, copyright 1973.**

9 Apr Tuesday: Located the first Japanese shrimping fleet quickly. There were 6 or 7 boats. Upon permission being granted by Mexican and Japanese authorities aboard, we boarded the largest boat of that particular fleet, after our letters from the Mexican Department of Marine had been presented and read. Large outfit, with crew of 50 or more in 14'-draft boat apparently built for shallow water work.

Mostly shrimps (of the invertebrates) were taken. All the large specimens examined were *Penaeus stylirostris* (Kingsley). One magnificent anemone, several sponges and/or tunicates, quite a few grass-like gorgonians, an arborescent gorgonian, one sea horse, several squid. In life, the sea horse was quite brilliantly red; turned gray in alcohol. *Stomolophus* in brilliant hues all over the surface. Many many fish, possibly several tons per haul, which were thrown back; the Japanese saved only the shrimps. We brought back one or two each of the smaller fish.

The men, both Japanese and Mexicans, were very kind. They gave us their choicest treasures, 2 dried sea fans, and one of the "lobsters" that had been brought aboard presumably that same day, since it was still moist and undecayed. The shrimps were beheaded, shelled, cooked, and possibly also canned, immediately. Very very efficient lot, both in handling boat and net, and in preparing the catch. Fish consisted of a great many small teleosts including pompano (and our boys were pretty mad that we didn't bring back more of them for food), catfish, and puercos. Eagle rays and butterfly rays. Maybe a hundred or so sharks, from 20" to 5 or 6' long, all thrown overboard, hammerheads, brown smooth hounds, etc.

Arbolito is their name for gorgonians; and *agua mala* for jellyfish.

The shrimps have ovaries distended. The Mexican Fish and Game Commission man aboard knew nothing about the names of the shrimps, said a study was in progress. Was very kind and fairly intelligent, but not intellectual and certainly no scientist. He said there was legal recognition of (I think he said) 7, 9 and 11 common shrimp, but he could differentiate no species. Had, however, a tremendous respect for scientific work. The respect that tolerant but ignorant people have. He thought the male-female succession was correct for the Mexican *Penaeus* as for the Canadian *Pandalus*.[1]

He wants copy of our *estudios*. We also promised to send him copy of Schmitt's *Marine Decapod Crustacea of California*, U.C. Press; and list of publications on shrimps.

With their many and their very large boats, with their industry and efficiency, but most of all by their intense energy, the Japanese very obviously will soon clean out the shrimp resources of Guaymas. In addition to which, they kill probably many hundreds of tons of fish per day, of which no human use is made, and for which only the scavengers, such as sea gulls, can be thankful. After sorting, the dead material is dumped back into the ocean. The eventual depletion is so obvious that before getting acquainted with the men, I thought there must be some skullduggery going on between the Mexican Fish and Game Commission Inspector and the Japanese captain. But when I got to understand the kindness and integrity (would you call it? honesty, maybe) of the inspector, I saw he was absolutely OK. Maybe collusion higher up. But, on the whole, I imagine the Mexican Department of Marine Industries hasn't yet realized the danger of depletion, or else hasn't realized it intensely enough to start doing anything about it. This is *not* Mexico for the Mexicans, at least not in the long run, anyway, because soon the Japanese will have cleaned out the fishing banks, a purely Mexican resource will be depleted and the Mexicans will have nothing but the taxes they collected. The first step should be some sort of evaluation, no matter how rough, so that catch limits could be imposed. If the fishery will, apparently, stand a 50,000 catch per year, that limit should be established as a starter; the requirement should be insisted upon that the region be combed not so intensively and completely. Part of the resulting taxes should finance a more careful investigation. If the shrimp are going to be depleted anyway., and to hell with the future, the way California sardines are going, and the way much United States timber has already gone, at least the depletion ought to be by Mexicans, or for the immediate benefit of Mexico. At least

[1]Sex reversal is unknown for shrimp of the family Penaeidae. Things have improved in Mexico since 1940; there are several professional biologists studying the various species of shrimp in the Gulf of California.

some of the needy Mexicans ought to get some of the food.[1]

But there again is the conflict of nations, of ideologies, of two conflicting organisms. And the units in those organisms are themselves good people, people you'd like to know, like the kind young Japanese captain. He didn't have any of the courtesy and formality and false front we associate with Japanese. He was just good people. And so were the crew.

The ship we were on was estimated by Tony to be 150 to 175' long, 600 tons. There were 12 boats in the combined fleets, including the 10,000-tonner. The smallest were 100 ton, larger than the largest Monterey purse seiner.

Enroute south, the boys have been having an exciting time with manta rays. Saw maybe a dozen or more. Two were harpooned but got away, the latter carrying two spears and breaking two lines, one of which was 1½" hemp rope. Now they have a 3¾" line attached, with a high breaking strain, maybe 20 tons. Pilot fish riding on the back of big manta ray.

At that night's anchorage S of Lobos Light, 5 miles from the entrance to Estero de la Luna, John caught a young male hammerhead shark with copepods, via hook and line.

10 Apr Wednesday: Low tide at Altate 6:45 AM, at Guaymas 8:15 AM, Mexican time; -0.1', at San Diego 4:45 PM Pacific Standard Time.

Up at 5:30. John and I left around 6 AM to collect in Estero de la Luna. A wet cool night. Outboard motor wouldn't start, so we had to row the entire distance, a matter of 3 or 4 miles, according to the chart and according to Tiny's estimate. I started rowing while John tried to start engine. Set a hindsight star about due S by the N star and rowed thus until fog blotted out stars, then the *Western Flyer* mast light by which I was at that time steering, then the boat itself. Then the fog closed in on us heavily from the other direction as well, and we were able to maintain our course only by

[1]At the present time three species of *Penaeus* are significant in the landings at Guaymas: *Penaeus stylirostris* (cameron azul), *P. vannamei* (cameron blanco), and *P. californiensis* (cameron cafe). Since World War II the fishery changed from canning to fresh or frozen shipments, primarily to the United States, and probably anyone who has dined on jumbo shrimp in a Pacific Coast restaurant has eaten one of these species, of which *P. stylirostris* and *californiensis* have been the most significant. The fishery has held up longer than Ricketts expected, but it is declining and may soon become insignificant. We have no way of estimating what the wastage of "trash fish" has done to the natural populations of the shrimping grounds, although much of this is thrown overboard and hence "recycled." The survival of a shrimp fishery depends in large extent on the maintenance of the estuaries and lagoons in which the young are nurtured.

According to the most recent information from the Fisheries administration provided by the courtesy of Sr. Pedro Mercado, the catch in recent years has been as follows:

1970

| Blue Shrimp: From September to December — 33,782 Kg. | Brown Shrimp: From September to December — 103,126 Kg. |

1971

| Blue Shrimp: 48,153 Kg. | Brown Shrimp: 48,153 Kg. |

1972

| Blue Shrimp: 133,381 Kg. | Brown Shrimp: 309,040 Kg. |

1973

| Blue Shrimp: From January to May — 14,171 Kg. | Brown Shrimp: From January to May — 235,456 Kg. |

keeping the boat at a given angle to the waves. We could only hope the wind didn't gradually switch the waves around, since then we might miss the point entirely and start rowing the long 100 miles around the whole Gulf.

A "wrong side of the bed" day from the start. I had slept poorly, dreaming I had been bereft of the still physically present girl friend. Got up once at 2:30 AM, thinking it was time to start, just about the time Carol screamed with nightmare, and I reassured her. Maybe she heard me and felt quieter. Then, when I started to jump from big boat into skiff, I fell instead. Then it was wet and cold. Then the fog closed down.

We weren't even sure originally of our right course for the estuary, a small mark to hit in that distance, even on a clear night. Fearful we'd get too far out to sea, we kept bearing E of N. Finally, with a fair wind kicking up the ocean a little, but at the same time improving our rowing speed, we heard suddenly a vicious whistling or hissing, and both thought at once of the dreaded *cordonazo,* the violent hurricane which, fortunately, doesn't occur at this time of the year. What with thinking about the possibility of the continuing fog keeping us ashore all day or maybe a couple of days, because in a fog it would be impossible for us to find the big boat even with a compass, we were apprehensive in the first place. But our hissing was only the breakers, which we soon got through to a low sandy shore with wave marks and shells cast up even on the highest ridges, and with the tracks of birds and animals all around. The entrance to the estuary was nowhere in sight. Finally, the fog lifted and the sun shone and we made out the entrance, maybe half a mile to the west.

Within, the estuary was an inland sea, with no shore visible from most places. There was a channel and fairly large boats with local knowledge could get in.

Biologically, it was fairly sterile. There were many small snails, from 1 to 5 examples each of several species of large snails, and some gorgonians with hydroids growing on submerged shells. Near the entrance (where some fishermen were working; they were unsmiling, sullen, willing to talk and be talked to, but with none of the joy that most Mexicans evidence at the chance of a conversation; they had 50-60 pounds of great wide mullet-like fish, took two to carry one between them), there were *Harenactis* with transparent and almost colorless tentacles spread out on the sand. Further in, there were *Cerianthus* in tubes, such as we had taken before. Scores of minute sand dollars of a new type, rather brilliantly colored (for a sand dollar) and with holes and elongate spines. A few small heart urchins. I dug a couple of larger ones, further in.

There were big holes of two types, but they went down too far for our search on this tide. Some big crustacean, I figured.

But the commonest animal of all was the same (?Enteropneustan) that we had found at San Lucas Cove and at Angeles Bay and that Carol had worked on. There were hundreds of the piles of castings. I was still unable to get any more of an animal than we had found there, but am not at all convinced we got the whole beast even once.

Several large, beautifully striped, Tivela-like clams. Many small, flat, pearly clams in the holes we dug in vain attempt to find inhabitant of big burrow. Hermit crabs in various gastropod shells, some large, were fairly common. We found one of the sand-burrowing brittle stars (Amphiodia?). Shells and sticks had barnacles, one type of which seemed to be new. One giant swimming crab with barnacles and seaweed.

But on the whole, the region was surprisingly sterile. Might have been

partly real, partly due to wind making for poor visibility, or partly psychological. I had a feeling that we mightn't be getting even a fair representation
of what was there, but I guess the fauna actually must have been sparse.

Mirage is very very bad here. A strange region. You can't see the shores of
these lagoons. No wonder the charts show dotted lines. Everything so
strange and indefinite, and wind always on the water. No wonder the Yaqui
fishermen (if it was Yaquis that I talked to) have such a bad reputation.
They live in an uncertain land.

Returning, a long hard trip. Must have taken nearly two hours, in spite of
John being able to start the motor this time. (Tex has spent more hours
working on that little outboard than he has on the big Diesel that goes day
and night with little attention, yet it still isn't dependable. In order to
operate an outboard dependably, you must either know that particular motor
or else be a good mechanic; with this, both—and still NG.)

I was thinking about Boodin's remarks. His reference to the essential
nobility of philosophy and how it has fallen into disrepute. But particularly,
p. XVIII of *The Realistic Universe* 1931: "Somehow the laws of thought
must be the laws of things, if we are going to attempt a science of reality.
Thoughts and things are part of one evolving matrix, and cannot ultimately
conflict" (in connection with his favorable disposition toward what he calls
pragmatism—a newer and far better light on pragmatism for me). But of
course so. In a unified field hypothesis (or in life, which is a unified field of
reality), everything is an index of everything else. And the truth of mind (the
way mind is) must be an index of the truth of things (the way things are).
However, one may stand in relation to the other as an index of the second or
irregular order, rather than as a harmonic or first order index. That is, the
two types of indices may be compared to the two types of waves (and indices
are symbols as primitive as waves). Type one: the regular or cosine wave, as
the tide, or undulations of light, sound, or any other type of energy,
especially where the output is steady and unmixed. These waves can be progressive in the sense of increasing or diminishing, or can be apparently stationary. (But deeply, some change or progression may be found in all oscillation, since all terms of a series must be influenced by the torsion of the first
term, and by the torsion of the end or the change of the series). These waves
are fairly predictable, as the tide. Type two: irregular, like the graphs of
rainfall in a given region, which fall into means which are functions of the
length of time during which observations have been made. These are unpre-
dictable individually; that is, you can't say whether or not it's going to rain
on a given day, but in ten years you can say there will probably be a certain
amount of rainfall.

Then I was thinking of the difficulty of explaining this to, for instance,
Tiny (when he tried to understand what I had to say about depleting and
sardine fluctuation, he got very mixed up and upset), as an index of people in
general. He would be happier if he could be relaxed and "easy"—go along
with—*until* he really understood what I was talking about. That may be
plenty difficult, but it's a lot easier and there's a lot less strain to it than
putting up barriers, with their impatience and intolerance, before a person
even understands what's being discussed. Then, if he had any valid
criticism, is the time for it. Criticism then becomes a constructive thing,
instead of a confusion.

I am again impressed with the inaccessibility of the shore. You can go to
places out in the ocean easily enough by boat. And you can get nearly anywhere on land by car, or by a combination of car and walking. But that

narrow stretch of country called the strand or the beach, which is neither land nor sea, but alternately one and then the other, and which is often beaten by surf, may be very difficult of access.

People who are afraid of having something put over on them must live a life of continual and quite difficult defense. I should think it would be very nerve-wracking. They insure themselves against doing more than their share of the work at too high a cost.

Talking to Sparky, I was reminded again how important short-wave radio is to these boys. Every night they talk to fishing boats at or near home, or to others who relay the message to Monterey. Which means a lot to family people such as Italians. And it's a source of much needed entertainment to them. We've twice received fairly important long distance phone or radio calls on business and once sent a wire clear from the wilderness.

Passing Mayo River mouth today, we saw 5 manta rays, big ones, in quick succession, mostly deep, but one so near the surface that Tony would have run him down if he hadn't submerged quickly.

11 Apr Thursday: Anchored 5 miles off Agiabampo shore last night, and ran in further with the big boat this morning. Left about 10 AM, arrived inside Agiabampo estuary about 10:30 AM. Returned about 1 PM. The tide when we returned was running so strongly against us through the channel, that two men had to row to help the outboard motor.

Within the entrance, the banks were heavily cut by currents. There were grapsoid crabs (but not Sally Lightfoot) high in the intertidal in sand burrows slanting 12 to 18". There were lots of conches with great stalked eyes, and hermits living in their cast-off shells.

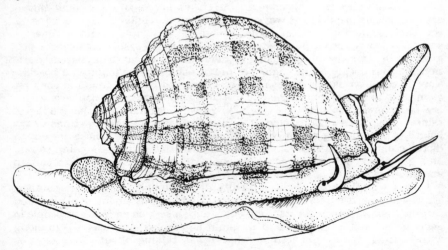

Cassis centiquadrata. **Drawing by Lynn Rudy.**

Further in, there were some *Chione* and a good many of the blue-clawed swimming crabs, *Callinectes* or similar.

In the eel grass, there were a few hermit crabs, not many, but one large and new to us, many sting rays and botetes and some other fish, but it was on the whole—the eel grass especially—a sterile area. I found some eel grass sexually mature, and took along some for identification. Lots of snail egg masses on the grass. What snail? We saw none of the animals. Also, what were the birds feeding on, on the bar in the middle of the little bay? One scale worm, magnificent specimen in *Cerianthus*-like tube. A good many worm tubes not investigated. Why isn't MacGinitie here? While we were collecting in the bay area to the N of the entrance, the wind was entirely still, and we could see well. There weren't many animals, at least not obviously, on the bottom.

On the way out, it seemed that the oystercatchers were hunting the fast and large grapsoid crabs. And what were the crabs hunting, I wonder?

Enroute across the Gulf: Tony just asked me to move his can of cigarettes away from the bridge, saying, "It draws the compass." I realized he said that in the way he'd say, "The point draws the waves," and I thought for a moment amusedly that an unthinking person would class these phenomena as equivalent, in the sense that they were equally true. Then I thought, "Why not, he's probably correct, they are."

The Sea of Cortez: and not an awful lot better known now than then.

12 Apr Friday: Arrived San Gabriel Bay, Espiritu Santo Island, about 10-10:30 AM, after running most of the night, but hove to for a few hours on account of fog. Left at once to go ashore, returning 2 or 2:30 PM, Mexican Standard Time. And on the last day of all—as on the first, the outboard motor absolutely balked, we had to row in; fortunately, this time, a short distance.

San Gabriel Bay consists of stretches of white coral sand alternating with boulder reefs. There is a fine big patch of coral almost emerging in the center of the bay. Mangrove islands and swamps on some of the bouldery patches. The coral is of the green and brown sorts, with many great heads. There are *Phataria* and club-spined urchins.

The sand beach had:

(1) Chitons, very very plentiful. By the thousand. At first, we found only a few and by accident, but Sparky and Carol discovered while they were in swimming that multitudes could be turned out of the deeper water, maybe 2 or 3' submerged, by following the small tufts of green algae attached to the front of each valve. They got a whole wash tub full.

(2) Hachas, with their fauna.

(3) *Harenactis*-like anemones, both solitary and clustered, possibly the same we have been seeing in many variations, as the hard anemone, from La Paz clear on up to Guardian Angel. All varieties, from typical *Harenactis*, solitary, elongate, with bulb buried in sand, down to short and clustered forms attached to stones or shells.

(4) *Callinectes*, lighter colored. Possibly a function of these vividly white coral sands.

(5) Holothurian, 1 worm-like, such as we took at Puerto Escondido. A few new snails. A sea porcupine or heart urchin, very nasty and with vicious sharp spines. Sparky had a pretty sore thumb for several days as a result of picking them up.

The rocky reef had anemones, limpets and barnacles. The one I investigated was being inundated by sand, and consisted largely of rocks and small boulders indurated below and being drowned above. The feature here, and the most characteristic animal was a membraneous tubed worm with tentacles like a serpulid. The purple and brown color of these tentacles was a feature of the intertidal landscape which changed suddenly to sand color when you stepped near and disturbed the animals so they withdrew their tentacles. Langustinas were being cast up by the million.

The mangrove swamp was a rich region. The roots of the trees were impacted with rocks that had a fine fauna of crabs and cucumbers. The large hairy grapsoid was highest, very active, hard to catch, and belligerent when caught. Autotomized readily. A *Panopeus*-like form was very common, and dopey. Many porcelain crabs and quite a few snapping shrimps but difficult to capture. The usual anemones and cockroaches not taken. Mosquitos. Oysters, 3 limpets and barnacles on the rocks. Barnacles on the mangrove roots. 1 *Callianassa* under rocks. A couple of new ophiurans. The mussel-like clam. A large sea hare turned up in the haul, and a few miscellaneous snails and clams. Most things here seem to be the same color as the coral sand, dazzling white. The last collecting trip of this series, and a very good one.

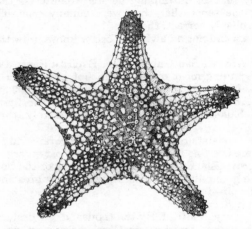

Oreaster occidentalis. **Drawing by Lynn Rudy.**

In connection with the unified field hypothesis, note the horror with which Tiny regards such "waste" as throwing dead fish overboard (as the Japanese were doing on that shrimp boat). (I couldn't tell him that, of course.) Every bit of that fish is eaten by scavengers. If by chance they miss any, the minute particles are utilized by detritus feeders, of which worms and cucumbers are most noticeable. Any microscopic portions—or even large portions, for that matter—so missed are reduced by the bacteria. So that what is one group's loss or death is another group's gain or life. Nothing is wasted. The equation always balances. The elements which the fish elaborated into an individuated physical organism, a microcosm, go back again into the undifferentiated macrocosm. There is no "waste"; there are, simply, forms of energy and/or food not utilizable by man. And any process that results in the forming of products not utilizable by man is called waste. The large picture is always clear; also the small picture of eater and eaten, and the large equilibrium of the life of a given animal being postulated on the presence of abundant larvae of just such forms as itself for food. Nothing is wasted. No star is lost. And, in a sense, there is no over-production, since every single living thing has its niche—a posteriori.

13 Apr Saturday: 11 AM, back on Pacific Standard Time, and back into the open Pacific, there was a tremendous clap of thunder. In an immediately menacing sky, I was above making things shipshape against the coming storm; picking up a couple of boxes of matches before the rain should soak them—we were short anyway. When the perfectly tremendous clap of thunder came, it sounded as though we had been shot; I nearly fell overboard. Below, Sparky had been taking a leak. That stopped that. But Tiny was best. He was sleeping and awoke suddenly to say, "What are they shooting at us for?" (I guess Navy training; there had been another boat on the horizon before he went to sleep.)

Tex just reported a fine dream about me. I was giving a very erudite lecture somewhere before a great hall of people. Very dignified lecture on food, how many varieties there were to it, how many ways it could be cooked, how much care people should take in preparing it. Suddenly I asked, "Oh, by the way, can I get one of the young gentlemen in the audience to go get me a sandwich?"

"Going along with" is merely an articulate expression for a process of relaxation whereby you go along with, rather than fight against, the pace of external events over which you have no control, or while you are developing a technique of control in the case of events that aren't inexorable.

Duality. In steering: a west-making tendency on the part of the waves or the wind is compensated by an east-bearing pressure on the wheel. The one is external influence over which you have no control, the other is a compensatory response directed from within, to the end that a straight course can be maintained.

This afternoon, I found myself humorously saying to Tony, as he spotted Margarita Island way ahead, "Is it where it ought to be?," and I have often said that of lighthouses at night. Now it seems to me that that idea is a good distinction between "ought" and "is." Of course the lighthouse is where it *is*; we, in a sense are where we are, too, but it is we who are "out" by relation to the lighthouse. Lighthouses are fixed; it's we who move (comparatively), and if the lighthouse isn't where it "ought to be," it's because we are out of where we want to be.

Immediately I came up on deck for my midnight to 3 AM shift with Tony, I had that unpleasant sense of presence of an unseen third person. As though a tall cloaked stranger were behind me, face muffled. Someone who couldn't be on the boat, since there were only seven of us and we were all accounted for, yet there he was. As though you forgot for a minute how many there were, and absent-mindedly allowed for an extra. I thought of death behind me in the gray night. It was murky, cloudy, slightly misty, everything was wet, you couldn't see the stars or the land. We couldn't pick up the lighthouses that should have come into sight, they weren't where they should be, and one of them never did appear. For a while, I thought of mentioning that sense of presence to Tony, but didn't, wisely, since he was already plenty strained with his navigation problem. Then I thought of John. Then I realized that in this whole superstitious crew there wasn't one person from whom I could have gotten comfort. All I'd have done in mentioning it would be to scare the hearer, or to arouse the antagonism or ridicule that is unaccepted fear. So the watch passed and nothing happened. Tony got six new gray hairs from changing course according to dead reckoning without being able to see the lighthouse from which he hoped to get bearings. They "weren't where they ought to have been." But the critical time passed with no trouble, I steering almost the entire shift while Tony, with even the riding lights turned off, strained eyes and ears for evidence of any possible oncoming danger.

Tiny is flying his kite again this afternoon. Just seems to satisfy some inpulse in him, so up it goes. He spent all morning making it, all afternoon flying it, from the turn table, or once from the crow's nest—of a boat coming full tilt up the Lower California coast.

Steering illustrates one of the important relations between technic and intention. With Tony standing over me, and I nervous of his observation, no matter how deeply I want the compass card to swing in the desired direction, no matter how great a price I would pay if my wish were fulfilled, no matter how intently under such circumstances an old-fashioned person would pray, it will not swing correctly unless I push the wheel in the right direction. The intensity of desire and the frenzy of the attempt have nothing to do with the desired results unless the technic is correct. If I push the wheel west strong and hard enough, that compass card is going to spin east, in spite of hell and high water.

But Ed is an illustration of the opposite relation. He had no predispositions toward music or toward playing the trumpet, except intense desire. His ear wasn't good, his sense of time was bad, he didn't know anything about the technic of music. A musical aptitude test would have demonstrated conclusively that music wasn't for him. Yet, it seems now that in time he'll become an extraordinarily good trumpet player, and he's already pretty good.

20 Apr Saturday, and subsequent: We got into San Diego maybe on Wednesday—I don't recall exactly, and have been pretty binzled ever since. There were moderate winds and stormy seas for the last 36 hours, and I was out for 22 of them.

Tony and I had the watch wherein we came in through the narrow pass S of Cedros and changed the course. Was already pretty rough, when I got up after my little sleep. Carol was already getting sick and went to her bunk in the morning. During the day, it got steadily rougher, typical Northwester; I was able to eat and to keep my wheel watch, but not much else. Even if you keep well, bad weather is terribly boring. You can't read or typewrite, you can't even talk pleasantly, for the labor of holding on. At 9 PM, I went up on top to take my wheel watch; quite a little spray was coming over and it was hard to hold on, and dangerous to climb the side ladder. Tony was steering, before his time, and he said he wouldn't want anyone else to guide the boat through the rough seas. The boat rode beautifully. Tony was able to ease her into waves so that she didn't take any green water and there was not even much spray when Tiny was hollering for him to "slow down for this one". Jack used to slow down for them, but Tony said the thing to do was to ease her into them and if they got too bad to run half-speed. The wind was only moderate, say 20 M.P.H., but the seas were higher than the wind would have indicated. I think three days of a gale would kill me, because I couldn't keep up my strength enough to eat. I was feeling rocky. Tony suggested that both John and I go below, take some sleeping pills and hit the hay—since it's difficult, for me anyway, to sleep when the boat is pitching badly, on account of the energy required to hold on. Between then and the following day, counting a couple of phenobarbitals already in me, I had taken 12 of those and nembutals, and didn't get up until 7:30 the following night, when we were nearly into San Diego. At 2 AM, Tony sent down, asking John to take the wheel, and he had to fight off his sleeping pill in addition to fighting the boat around in the stormy seas.

All that medicine ought to have slugged me, but still I woke up when spoken to, or when the engine stopped or the bell rang that indicated over-heating, or even when my name was mentioned. But when I dressed, passed customs and medical inspection and went ashore to eat steak, I was drunken boy. I couldn't see or walk or talk clearly. We got into town late, due to rigorous customs inspection, more intense than at any other time I have come in from either Canada or Mexico or Alaska. The boys tried to smuggle some sea stores and the inspectors, finding some of them, slapped a $38 fine against the boat and made a pretty thorough search. I suppose we should have got in touch with the agent first thing. The woman said they were available night or day, but there would be overtime if we came in after 5 or before 6.

John and Carol went to a hotel for a decent night's sleep, I went back to the boat where I slept through that night also.

Awoke early, helped clean up the boat, Tiny and I working fairly briskly in the galley; had a little breakfast beer. Intended then to type, but John came down and we started drinking Scotch whiskey. All that day we drank. Tiny and Sparky came to hotel and had drinks and dinner with us, I first luxuriat-ing in hot shower with plenty of fresh water. Then Tiny's girl friend showed up, then Maxie Wagner, and we took over the bar. Later went to the Paris Inn, where I got sad and walked back to boat about 2 AM. Got in quietly a little before Sparky rolled along, wearing Maxie's hat, which woke up the boat.

The following day, Carol and I had been considering going back by land, but she ended up by deciding to take it on the chin and go by boat. Alberta was going to drive back to Los Angeles anyway, and offered to take Maxie and me.[1] I looked up the weather report, found another Northwester moving down from the coast of Oregon and figured to get a train in Los Angeles. I never have liked being bounced around in small boats and avoid it when I can; seasickness, even if you avoid nausea as I did this time, is pretty un-pleasant.

We drank beer on the way up—Alberta and I, and whenever we'd stop, Maxie would have a double slug of rum. He was due back at the studio at 5 PM, we got into Hollywood about 6 PM, after he had called the lot, and we hung around, drinking and talking and meeting some quite nice people, like the guy who made "Grass" and "Chang," until Max got shaved and dressed, and got me a check cashed. Got to RKO lot about 9 PM; interesting place and people, and what drunks! And beautiful girls who acted like clever floozies, one of them jumping on Maxie's leg and giving him an imitation screwing that was very realistic. We hadn't eaten, wanted to go, so some of them asked us to bring back a bottle of Scotch and gave us paycheck vouchers to identify us for return. Instead, Alberta and I had been getting acquainted and liking each other, and she said, "Wouldn't it be amusing if you didn't show up until after the boat?" I said that's just about what would happen, and then she said if I'd stay over, we'd go down to San Pedro to the *Sea Giant* the following night and call up the ship to kid them along, they expecting me already to be in Pacific Grove. So we had a good dinner and lots more to drink and started making the rounds of Hollywood night clubs, which are very good and very cheap. I found Carta Blanca beer every-where. Alberta knew one of the entertainers at Seven Seas and we drank and danced around until I thought of the possible urgent need that guy might

---

[1] Alberta and her friends are unidentifiable at this late date.

have for his paycheck voucher. So we went back to the bar where that gang hung out—Alberta has a marvelous sense of direction. I'd never have found it—and there they were. Maxie said, "I knew Eddie would come back," and the guy with the recovered voucher hugged and kissed us. So then we went to another place where there was a marvelous Negro orchestra with a piano player, King Cole, whom it was a pleasure to watch. We put the place to sleep, finally, apparently first insulting some minor movie director who figured people should know him. I don't know any of the names even, and when he got put out, Alberta said it would be all right with us if he went back to his own table. Which Maxie said was a fine thing, because the guy was too much toadied to. Jack Wagner is a good man.

So we got to Alberta's sister's place pretty late, and didn't get up until late next day. Then we persuaded her brother-in-law, who is a street-car conductor, nice young kid just out of Missouri, to take the day off, and we all got pleasantly binzled again, and they were very good to me and took me to see some of their relatives. Part Indian Oklahoma people. Always in some drunken driving trouble. Compton is terribly strict, opposite of Hollywood. Their Aunt Lizzie was fine; wish John could have been there; I had a sense of love for her in the sense that I loved that old, old Russian woman in Seattle, who couldn't speak any English, that time Xenia and I went there for Easter morning breakfast after midnight service with Jack and Sasha. Then over to look up *Sea Giant*, and nobody knew where it was. We went from Terminal Island to San Pedro, a long way around, only to find it was out fishing. So Alberta located another Monterey boat, the *New Roma*, and the captain, Buster, a very nice guy, made us welcome, gave us still more beer, which by that time we very obviously didn't need, and started his motor for power to broadcast to the *Western Flyer*. They had already closed down their receiver, however, Sparky saying subsequently that he thought Carol might be disturbed by very extensive conversations. Buster promised to try to contact Sparky at 8, the following morning, to tell him we were there and partly maybe to forewarn Tiny, in case he'd be sore at Alberta not telling him what she was up to. So back to their house in Compton again, where, way after 10, we cooked a big dinner and went to bed. Lucille was toying with the idea of eating the fine Italian salad that Alberta fixed to go with the best steak I could get—and not very good that time of night—said it usually made her sick. But she ate it and was promptly sick as a horse.

In the morning, up late again, leisurely lunch after sunning awhile on Long Beach beach. Left for Pacific Grove about 5:30, I driving most of the way, a safe steady 65 or 70, car was new. Good dinner at Santa Barbara and beer after that, whenever we wanted it. We closed the bar at San Miguel and brought a little beer along, but by the time we got to the lab after dawn, we were cold and tired, and I was worried about how cold the lab would be, and figured that my blankets would all be on the boat, and we didn't have money enough to stay out comfortably one more night and have meals in the morning. But the lab was neat and pretty; I started the furnace. Tal, bless her heart, had brought back my bed, so we had some music and went to sleep for a couple of hours before trying to route out Tiny who had been out all the night before. Frances called up about 8 AM and John a little later.[1]

22 Apr Monday: The day on which we were supposed to return, I having cut it by one day and the others by two. Sparky and I unloaded the boat, I

[1]Frances Strong, Ed's sister.

got Ed to help, and what with the Scotch whiskey I had been trained on, I found it plenty hard. Took four truckloads and one more load of groceries in the back of the Ford. In the afternoon, Alberta and Tiny came over, she en route back to Los Angeles. I sorted stuff out so I could get around, picked up Tal, we had some beer, and went down to the boat for some final errands.

Trip covered approximately 25-30 collecting stations all in the Gulf, upward of 4,000 miles, and two days less than six weeks. We took probably the greatest lot of specimens ever to have been collected in the Gulf by any single expedition, certainly the greatest per individual, since there were only 2 to 6 of us, and other trips have had whole corps of scientists, and trained personnel to run the equipment.

I had kept up in good spirits throughout, but feel depressed and lonely now. Part probably hangover, part let-down from the last few days which were fairly happy, but most probably due to seeing how, when people come back from a trip, everyone has some one person who sidetracks everything else just for him. And I keep recalling that in the past year I have had only people with whom I was No. 2 person; I have been companions with terribly nice people like Jan and Alberta—and had a fine time—but their depths were for someone else, and they had little or nothing to give me, or with people like Lee or Marge or Muriel who haven't much to give anyone. I suppose the answer is that it's nice to be loved best and only, and who hasn't that lacks an important part of life. So, in one sense, every place is alike for me and there's no point to my coming back; I felt that most strongly when I came back from Alaska after four months. But all things pass, including that feeling; and the good feelings; and all things.

26 Apr Friday, 6 PM: Finished, a big job. And sorting the specimens, a bigger one now before me.

Zoogeographical summing up: at least three regions in the Gulf.

1. The SW portion, along the Baja California shore from Cape San Lucas to maybe San Jose Island (the first place the tides started to be "wrong" and the water was so cold). Tropical fauna; corals, sea fans and arborescent gorgonians, ornate starfish, club-spined urchins, highly-ornamented spiny lobster. Very rich in a tropical sense.

2. The W and NW portion of the Baja California shore. Much like Pacific Grove; barnacles, limpets, anemones, *Panulirus interruptus,* no starfish except *Heliaster* and a few *Linckia.* Very rich in a northern sense.

3. The E portion along the Sonora shore. Depositing shore, lagoon region, oysters and shrimp. Rather sterile.

IIIC. The Log of the *Western Flyer*

Tony Berry's "Log" of the *Western Flyer* is a casual document that possibly might not have met standards for insurance had the boat cracked up at Cape San Lucas after midnight (as it came very close to doing); and, it must be said, is not all that we would have wished it to be in retrospect. Nevertheless it is a concise statement of the whereabouts of the *Western Flyer* from day to day between March 14 and April 18, 1940. Now and then Tony had trouble with Spanish names, and garbled them. Some of these have been correctly —and pedantically—stated in their correct form in brackets. Once, early in the trip, the "scientists" were confused about where they were and thought they spent an overnight anchorage on March 20 at Pescadero Point; but it was actually Coyote Point. On the map we have indicated all the localities visited or mentioned during the trip; also the dates, especially of overnight stops, according to this log.

Left to right: Tiny, Ed, Carol and John Steinbeck.
Courtesy Mrs. William H. Brown.

Steamer   Western Flyer   Voy   270 miles   Cedros

Sailing From   San Diego   To   Mexico And Return

BRIDGE COMPASS	DISTANCE BY LOG	TIDE	WIND	BARO- METER	WEATHER & REMARKS
March 14, 1940					
2:10 PM	Left San Diego 1				
3:10 PM	Buoy off entrance to San Diego.			SE 3/4 S	
3:45 PM	Change course to Cedros.				
4:20 PM	Coronado Island (S beam).				
8:40 PM	Todos Santos Island.			6-1/2 hrs	
March 15, 1940					
5:30 AM	San Martin Island.				
8:30 PM	Cedros Island light.			(S)	
12:30 AM	Pt. Eugena [Punta San Eugenio].			27-1/2 hrs	
March 16, 1940					
1:00 AM	Change course.			SE 3/4 E	
1:00 PM	Running into fog.				
7:00 PM	Run out of fog.			22-1/2 hrs	
10:00 PM	Cape Lazarius [Cabo San Lazaro]. Light outside of us; about 15 miles off course.			5-1/2 hrs	
March 17, 1940					
3:55 AM	Changed course to SE 3/4 E				
8:50 AM	Cape Lazario Light above. Changed course to SE E 3/4			5 hrs	
9:20 AM	Cape Tosco Pt. abeam.			2 hrs	
10:30 AM	Same course. Lots of Skipjack and Tuna. Breezing & jumping.			13-1/2 hrs	
12:00 PM [Midnight]	Arrived at Cape Lazo [Falso?]				
12:05	Changed course for Cape Lucas				
12:45	Slowed down and forward slowly, all of a sudden shore ahead, dropped sounding line 14 fathoms, but boy, you could throw a rock on the shore. A close call I calls it.				
March 18, 1940					
	Laid at Cape San Lucas all day. Entered and cleared for La Paz. Saw the cannery and town.				
March 19, 1940					
5:30 AM	Left San Lucas for Pulmo Point for the scientist to get specimens.				
10:45	Arrived at Pulmo Point and dropped the anchor.				
March 19, 1940					
3:30 PM	Left Pulmo Point.				
6:00 PM	Dropped anchor by Pescadero Pt.				
March 20, 1940					
5:30 AM	Left Pescadero Pt.				

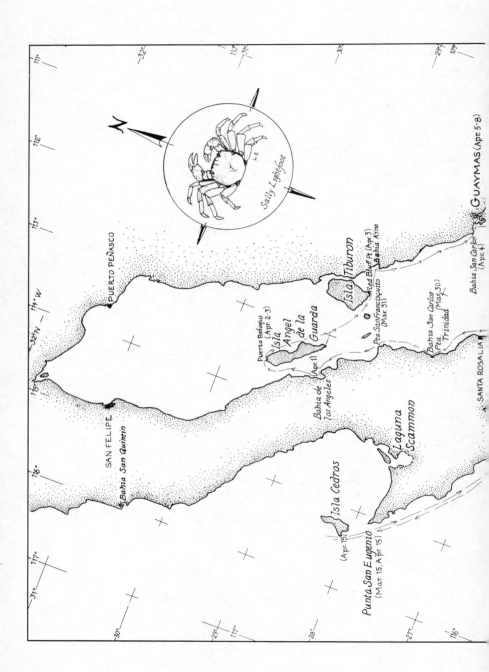

N

Sally Lightfoot

L.E.

PUERTO PEÑASCO

SAN FELIPE

Bahia San Quintin

Puerto Refugio
(Apr. 2-3)

Isla
Angel
de la
Guarda

Isla Tiburon

Red Bluff Pt. (Apr. 3)
Bahia Kino

Pta. San Francisquito
(Mar. 31)

GUAYMAS (Apr. 5-8)

Bahia San Carlos
(Apr. 4)

Bahia de
los Angeles
(Apr. 1)

Bahia San Carlos
Pta. (Mar. 30)
Trinidad

SANTA ROSALIA

Laguna
Scammon

Isla Cedros

(Apr. 15)

Punta San Eugenio
(Mar. 15, Apr. 15)

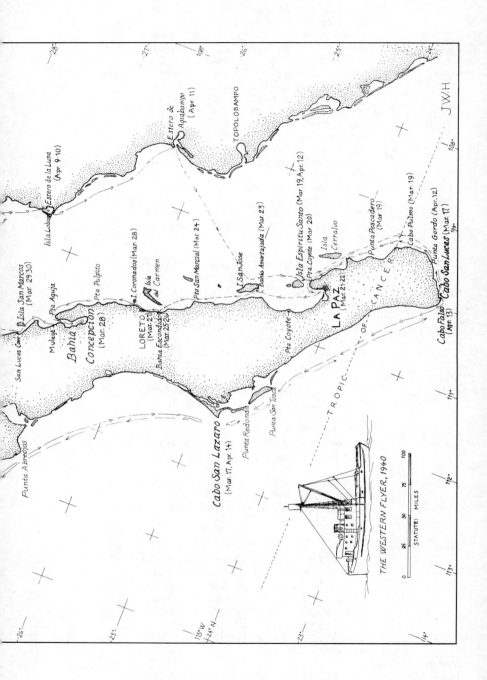

Punta Abre Ojos

Isla San Marcos (Mar. 29-30)
San Lucas Cove
Estero de la Luna (Apr. 9-10)
Isla Lobos
Pta. Aguja
Mulege
Bahía Concepcion (Mar. 28)
Pta. Pulpito
I. Coronados (Mar. 28)
LORETO (Mar. 27)
Isla del Carmen
Bahía Escondido (Mar. 25-26)
Pta. San Marcial (Mar. 24+)
Estero de Aguiabampo (Apr. 11)
TOPOLOBAMPO
I. San Jose
Bahía Amortajada (Mar. 23)
Isla Espiritu Santo (Mar. 19, Apr. 12)
Pta. Coyote (Mar. 20)
Isla Cerralvo
LA PAZ (Mar. 21-22)
Pta. Coyote
Punta San Tosol
Punta Redonda
Cabo San Lazaro (Mar. 17, Apr. 1+)
Punta Pescadero (Mar. 19)
Cabo Palmo (Mar. 19)
Punta Gordo (Apr. 12)
Cabo Falso (Apr. 13)
Cabo San Lucas (Mar. 17)
TROPIC OF CANCER

J.W.H.

THE WESTERN FLYER, 1940

STATUTE MILES
0   25   50   75   100

	The boat *Pacific Queen* was icing fresh fish here. Also the *Vashon* came in to anchor. Headed for Espiritu Santo Island.
11:45 AM	Arrived at Espiritu Santo Island. They collected quite a few specimens and are well satisfied. On the way to this island, we passed the *Miss California* and also a big black yacht, could not see the name. We are anchored here for the night, also I talked to the *Sea Rover;* he says there are about 15 boats on Espiritu Santo bank. Sparky and I have a blowfish apiece. The weather is lovely and I am sorry my wife isn't here.
7:00 PM	Had to move from anchorage. S wind blowing hard.
9:00 PM	Moved to Coyote Point [N.B. This is the "Pescadero Pt." of *Sea of Cortez*, pp. 82 and 91.]
March 21, 1940	
8:30 AM	Started from Coyote Point to go to La Paz.
12:00 AM	Arrived at La Paz. Officials came aboard.
March 22, 1940	Laid at La Paz today. Went ashore to church. Lot of junk souvenirs for sale.
March 23, 1940	
10:15 AM	Left La Paz for Amortajada Bay.
2:25 PM	Arrived at Amortajada Bay.
2:30 PM	Dropped anchor. Went ashore and got lot of sea shells and explored around.
March 24, 1940	
8:00 AM	Got up and looked around. Weather's fine. Some of the boys went ashore again. Sparky went ashore to get more shells.
12:10 PM	Left Amortajada Bay for Pt. Marcial.
4:10 PM	Arrived at San Marti Bay [Bahia San Marcial]. Dropped anchor for the night.
March 25, 1940	
12:10 PM	Left San Marti Bay for Puerta Escondito [Escondido]. Prettiest place I have seen. A natural bay and harbor. Landlocked on all sides.
March 26, 1940	
	Laid at Puerta Escondito on anchor. Not much doing today. The boys had a celebration last night. Quite a few hangovers today. Also, we ran out of water in one tank today. The Mexicans around here have their hands out all the time for money. Started to run on stern fuel tanks yesterday.
March 27, 1940	
11:00 AM	Left Puerta Escondito for Loreto. Stopped

	outside of Loreto for 2 hrs. Everybody but Tex and I went ashore.
1:00 PM	Left Loreto for Coronados Island.
2:10 PM	Dropped anchor in a little bay on the southwest side of Coronados Island. Tex, Sparky, Tiny and I went swimming on the whitest beach made all out of crushed seashells.

March 28, 1940

9:10 AM	Left Coronados Island anchorage for Conception Bay.
11:30 AM	Abeam of Point Pulpito.
4:30 PM	Arrived at Pt. San Rosalia in Conception Bay. [This Pta. Sta. Rosalia is on the east shore of Bahia Conception at about 26°41' N.] Good pickings for the hunters.
4:35 PM	Dropped anchor for the night.

March 25, 1940

12:00 AM	Left Pt. Rosalia for [San] Marcos Island.
4:00 PM	Dropped anchor off San Lucas Cove. Nice place, but not good for swimming.

March 30, 1940

10:00 AM	Left San Lucas Cove to San Carlo Bay.
5:30 PM	Dropped anchor off Trinidad Pt. Went ashore swimming.

March 31, 1940

12:15 PM	Left for San Francisqueta Bay [San Francisquito].
5:30 PM	Dropped anchor. S. wind blowing like hell.

April 1, 1940

9:00 AM	Left San Francisqueta Bay for Angeles Bay [Bahia de los Angeles]. Arrived at Angeles Bay; quite a tricky bay to get into. Lots of small islands inside this bay. A camp ashore, lots of trucks and an airplane on the beach, some kind of a construction camp, I presume. NW wind blowing, first chop we have had since we left Cape San Lucas.

April 2, 1940

9:00 AM	Left Angeles Bay for Puerto Refugio. NW wind blowing.
2:00 PM	Dropped anchor at Angel de la Guardia Island.

April 3, 1940

7:30 AM	Left Puerto Refugio at Angel Island.
5:00 PM	Dropped anchor off Tiburon Island at Red Bluff Point. Weather fine.

April 4, 1940

8:30 AM	Left Red Bluff Point for Guaymas.
5:00 PM	Stopped at Puerto San Carlos Bay. Dropped anchor for the night. Mosquitoes galore. They can give this country back to

the Indians.

April 5, 1940

7:30 AM Left Puerto Carlos for Guaymas.

10:00 AM Arrived at Guaymas. Pilot came aboard and custom officials.

April 6, 1940 Anchored at Guaymas. Everybody ashore.

April 7, 1940 Anchored at Guaymas.

April 8, 1940

5:00 PM Anchored at Guaymas. Waiting for further orders.

5:30 PM Pulled out of Guaymas to anchor off Isle of Pajaros [?]. Cleared customs for San Diego.

April 9, 1940

8:30 AM Left anchorage for shrimp fishing boats. There are 12 Japs' boats here. All big boats. They are sure killing a lot of other fish. John and Ricketts went out.

1:00 PM Started for Lobos Island anchorage. On the way, we tried to spear at least 50 Manta Ray. Lost all our harpoons.

5:00 PM Dropped anchor.

April 10, 1940

10:00 AM Still on anchor. The specimen hunters went to the Estero [Estero de la Luna] Lagoon early this morning, not back yet.

12:95 AM Left anchor for Agiobompo [Estero de Agiobampo].

9:15 PM Dropped anchor in 10 fathoms of water. Figure we are about 5 miles offshore. Off of Agiobompo.

April 11, 1940

7:00 AM We moved into shore close to the lagoon. We were about 5 miles offshore. They went ashore.

3:00 PM Left Agiobompo. Laid a course SW X S 1/2 S to San Jose Island.

April 12

2:00 AM San Jose Island on the bow, changed course to SSE. Run one hour and a half, then we drifted till 7:00 AM.

7:00 AM Started up again for Espiritu Santo Island.

April 12, 1940

10:30 AM Arrived at San Gabriel Bay off of Espiritu Santo Island.

12:15 AM Left San Gabriel Bay for Cape San Lucas.

3:30 PM Gorda Point (nice weather).

6:45 PM Pescadero Point.

9:30 PM Turned course for Los Frailies [Frailes].

11:45 PM Turned for Cape San Lucas.

April 13, 1940

5:00 AM Abeam Cape Falso. Set course for NW X

	W 1/2 W.
11:00 AM	A big steamer passed us about 4 miles outside of us.
11:30 AM	Caught three yellowfin tuna on the gigs.
8:00 PM	Abeam Pt. Tosco.
1:00 AM	Kind of hazy, could not see Redondo Light at 10:00 PM.
April 14, 1940	
1:30 AM	Changed course to NW 3/4 W. Did not see Cape Lazarus Light. Heavy haze inshore; figure we are about 10 to 15 miles off Cape Lazarus.
1:11 AM	Steamer inside of us about 4 miles headed toward Cedros. We should see Abrejos [Punta Abreojos] Point about 4 PM, I hope. Hazy weather on Abrejos Point. *Bremen* is 3 miles inside of us. Looks like we are going to have company.
April 15, 1940	
5:15 AM	Abeam Point Eugenia. *Bremen* in front of us.
8:45 AM	Abeam Cedros Light. Change course to NW 1/2 N.
April 16, 1940	
1:30 AM	San Martin Island. Went inside of island to eat, as weather is rough outside.
12:00 PM	Todos Santos Island Light.
5:00 PM	Abeam of Coronados Island.
7:05 PM	Tied up alongside of Quarantine Wharf in San Diego.
April 17, 1940	
April 18, 1940	Laid in San Diego.
2:00 PM	Left for Monterey.

Ed Ricketts at the Great Tide Pool, Pacific Grove, California. Courtesy Ed Ricketts Jr.

IIID. Essay on Non-teleological Thinking [1]

Non-teleological, rational, or "is" thinking, as contrasted to the more usual cause-effect methods. An inductive presentation. [2]

During the '31 depression, we lived close to a destitute and rather thriftless 132
family. My wife used to remark that they looked to the county authorities for support because they were shiftless and negligent; that "if they'd perk up and be somebody, they'd be alright." Her viewpoint was undoubtedly correct enough so far as it went. But I used to wonder what would happen, assuming that people of this sort could and would change their habits, to those with whom they would exchange in the large pattern,—those whose jobs would be usurped, since at that time there was work for, say, only 70% of the total population, leaving the remainder as government wards.

My attitude had no bearing on what might be, or was to be in the future, or could be if so-and-so came about; it merely considered conditions "as is." No matter what the situation might be with regard to the ability or aggressiveness of the separate units, at that time there were great numbers necessarily out of work, and the fact that those numbers comprised the incompetent or maladjusted or unlucky units is in one sense beside the point. No causality is involved in that; collectively, it's just "so." The units may be blamed as individuals, but as members of society they cannot be blamed. Any given individual very possibly may transfer from the underpriviledged into the more 133
fortunate group by better luck or by improved aggressiveness or competence, but all cannot be so benefited whatever their strivings, and the large population will be unaffected. The 70-30 ratio will remain, merely with a reassortment of the units. And no blame, at least no social fault, imputes to these people; they (or some similar units) are where they are "because" natural conditions are what they are. And so far as we selfishly are concerned, we can rejoice that they, rather than we, represent the low extreme, since there must be one.

I

So, if I am very aggressive, I should be able to obtain a position even under the most depressed economic conditions, but only because there are others, less aggressive than I, who serve in my stead as potential government wards. In the same way, the sight of a half-wit need never depress me, since his extreme, and the extreme of his kind, so effects the mean standard of sanity that I, hatless, coatless, often bewhiskered, thereby will be regarded only as a little odd. And similarly, I cannot enthuse over the success manuals that tell our high school graduates how to obtain employment, there being jobs for only half of them!

This type of thinking unfortunately annoys many people; it may especially

[1]Typed by Toni, March 1941, original to John. [EFR]

This version of "Non-teleological Thinking" was prepared for Steinbeck as he was writing up the trip, and forms a substantial part of pages 132-150 of *Sea of Cortez*. The appropriate page numbers of the book as originally published by Viking are indicated in the margin.

[2]"How does a hen know the size of an egg cup when she lays her egg?" (Heard on the Chase & Sanborn Hour, October 1, 1939). [EFR]

arouse the anger of women, who regard it as cold, even brutal, although actually it would seem to be more tender and understanding, and certainly less blaming, than the more conventional methods of consideration. And the value of it as a tool in increased understanding cannot be denied.

As a more extreme example, consider the sea-hare *Tethys*, a shell-less flabby sea slug or snail, faintly resembling a rabbit crouched over, which may be seen crawling about occasionally in tidal estuaries. A California biologist determined that more than 478 million living eggs may be produced by a single animal in a single breeding season; and the adults may occur by the hundred! Obviously, all these eggs cannot mature, all this potential cannot become reality, else the ocean would soon be occupied exclusively by sea hares. In a few generations, they would overflow the earth; there would be nothing for the rest of us to eat; and nothing for them unless they turned cannibal. On the average, probably no more than the Biblical one or two can attain full maturity. Somewhere along the way, all the rest will have been eaten by predators whose life cycle is postulated upon the presence of abundant larvae of sea hares and other forms as food. Now, picture the combination mother-father hare (the animals are hermaphroditic, with the usual cross fertilization) parentally blessing its offspring with these words: "Work hard and be aggressive, so you can grow into a nice husky *Tethys* like your ten-pound parent." Imagine it, the hypocrite, the Pollyana, the genial liar, saying that, en masse, to its millions of eggs, with the dice loaded at such a ratio! 99.999% are destined inevitably to fall by the wayside. Any given individual has almost no chance at all. Never-the-less, the race survives, and there is a semblance of truth in the parent sea-hare's advice, since even here, with this almost infinitesimal percentage, the race is still to the swift and/or the lucky.

Teleological thinking, as exemplified by my wife's notions about our improvident neighbors—correct enough in itself, but now seen to be only part of the picture, is associated with the evaluating of causes and effects. It considers changes and "cures," what "should be," the presumed bettering of present conditions (often, unfortunately, without achieving more than a most superficial understanding of those conditions).

Non-teleological ideas derive through "is" thinking associated with natural selection as Darwin understood it. They consider events as outgrowths and expressions, rather than as results; conscious acceptance as a desideratum and certainly as a prerequisite to all else. In their intolerant refusal to face things, teleological notions frequently substitute a fierce and sometimes hopeless attempt to change conditions which are assumed to be undesirable, in place of the understanding acceptance which would pave the way for a more sensible attempt at change if that still seemed desirable. Non-teleological thinking concerns itself not primarily with what should be or could be or might be, but, rather, with what actually "is," attempting at most to answer the questions what or how, instead of why—a task in itself rigorously difficult.

An interesting parallel to these two types of thinking is afforded by the microcosm with its freedom or indeterminacy, as contrasted to the morphologically inviolable pattern of the macrocosm. Statistically, the electron is free to go where it will. But the destiny pattern of any aggregate, comprising uncountable billions of these same units (as for example, the eventual disintegration of a stick of wood or a piece of iron, through the departure of the comparatively immortal electrons), is fixed and certain, however much that inevitability may be delayed by much deferring of the operation of the second law of thermodynamics as is conferred by painting and rust-proofing.

II

Examples sometimes clarify an issue better than explanations or defini-
tions. Here are three situations considered contrastedly by the two methods.

a. Why are some men taller than others?
136

Teleological "answer": because of the under-functioning of the growth-
regulating ductless glands. This seems simple enough. But the simplicity is
merely a function of inadequacy and incompleteness. The finality is only
apparent. A child, being wise and direct, would ask immediately, if given this
answer: "Well, why do the glands under-function?," hinting instantly toward
non-teleological methods, or indicating the rapidity with which teleological
thinking gets over into the stalemate aspects of first causes.

There can be no "answer" in the non-teleological sense. There can be only
pictures which become larger and more significant as one's horizon increases.
In this given situation, the steps might be something like this:

(1) Variation is a universal and truly primitive trait. It occurs in any group
of entities, razor blades, measuring rods, rocks, trees, horses, matches,
or men.

(2) In this case, the apropos variations will be toward shortness or tallness
from a mean standard: the height of adult men as determined by the
statistics of measurements or by common sense observation.

(3) In men varying toward tallness, there seems to be a constant relation
with an under-functioning of the growth-regulating ductless glands, of
the sort that one can be regarded as an index of the other.

(4) There are other known relations consistent with tallness, such as compensatory adjustments along the whole chain of endocrine organs. There
may even by other factors, separately not important, or not yet discovered, which in the aggregate may be significant.

(5) The men in question are taller because they fall in a group within which
there are the above-mentioned relations. In other words, "They're tall 137
because they're tall".

This is the statistical or "is" picture to date, more complex than the teleological "answer"—which is really no answer at all—but complex only in the
sense that reality is complex, actually simple, inasmuch as the simplicity of
the word "is" can be comprehended.

Understandings of this sort can be reduced to this deep and significant
summary: "It's so because it's so." But exactly the same words can also
express the hasty or superficial attitude. There seems to be no explicit method
for differentiating the deep and participating understanding—the "all-truth"
which admits infinite expansion or change as added relations become
apparent, from the shallow dismissal and implied lack of further interest
which may be couched in the very same words.

b. Why are some matches larger than others?

Examine similarly a group of matches. At first, they seem all to be of the
same size. But to turn up differences, one needs only to measure them carefully with calipers, or to weigh them with an analytical balance. Suppose the
extreme comprises only a .001% departure from the mean (it will be actually
much more), even so slight a differential we know can be highly significant, as
with the sea hares. The differences will group into plus-minus variations from
a hypothetical mean to which not one single example will be found exactly to

conform. Now the ridiculousness of the question becomes apparent. There is no *particular* reason. It's just so. There may be in the situation some factor or factors more important than the others. Due to the universality of variation, even in the factors themselves that "cause" variation, there surely will be, some maybe predominantly so. But the question as put is seen to be beside the point. The good answer is "it's just in the nature of the beast"; and this needn't imply belittlement; to have understood the "nature" of a thing is in itself a considerable achievement.

138

But if the size variations should happen to be quite obvious, and especially if uniformity were to be a desideratum, then there may be a particularly predominant "causative" factor which could be searched out. Or if a person must have a stated "cause"—and many people must, in order possibly to get an emotional understanding (really a sense of relation of the situation) and to give a name to the thing so it can be "settled" so as not to bother them any more—he can examine the automatic machinery which fabricates the products, and discover in it the variability that results in variation in the matches. But in doing so, he will get involved with a larger principle or pattern, the universality of variation, which has little to do with causality as we think of it.

c. Leadership.

Teleological notion: that those in the forefront are leaders in a given movement and actually direct and consciously lead the masses, in the sense that an army corporal says "Forward march" and the squad marches ahead. One speaks in such a way of church leaders, of political leaders, and of leaders in scientific thought, and of course there is some limited justification for such an idea.

Non-teleological notion: that the people we call leaders are simply those who, at the given moment, are moving in the direction behind which will be found the greatest weight, and which represents a future mass movement.

For a more vivid picture of this state of affairs, consider the movements of an amoeba under the microscope. Finger-like processes, the pseudopodia, extend at various places beyond the confines of the chief mass. Locomotion takes place by means of the animal flowing into one or into several adjacent pseudopodia. Suppose hypothetically that molecules which "happened" to be situated in the forefront of the pseudopodium through which the animal is progressing, or into which it will have flowed subsequently, should be endowed with consciousness and should say to themselves and their fellows: "We are directly leading this great procession, our leadership 'causes' all the rest of the population to move this way, the mass follows in the path we blaze." This would be equivalent to the attitude with which we commonly regard leadership.

139

III

As a matter of fact, there are three distinct types of thinking, two of them teleological. Physical teleology, the type we have been considering, is by far the commonest today. Spiritual teleology is rare. Formerly predominant,now it occurs metaphysically, and in most religions especially as they are popularly understood, but not, I suspect, as they were originally enunciated or as they are still known by the truly adept. Occasionally, the three types may be contrasted in a single problem. Here are a couple of examples:

A. Van Gogh's feverish hurrying in the Arles epoch, culminating in epilepsy and suicide.

Teleological "answer": Improper care of his health during times of tremendous activity and exposure to sun and weather, brought on his epilepsy and
death.
Spiritual teleogy: He hurried because he innately foresaw his imminent death,
and wanted first to express as much of his essentiality as possible.
Non-teleological picture: Both the above, along with a good many other symp-
toms and expressions (some of which could probably be inferred from his
letters), were part of the same under-lying pattern, perhaps his "lust for life."

B. The thyroid-neurosis situation.

Teleological "answer": Over-activity of the thyroid gland irritates and over-
stimulates the patient to the point of nervous breakdown.
Spiritual teleology: The neurosis is causative. Something psychically wrong   140
drives the patient on to excess mental irritation which harries and upsets the
glandular balance, especially the thyroid, through shock-resonance in the
autonomic system, in the sense that a purely psychic shock may spoil one's
appetite, or may even result in violent illness. In this connection, note the
army's acceptance of extreme homesickness as a reason for disability
discharge.
Non-teleological picture: Both are discrete segments of a vicious circle, which
may also include other factors as additional more or less discrete segments,
symbols of an underlying but non-teleological pattern which comprises them
and many others, the ramifications of which are n, and which has to do with
causality only reflectedly.

IV

Teleological thinking may even be highly fallacious. Consider the situation
with reference to dynamiting in a quarry. Before a charge is set off, the foreman toots warningly on a characteristic whistle. People living in the neighborhood come to associate the one with the other, since the whistle is almost
invariably followed within a few seconds by the shock and sound of an explosion for which one automatically gets ready. Having experienced this many
times without any closer contact, a very naive and unthinking person might
justly conclude, not only that there was a cause-effect relation, but that the
whistle actually caused the explosion. A slightly wiser person would insist
that the explosion caused the whistle, but would be hard put to explain the
minus t element. The normal adult would realize that neither the whistle
caused the explosion nor the explosion caused the whistle, but that both were
parts of a larger pattern out of which a "why" could be stipulated for both, but
more immediately and particularly for the whistle. Determined to chase the
thing down in a cause-effect sense, an observer would have to be very wise   141
indeed who could follow the intricacies of cause through more fundamental
cause to primary cause, even in this largely man-made series, about which we
presumably know most of the motives, causes and ramifications. He would
finally end up in a welter of thoughts on production, and ownership of the
means of production, and economic whys and wherefores about which there is
little agreement.

The example I have quoted is the most obvious and simple I can recall. Most
things are far more subtle than that, and have many of their relations and

most of their origins far back in things more difficult of access than the tooting of a whistle calculated to warn by-standers away from an explosion. We know little enough even of a man-made series like this—how much less of purely natural phenomena about which also there is apt to be teleological pontificating!

Usually it seems to be true that when even the most definitely apparent cause-effect situations are examined in the light of wider knowledge, the cause-effect aspect comes to be seen as less, rather than more significant, and the statistical or relational aspects assume larger importance. It seems safe to assume that non-teleological is more "ultimate" than teleological reasoning. Hence the latter may prove to be limiting and constricting except when used provisionally. But while it is true that the former is more open, for that very reason its employment necessitates greater discipline and care, in order to offset the dangers of inadequate control and looseness.

Frequently, however, a truly definitive answer seems to arise through teleological methods. Part of this is due to a wish fulfillment delusion. When a person asks "why?" in anything, he usually deeply expects, and in any case receives, only a relational answer in place of the definitive "because" which he thinks he wants. But he customarily accepts the actually relational answer (it couldn't be anything else unless it comprised the whole, which is unknowable except by "living-into"), as a definitive "because." Wishful thinking probably fosters that error, since everyone continually searches for absolutisms (hence the value placed on diamonds, the most permanent physical things in the world), and imagines continually that he finds them. More justly, the relational picture should be regarded only as a glimpse, a challenge to consider also the rest of the relations as they are available, to envision the whole picture as well as can be done with present abilities and data. But one accepts it instead as a real "because," considers it settled, having named it, loses interest and goes on to something novel.

Chiefly, however, we *seem* to arrive occasionally at definitive answers through the workings of another primitive principle: the universality of quanta. No one thing ever merges gradually into anything else, the steps are discontinuous, but often so very minute as to *seem* truly continuous. If the investigation is carried deep enough, the factor in question, instead of being graphable as a continuous process, will be seen to function by discrete quanta, with gaps or synapses between, as quanta of energy, undulations of light. The apparently definitive answer occurs when cause and effects both arise on the same large plateau which is bounded a great way off by the steep rise which announces the next plateau. If the investigation is extended sufficiently, that distant rise, however, will inevitably be encountered, the answer which formerly seemed definitive now will be seen to be inadequate, and the picture will have to be enlarged so as to include the ripple next further out.

Everything impinges everything else, often into radically different systems, although in such cases faintly. I doubt very much if there are any teleologies, or between the two teleologies. But there can be no conflict between any of these and the non-teleological picture. For instance, in the condition called hyperthyroidism, the treatments advised by believers in the psychic or neurosis etiology very possibly may conflict with those arising out of a belief in the purely physical cause. Or even within the physical teleology group, there may be conflicts between those who believe the condition due to a strictly thyroid upset, and those who consider causation derived through a general imbalance of the ductless glands. But there can be no conflict between any or all of these factors and the non-teleological picture, because the latter includes them—evaluates them relationally or at least attempts to do so, or maybe only accepts them as time-place truths. Teleological "answers" necessarily must be included in the non-teleological method—since they are part of the picture—even if only restrictedly true, and as soon as their qualities of relatedness are recognized. Even erroneous beliefs are real things, and have to be considered proportional to their spread or intensity. "All-truth" must embrace all extant apropos errors also, and know them as such by relation to the whole, and allow for their effects.

V

The criterion of validity in the handling of data seems to me to be this: that 144 the summary shall say significantly and understandingly, in substance "It's so because it's so." Unfortunately, the very same words might equally derive through a most superficial glance, as any child could learn to repeat from memory the most abstruse of Dirac's equations. But to know a thing emergently and significantly is something yet again, even though the understanding may be expressed in the self-same words which were used superficially. In the below example (abstracted from the article on Ecology by Elton, Encyl. Britt., XIV Ed., 7:916), note the deep significance of the emergent as contrasted to the presumably satisfactory but actually incorrect original naive understanding. In Norway, an important game bird, the Willow Grouse, was becoming scarce, so that protective regulations were required, and a bounty was placed on its chief enemy, a hawk which was known to feed heavily on them. Quantities of the hawks were exterminated, but despite these drastic measures, the grouse disappeared more rapidly than ever. The naively-applied usual remedies failed, but instead of becoming discouraged and quietistically letting this bird become extinct, the authorities enlarged the scope of their in- 145 vestigations, with the result that the anomaly was explained. An ecological analysis into the relational aspects of the situation disclosed that a parasitic disease, coccidiosis, was endemic among the grouse, which, in its first stages, so reduced the speed of their flight that they became easy prey for the hawks. Thus, the hawks, in living largely off the slightly ill birds, prevented them from developing the disease in its full intensity and so spreading it more widely and quickly to otherwise healthy fowl. The enemies of the grouse population, by checking the epidemic aspects of this disease, were in this case actually friends in disguise.

In summarizing the above situation, the measure of validity wouldn't be to assume that, even in this well-understood factor (coccidiosis), we have the real "cause," but to say, rather, that in this phase we have a highly significant and probably preponderantly important relational aspect of that specific picture.

However, many people are unwilling to chance the sometimes ruthless appearing notions which may arise through non-teleological methods. They fear even to use them in that they may be left dangling out in space, deprived of such emotional support as had been afforded them by their unthinking belief in the institutions of tradition; religion, science, in the security of the home or the family, or in a comfortable bank account. But for that matter, emancipations in general are apt to be held in terror by those who have not yet achieved them, but whose thresholds toward them are becoming significantly low. Think of the horror, or at best tolerance, with which little girls regard their brothers who have dispensed with the Santa Claus belief, or the devout young churchman, his university senior who has grown away from depending on the security of religion.

146   As a matter of fact, in employing this type of thinking with other than a few close friends, I have been referred to as detached, hard-hearted, or even cruel. Quite the opposite seems to me to be true. Non-teleological methods more than any other, seem to me to be capable of great tenderness, of an all-embracingness. Consider, for instance, the fact that, once a given situation is deeply understood, no apologies are required. There are ample difficulties even to understanding conditions as "is." Once that has been accomplished, the "why" of it (seen now to be simply a relation, although probably a near and important one) seems no longer to be preponderantly important; it needn't be condoned or extenuated, it just "is," it is seen relatedly merely as part of a more or less dim whole-picture. As an example: a woman near us in the Carmel woods was upset when her dog was poisoned—frightened at the thought of passing the night alone after years of companionship with the animal. She phoned to ask if, with our windows on that side of the house close, we could hear her ringing a dinner bell as a signal, during the night, that marauders had cut her phone wire preparatory to robbing her. Of course that was, in fact, a ridiculous and improbable contingency to be provided against; a man would call it a foolish fear, neurotic. And so it was. But my wife said kindly, "We can hear the bell quite clearly, but if desirable, we can adjust our sleeping arrangements so as to be able to come over there instantly in case you need us," without even stopping to consider whether or not the fear was foolish, or to be concerned about it if it were, correctly regarding all that as secondary. And if the woman had said, apologetically (as she may have done, I forget), "Oh, you must forgive me; I know my fears are foolish, but I am so upset!," the wise reply would have been: "Dear person, nothing to forgive. If you have fears, they *are*, they are real things, and to be considered. Whether or not they're foolish is beside the point. *What* they are is unimportant alongside the fact

147 that they *are*." In other words, the "badness" or "goodness," the teleology of the fears was decidedly secondary. The whole notion is conveyed by a smile or by a pleasant intonation more readily than by the words themselves. Teleological treatment, which I should have been tempted to employ under the circumstances, especially if I didn't like the woman, would first have stressed the fact that the fear was foolish. —Would say, with a great show of objective justice: "Well, there's no use in *our* doing anything; the fault is that *your* fear is foolish and improbable. Get over that, then if there's anything *sensible* we can do, we'll see," with smug blame implied in every word. —Or, more kindly, would try to reason with the woman in an attempt to help her get over it—the "business" of propaganda directed toward change even before the situation is fully understood (maybe as a lazy substitute for understanding, which is a difficult thing). Or, still more kindly, the teleological method would try to understand the fear causally. But with the non-teleological treatment, there is only the love and understanding of instant acceptance; after that fundamental may have been achieved, the next step, if any should be necessary, more sensibly can be considered.

    Strictly, the term non-teleological "thinking" ought not to be applied to what I have in mind. Because it involves more than thinking, that term is inadequate. Modus operandi might be better—a method of handling data of any sort. The example quoted just above concerns feeling more than thinking. The method extends beyond thinking, even to living itself; in fact, by inferred definition, it transcends the realm of thinking possibilities, it postulates "living into."

    In the destitute neighbor illustration (I), thinking, as being chiefly concerned, was the point of departure, "the crust to break through." There, my wife handled the situation in the inadequate teleological manner, I in the non-teleological, which also included her viewpoint as correct but limited. But when it came to the feeling aspects of a human relation situation, my wife probably ameliorated the woman's fears in a loving, truly mellow and adequate fashion, whereas I would have tended to employ a more sophisiticated teleological method. 148

Incidentally, there is in this connection a remarkable etiological similarity to be noted between cause in thinking, and blame in feeling. One feels that one's neighbors are to be blamed for their hate or anger or fear. One thinks that poor pavements are "caused" by politics. The non-teleological picture in either case is the larger one, that goes beyond blame or cause.

And the non-causal or non-blaming viewpoint seems to me to represent very often relatively the "new thing," the Hegelian "Christ-child" which arises emergently from the union of two opposing viewpoints, such as those of physical and spiritual teleologies, especially if there is conflict as to causation between the two or within either. The new viewpoint very frequently sheds light over a larger picture, providing a key which may unlock levels not accessible to either of the teleological viewpoints. There are interesting parallels here: to the triangle, to the Christian ideas of trinity, to Hegel's dialect, and to Swedenborg's metaphysic of divine love (feeling) and divine wisdom (thinking).

VI

The factors we have been considering as "answers" seem to me to be merely symbols or indices, relational aspects of things or of a thing (of which they are integral parts), not in itself to be considered in terms of causes and effects. The truest reason for anything being so is that it *is.* This is actually and truly a reason, more valid and clean than all the other separate reasons, or than any group of them short of the whole. Anything less than the whole forms part of the picture only, and the infinite *whole* is unknowable unless by "being" it, by living into it.

A thing may be *so* "because" of a thousand and one reasons of greater or lesser importance, such as the man oversized because of glandular insufficiency. The integration of these many reasons which are in the nature of relations rather than reasons, is that he *is.* The separate reasons, no matter how valid, are only fragmentary parts of the picture. And the whole necessarily includes all that it impinges as object and subject, in ripples fading with distance and intensity-decrease. 149

The frequent allusions, in this discussion, to an under-lying pattern, have no implication of mysticism—except inasmuch as a pattern which comprises infinity in factors and symbols might be called mystic. But infinity as used here also occurs in the mathematical aspects of physiology and physics, both far away from mysticism as the term is ordinarily employed. Actually, the underlying pattern is probably nothing more than an integration of just such symbols and indices and mutual reference points as are already known, except that its power is n. Such an integration might include nothing more spectacular than what we already know. But, equally, it *could* include anything, even events and entities as different from those already known as the tensors and spinors and the ideas of electrical charges in mathematical physics differ from the mechanical-model world of the Victorian scientists.

In such a pattern, causality would be merely a name for something that exists only in our partial and biased mental reconstructings. The pattern which it indexes, however, would be real, but not intellectually apperceivable in its entirety because it goes everywhere and is everything and cannot be encompassed by finite mind or by anything short of life, which it is.

The psychic or spiritual residua remaining after the most careful physical analysis, or the physical remnants obvious particularly to us of the twentieth century in the most honest and disciplined spiritual considerations of medieval philosophers, all bespeak such a pattern. Those residua, those most minute differentials, the 0.001 percentages which suffice to maintain the races of sea animals, are seen finally to be the most important things in the world, because they are everywhere. The differential is the true universal, the true catalyst, the cosmic solvent. Any investigation carried far enough will bring to light these residua, or rather, will leave them still unassailable as Emerson remarked a hundred years ago in "The Oversoul"—will run into the brick wall of the *impossibility* of perfection while at the same time insisting on the *validity* of perfection. Anomalies especially testify to that framework, they are the commonest intellectual vehicles for breaking through; all are solvable in the sense that any *one* is understandable, but they lead with the power *n* to still more and deeper anomalies.

This deep underlying pattern inferred by non-teleological thinking crops up everywhere—a relational thing surely, relating opposing factors on different levels, as reality and potential are related. But it may not be considered as causative, it just exists, it *is*, things are merely expressions of it. And they *are* it, also. As Swinburne, extolling Hertha, makes her say "Man, equal and one with me, man that is made of me, man that is I," so all things which are *that*, equally can be extolled. It materializes everywhere in the sense that Eddington finds the non-integer,—"number" appearing everywhere, in the background of all fundamental equations (*The Nature of the Physical World*, pp. 208-10), in the sense that the speed of light, constant despite compoundings or subtractions, seemed at one time almost to be conspiring against investigation.

The whole is necessarily everything, the whole world of fact and fancy, body and psyche, physical fact and spiritual truth, individual and collective, life and death, macrocosm and microcosm (the greatest quanta here, the greatest synapse between these two), conscious and unconscious, subject and object. The whole picture is portrayed by *is*, the deepest word of deep ultimate reality, not shallow or partial as reasons are, but deeper and participating, possibly encompassing the oriental concept of "being."

IIIE. Morphology of *The Sea of Cortez*

There is a dual structure of thought and beauty. Contributions from the one side are largely mine, from the other, John's. The structure is a collaboration, but shaped mostly by John. The book is the result.

A universal thesis was stated in the introduction—the way things are. The trip is shown to have been an example of that thesis. The idea is on pp. 1, 3 and 4, the fullness of its expression on pp. 149-50-51, and on p. 217 and elsewhere, its summing up on pp. 270-71.

(1) The design of a book is the pattern of a reality controlled and shaped by the mind of the writer...(p.2)...We wanted to see everything our eyes would accommodate, to think what we could, and, out of our seeing and thinking, to build *some kind of structure* in modeling imitation of the observed reality. We know that what we would see and record and construct would be warped, as all knowledge patterns are warped; first, by the collective pressure and stream of our time and race, second, by the thrust of our individual personalities. But, knowing this, we might not fall into too many holes—we might maintain some balance between our warp and the separate thing, the external reality. The oneness of these two might take its contribution from both. For example: the Mexican sierra...etc....(p.3). We said, "Let's go wide open. Let's see what we see, record what we find, and not fool ourselves with conventional scientific strictures. We could not observe a completely objective Sea of Cortez, anyway, for in that lonely and uninhabited Gulf, our boat and ourselves would change it, the moment we entered...realizing that we become forever a part of it...that the rocks we turn over in a tide pool make us truly and permanently a factor in the ecology of the region. We shall take something away from it, but we shall leave something too. Perhaps out of the two approaches, we thought, there might emerge a picture more complete and more accurate than either alone could produce..."
(149) Close of non-teleological thinking essay: "The frequent allusions to an underlying pattern have no implication of mysticism—except inasmuch as a pattern which comprises infinity in factors and symbols might be called mystic...In such a pattern, causality would be merely a name for something that exists only in our partial and biased mental reconstructings. The pattern which it indexes, however, would be real, but not intellectually apperceivable, because the pattern goes everywhere and is everything and cannot be encompassed by finite mind or by anything short of life—which it is...(p.150)....
But it must not be considered as causative, it simply exists, it *is*, things are merely expressions of it as it is expressions of them. And they *are* it, also. ...(p. 151).... This little trip of ours was becoming a thing and a dual thing, with collecting and eating and sleeping merging with the thinking-speculating activity. Quality of sunlight, blueness and smoothness of water, boat engines, and ourselves were all parts of a *larger whole* and *we could begin to feel* its nature but not its size."
(p. 270) "Some creative thing had happened, a real tempest in our small teapot minds...the shape of the trip was an integrated nucleus from which weak strings of thought stretched into every reachable reality, and a reality which reached into us through our perceptive nerve trunks. The laws of thought seemed really one with the laws of things...drawings, incompleted and imperfect of how it had been there. The real picture of how it had been there was in our minds. ...they were all one thing and we were that one thing too."

IIIF. "Forgotten Village" Antiscript

This antiscript is a reaction to the book version of *The Forgotten Village*, which consists of a brief introduction by John Steinbeck, and captions from the narration, "With 136 photographs from the film of the same name." Probably Ed never saw the film itself. A startling aspect of the film is the resemblance of the doctor to Ed in stature, build and manner of holding his head and moving about. Compare, for example, the scene on page 119 of the book with the photograph of Ed taken by Willard Bascom in this volume. Ed did not, apparently, notice this resemblance which comes out more strongly in the film, nor did he comment on the usual inept stage business of a microscope set at lower power and tilted to observe bacteria in a water drop preparation. The casting was not deliberate; according to Herb Kline, the only person they could find for the doctor was the visiting *interne* or sanitarian himself.

The *interne* of *The Forgotten Village*.
The Forgotten Village, p. 119, Viking
Press, 1941.

Ed Ricketts, 1947.
Courtesy Willard Bascom.

THESIS AND MATERIALS
for a
SCRIPT ON MEXICO

which shall be motivated oppositely to John's
"FORGOTTEN VILLAGE"

I.   Thesis

II. Materials for a Script.
   A. Plan
   B. Prelude
   C. Part I: The Way Things Have Been
   D. Part II: The New Thing Creeping In
   E. Part III: The Result—The Debacle
   F. Postlude

I. Thesis

There are two types of entities:

THE REGION OF OUTWARD POSSESSIONS

(1) The outer or intellectual-material things, related to the realm of physical and mental acquisitions: communication and transportation; education in the formal and usual sense, as emphasizing the acquisition of facts and skills, and in which the teaching is by rule, more or less impersonal, and in quantity production; sanitation, medicine and surgery; engineering, the planning and executing of functional and efficient buildings, cities, highway systems, radio networks, etc.; development and refinements of measuring methods, mathematics, logic and science; finance and economics.

The realm of thinking and of the physical world. The emphasis is on change, acquisition, progress. Symbols are: high-tension lines, modern highways, modern schools.

THE REGION OF INWARD ADJUSTMENTS

(2) The inward things. Entities of this sort are associated so frequently with the stagnation of present-day religion, or considered so rarely in a consciously disciplined fashion as to require some discussion even to define them roughly. The most obvious examples are in the field of human relationships, involving friendship, tolerance, dignity or love, but there are larger relationships, between human society and the given individual, between man and the land, and between man and his feeling of supra-personal participation from within. I have tried to indicate the modern feeling for some of these relationships by the quotations below. Teaching in the old sense is another example, wherein there was emphasis on inward structures, "something to tie to in a crashing world," a sense of verities, usually established through personal relationship between master and pupil.

Although now obscure, ideas of this sort are not without their modern protagonists. A weekly magazine has twice recently questioned whether "the other side" may not have values, the loss of which involves a price too high to pay for the acquisition of material benefits:

"The life of an English village is based on the premise that contentment is better than efficiency. It asserts that a mass production assembly line is less important to a man than liking his own village and his fellow villagers."

And again, speaking of a Chinese village now being modernized:

"Before the war, it was one of the most *backward* places in China.... Today, with the best brains...[in the country] within its borders, Szechwan Province is one of the most *progressive* parts of China. Philosophers may question whether what Lung Chuan I has may not be better than what it will get from the West. For one thing, its kind of civilization has survived a long time. Whether Western civilization will do better can only be answered in 5000 A.D. China is going to find out." (Italics are mine.) (Life, Nov. 24, 1941.)

A professor of economics contrasts the *scale* of living with the *standard* of living:

(Elizabeth E. Hunt, 1938, Consumption in Our Society, McGraw Hill, N.Y. p. 265.)

"In some cases, the scale as an indication of the standard is poor indeed. In practical life, some social investigators have fallen into error in assuming the standard to be no more than the scale. They have made recommendations for "reform" based on a very incomplete understanding of the whole standard-of-living pattern. The following example shows this . . .

"A group of farm families lived in a hilly and infertile region of the South. The material goods they consumed were very meager. They were poor. They were unable to produce enough to purchase what the investigators held was a decent American scale of living. The people had no washing machines and no bathrooms. Their children went barefoot. The variety of food was limited to pork and cornmeal, the vegetables they raised, and the fruit they gathered in the pastures. The investigators proposed that the government take over the land of these farmers and the farmers be helped to migrate to more fertile farms or to take up industrial labor in the city.

"What the investigators failed to take into account was the fact that to some of these families the life they led was a life they preferred to its alternatives. Fertile fields and fat pay envelopes were not what they most wanted. Bathrooms and washing machines were good, to be sure, but the price their critics would have them pay was too high.

"Their standard included things that the investigators did not measure or even notice. These families liked the beauty of the hills around them; they liked picking raspberries in the briar patch; they enjoyed their isolation; they did not want ease; some of them even took satisfaction in the struggle itself. Their scale appeared as one thing, their standard very different. Working on fertile lands or in factories, they would gain certain things easily measured and lose others, measured not so easily; and the latter, to them, were more important.

"In the same way, and in even more marked degree, governments may interfere with the lives of subject races who are technologically backward and, in the effort to raise their scale, break down their standard. The change may be so rapid and so extreme that the subject peoples lose their zest for living or even their hold on life. The history of the government's effort to raise the scale of the Indians affords many examples of this. We gave them money, food, our own type of education and religion; they lost their sense of cultural security on which their standard of living depended. For the sake of a higher scale, standard was sacrificed."

Applying this parallel to present-day Mexico, it would seem that the active and articulate middle class already prefers the fat pay envelope. Many of the people are stage-struck with technological progress and tend to hasten the march of their already committed nation.

Finally, even the presumably hard-boiled editor of a very practical newspaper is constrained to write about these spiritual entities in a Memorial Day editorial:

"There is no sorrier nor more unmanly propaganda than that that libels the dead of America's wars . . . with the inference that these dead have died in vain.

"It is not for war itself nor for causes of war, that free men give their lives. It is for things they believe in, rightly or wrongly, for causes they consider to be just, for ideals that are in their own minds, or even for the sake of carrying a man's part among their fellows in suffering and in danger—these things are not vain things for which men have died.

"Conscientious objectors to war, religious 'heretics,' political dissenters have also given their lives for their beliefs. Socialists, fascists, communists, republicans, jacobins, royalists—all have their roll of honor. To be willing to suffer and die for his traditions, his country, and his love of liberty is perhaps the most god-like attribute of man. In that, he is eternally right and forever to be honored—no matter how misled, misguided, cheated, or wrong in fact or principle. However such men die, they rise superior to those that live in vain."

(Peninsula Herald, Monterey, California, May 30 [1938?].)

This "other side," which in the East even the bravest men are proud to own, is with us rarely discussed by practical men. It is associated too often with feminine traits, with the unconscious—the realm of feeling. The emphasis is on acceptance, on appreciation of what *is,* as contrasted with propaganda for change. A symbol is hard to suggest. Perhaps the "deep smile," mentioned further along, comes nearest.

Having (I hope) indicated the validity of entities of the second or spiritual order, as contrasted to those of the first order, the foundation will have been laid for the materials I have in mind. The argument for a script on Mexico, with a motif diametrically opposite to that of John's "Forgotten Village," but equally true and equally significant factually, could be developed somewhat along the following lines:

(1) In the past, the majority of the Mexican people have put more of their life energy into things of the second order (love, friendship, appreciation) than into the problems of getting themselves fine homes and other material acquisitions in general, good health through medicine, etc., thus achieving among their countrymen to the north the reputation for being lazy and careless.
(2) The majority of people of the European nations have put their energy into things of the first order, and so have beautiful bathrooms and aseptic operations, but lack the Mexican's natural development in the arts of friendship, appreciation, and human relations in general.
(3) The spirit of the first order is dominant in the so-called progressive nations, and it tends to spread from its centers of nurture into previously uninfected regions, a true zeitgeist. It arrives coincident with the spread of high tension wires, modern schools, the automobile age; but its receptor must be already there, potential in the minds of the people who espouse it. And the spread of this spirit is so rapid and devastating that it upsets the age-old relation between man and the land, and between man and man.

The tragedy is that, whatever as individuals we think about it, whether or not we approve, the modern thing exists. Here it is. And it's furthermore still in the ascendency as a present reality. We must deal with it, and refusing to face it cannot minimize its increasing inroads. Although history shows that only most rarely the two things may co-exist racially (the Periclean Age in Greece), we may at least hope to avoid the extreme imbalance of the Hindu—all inner with an utter lack of material progress, or that of the material American culture with its dearth of inner values. Why the two should co-exist so rarely is difficult to understand. Probably the life energy of a race is more circumscribed (restricted) than that of the individual, who seems to be able to build it up pretty much as he will. Developing co-ordinately is probably equivalent to walking the knife edge. By intent, discipline and skill, the individual with his free-will and determinancy may achieve it. But to postulate that goal for the race would be for us to assign the free-will of the molecule to the inevitable destiny of the molecule-group. Whatever may be the individual divergences of rare constituents, the group, having started in one direction, tends to develop along those lines until it exhibits the law of diminishing returns, or until it contacts powerful opposite influences such as technologically backward races seem to have found in the spirit of American progress.

II. Materials for a Script

A. Plan.

The chief character in John's script is the Indian boy who becomes so imbued with the spirit of modern medical progress that he leaves the traditional way of his people to associate himself with the new thing.

The working out of a script for the "other side" might correspondingly be achieved through the figure of some wise and mellow old man, who has long ago developed beyond the expediencies of economic drives and power drives, and to whom for guidance in adolescent troubles some grandchild comes (as the young girl to the Philosopher in James Stephens "Crock of Gold"). A wise old man, present during the time of building a high speed road through a primitive community, appropriately might point out the evils of the encroaching mechanistic civilization to a young person.

B. Prelude.

Picture of some non-expedient artist such as Goitia or Orozco, finishing, with fatigue, but with the sense of a good job well done, a mural that has been conceived and executed in love and with integrity, painting in the final inscription:

"La verdadera civilizacion sera la harmonia de los hombres con la tierra y de los hombres entre si."

Literally: "The true civilization will be the harmony of the men with the land and of the men among themselves." In a better English style, it would read: "True civilization will secure harmony between men and the land, and between men among themselves."

Actually, it was Rivera who made use of this phrase on one of his murals, I think, on one of the Ministry of Education murals.

C. The Way Things Have Been.

1. The curiously illuminating smiles, of especially the younger poor country people, on the rare occasions when you are able to get contact with them, as evidence of their internal adjustment and happiness in a life normally involving almost unbelievable rigors of proverty and disease (despite which they exhibit stamina probably unattainable by the vigorous American who describes them as lazy), as in:

(All this as contrasted with the inwardly shallow lives of the outwardly rich tourists as they drive by, bored, or condescending, or dewey-eyed with romance, or vicariously seeking something they've been told they can find here.)

a. Some of the children we passed and waved to, and many of the young men to whom we threw cigarettes, along the main highway to Mexico City. These deep smiles are so illuminating as to comprise in themselves important experiences for the observer. An American would do well to trade his material possessions and his health for such transcendent joy.

b. The indescribably poor Indians in the Comancho procession at Puebla, who, stumbling over a sidewalk obstruction in the great crowd where we were taking movies, would laugh heartily and enjoyably, instead of being irritated.

2. Their rich relational life, as evidenced by:

(a) The genuine and contagious joy with which friends greet each other.

Even the men were sincerely glad to see one another, not regarding each other so much as we do, merely in terms of possible social or financial advancement. More like the pure camaraderie of slightly drunk Americans, but more quiet and apparently more real.

(b) Captain Corona in Guaymas remarking to us with courtly sincerity in the presence of his wife, that finding and marrying her was the finest move he made ever in his life.

(c) The Indian who, with his small son, was loitering about aboard the *Western Flyer*. When he saw a group of Mexicans taking leave of us with expressions of real regret, he said to me with a smile, "Good friends." I suddenly realized the significance of what he was saying, agreed with him, and told him that such a thing occurred not so often in the United States as it did here.

(d) The hand-operated, incredibly junky merry-go-round for infants, near the poor peoples' market in Guadalajara. Little children were fastened into seats—everything was improvised, poor, and home-made—hung on chains from a May-pole canopied with native religious paintings. Then the operator swung the whole thing around by hand from the inside. I suppose one centavo per ride. Little girls came, themselves little more than infants, with infant sisters and brothers. It was such a joyful occasion! I would have given a great deal to be able gracefully to treat some of those children to a ride, who looked on so wistfully. If I could—without changing the simplicity of the picture. In this intent, I wasn't alone. In the scattered group of older spectators, there was wrinkled Indian with a superating eye. He saw me watching, as I saw him, and he smiled at me. Probably both of us wanted just one thing more than anything else in the world right then: to give those youngsters, all the children in Guadalajara, all the people everywhere in the whole world, a ride on that wonderful, on that unbelievably beautiful contraption. But I couldn't participate without spoiling what I most admired. And *he* couldn't; he hadn't any money.

3. Their inherent honesty, in a sense deeper than we use the term. The fiction that the Mexican is fundamentally dishonest is in part fostered by Americans (Although I remember sixteen years ago driving with a loaded touring car into Ensenada and asking an American restaurant owner if it was safe for us to park in front of her place while we had dinner. "Lord, yes," she said, "you're not in the States. Leave your car parked here several days if you want, nobody'll take anything."). But Americans will document this idea, especially those who have lived (as Americans) for many years in the big Mexican cities without once having touched the heart of the country— or anything else, for that matter—except in the most superficial manner (vide the American business man I talked to on Election Day over by the Green Cross Hospital on Election Day, 1940). But even the Mexicans themselves, especially the upper class, keep this fiction alive, in pretty much the same way that Chicagoans boast about the wickedness of their city. With some semblance of truth, they point out that everything removable may be stripped from an unguarded parked car; they're proud of the fact that strangers who walk into certain sections of the city may get into trouble. Their pride in these things is such that they want to believe them whether or not they are factually true.

And of course there is some truth in all of it. Petty thievery, as the Communist gal at the University assured me, may be more prevalent in Mexico City than in most United States towns. But the fact of the matter is that people so diverse as Mark Marvin, Carlos Cabello and Ed Ricketts have been treated better and more honestly in Mexico as a whole, than they have been in the States. And even the people who foster the tradition, act out of knowledge of its incorrectness:

(1) In the crowded street near Sanborns, at the 6 PM rush hour, Mark gave one peso to a young boy he'd never seen before, with the request that he get an American paper and return with the change. Four out of five Mexican kids would fulfill that trust; one out of two Chicago kids would *not*. (Yes, the boy returned!)

(2) Carlos is more careless about locking the car than I am (except in the heart of Mexico City, where he says it's different). When I check up on him, he says, "Listen, Ed, the people in this town are honest, I know them, they won't steal anything from us." (As though I thought they would! Just following Herb's instructions [Herbert Kline, Director and Producer, "The Forgotten Village"].) And Carlos is quicker than I to pick up people along the road. The idea (even if true, and even if Herb insists on it) that giving Mexicans a lift is bad business, ought to be disregarded, because it results in contacts whose value far outweighs its risk of dire consequences. In fact, I, who most disapproved of this proscription, was the only one who paid any attention to it.

In its results, the fictions that everything must be watched is a pretty good thing—so long as you don't believe in it implicitly (and it is true to some extent). It provides not very remunerative occupation to a great many Indians who would otherwise (presumably) starve, and to lots of children. Lovely children! And in the process, many small amounts of money change hands. It provides a function in life for old women who lock courtyard gates —and then re-lock them—if you come home after 10 PM, charging you ten centavos. Everyone knows you have no business being out after 10 PM, anyway! If this idea were to be repudiated suddenly, it would cause a real upset in the economic life of Mexico (and probably of France and of Spain, unless the war has changed all that), and would work a real hardship on a good many old or infirm people who have no other means of income.

D. The New Thing Creeping In.

The gradual influence of the "new thing," which was at first outside the country, but which is now working from within, in corrupting the old life and in upsetting the age-old relation between the people and the land and between the people themselves, as evidenced by:

(1) The nieve seller at Puebla.

The day of the Comancho meeting, a nieve seller was operating in the plaza. Sasha [Alexander Hackensmid, Director of Photography, "The Forgotten Village"] and I, faced with an indeterminate wait, were observing the way he did business. From his back-pack headquarters, set up in one corner of the park, he would fill with nieve his stock of 15 or 20 glasses, stick a spoon in each dish, and then start dispensing them around the park from his handtray. He would hand a glass of this cheap snow-ice-cream to whomever beckoned for one. We wondered how he could possibly keep track of his dishes and of the five centavos due him, since he took no money at the time. We discovered it was very simple. He didn't keep track at all; the customer did! When the customer had eaten the ice—slowly, because things of that sort didn't happen every day, and were to be relished fully when they did— he sought out the nieve-seller's headquarters, returned the glass and spoon and paid him the five centavos. We watched and waited, confident that in a holiday group of careless Mexicans, the inevitable was only a matter of time.

Sure enough! A poorly dressed country-fellow walked up confidently, relaxed and happy, set his glass and spoon on the tray, started to dig for his five centavo piece. At first, everything was fine—just a matter of a misplaced coin. Then the truth dawned on the nieve-seller, on the buyer, and on us, all at the same time. That piece of money had already been spent, earlier in the day. The nieve-seller went about his business, purposefully, permitting his customer to get accustomed to the predicament, unembarrassed by attention. Finally, he walked away, as I believe, to let the man get some composure. Then when he came back, Sasha and I could see the pantomine, and I thought we could safely reconstruct the substance of what was said. "Perfectly all right," said the nieve-seller, "these things happen to anyone. Why, I remember once when I...etc., etc..... If you're in town of a Sunday or feast day in the next few months, and have the money, look me up, I'll be right here in the Plaza. If you're not, or if you're broke, perfectly all right, think nothing of it." And so on, until they parted, best of friends.

I kept thinking: What if the nieve-seller tried to conduct business with Americans along those lines, or even with United States resident Mexicans, who had acclimated themselves to our ways? Your brisk, ethical American would not only not bother to pay the nieve-seller (since doing so would entail some trouble), he wouldn't even bother to return the glass and spoon. "Such lack of business acumen!," the American would think. He'd set down the glass and the spoon, that precious stock-in-trade of a poor huckster, wherever he'd happen to be. He wouldn't mean to cheat the man. He'd say to himself, "Hell, it's only a small amount, less than a cent in *real money,* anyway." He'd just neglect to attend to that small matter. And the nieve-seller, who dealt formerly only with Mexicans, who have, in any case, such a reputation for small thievery, would have to adopt a C.O.D. policy when dealing with Americans. Or else he'd have to retire bankrupt from his business, with an attitude of cynicism toward the "honest" *norteamericanos,* to boot.

(2) A new road being forced through an unwilling country (as I have seen happen in Santa Tomas Valley in Northern Lower California) by a non-resident socialist government which believes in good roads and rapid communication, whether the district wants it or not. A wise old man, seeing this, would realize that the sudden change would destroy a lovely old way of life, and that the school teacher or government official who was the instrument of the change would be all the more dangerous if he were a good man who himself had the fire of zeal for the new thing. The old harmony between the people and the land would be upset by the new high speed road with its strange people passing by, with its trespassers and picnickers, and by the changed economy incident to a high speed road. The good relations between parent and child would be upset by the boys hitch-hiking into Ensenada to the movies and pool halls, and by the gals getting themselves screwed by flashy strangers in shiny cars.

(Alongside of this contrast are Orozco or Goitia, honest and fierce, uncorrupted by the new thing, painting a mural in which a mechanical man is shown strangling the Mexican race (as Orozco actually did portray in his Belles Artes mural).)

(3) The children in a primitive community, before and after the high speed road has come through. The first is exemplified by such a town as Loreto, where one boy was genuinely interested in showing the strangers through the mission and the school and the town, not primarily expediently or for money, but because he had a warm heart and because he liked the stranger.

The second type is illustrated by the kids at Tijuana, interested chiefly in what they can get out of you, in some cases becoming thieves and rascals. In an inward sense, the Mexicans are more advanced than we are, but they can be corrupted by a virus so powerful as that of the present United States mechanistic civilization.

E. The Probable Results.

Humorous interplays: Their naive use of the machine in which they are (already today) most vitally interested. It's a beautiful new toy, and they cling to it, despite the fact that it takes the smile and the slow pace out of them, upsets their relation with the land and with each other, and substitutes the irritated nervous pace of Western man.

A debacle, per remarks of what's his name, the very tall movie director who did *Grass* and *Chang.* Just returning from the interior of Guatemala, a couple of years back, he said it was his hope that there would be no compulsory education there ever, to change that sturdy primitive simplicity and hospitality. Said that he was in Persia before and after the spread of education—went in the second time by plane, and that the very great change could be attributed to no other obvious factor. That the new thing had come in there without benefit of road or power line (but of course the airplane and its basing facilities is a pretty modern transportation method, and I should expect that it could change the country fastest of all).

Mexico City camiones, driven like a bat out of hell, radiator invariably boiling—cap thrown away after the engine has boiled the first few times. It's the ideal of every Mexican boy to be driver of an emergency vehicle, and very many of them are!

After this change had taken place—and it's happening pretty rapidly in Mexico, I should expect to see:

The fine plumbing that doesn't work at night, account of low water pressure. As Carol says of the *bombas,* the pressure pumps: "They can't go day *and* night."

The *lack* of the deep smile in the common people as evidence of their lack of inward adjustment and happiness in the midst of a life now of comparative ease, health and financial security.

(a) The woman in the home now would be making tortillas from packaged cornmeal, with a not-too-good electric mixer, Goats milked by an electric milking machine, worker in a hurry, co-op dairy closes at a certain time and 100% production must be in before then. Smile gone.

My incident of the Lomas de Chapultepec line of camiones suddenly ceasing operations. No one seems to know why. The people told me, "They just stopped going by," and didn't seem even surprised! (There was a strike. I kept at it until I found out. But still I'm not entirely sure!)

(b) A Mexican in a co-op factory, as a putter-on of a single bolt in a quantity production line. Smile gone. A nervous irritability (foreign to him and to his race) now in its place, as the foreman gives them a pep talk on the Five Year Plan, so speeding them up toward still greater heights of production "so that everybody'll have enough of everything" (except adjustment and happiness). Impossible for him to quit now. He's acclimated to the new thing, accustomed to his present scale of living, and has now no other means of support for his family. There is also the social pressure of his fellows. And of his superior: "The State needs you."

An American rushing suddenly into a store to phone, only to be told by the store-keeper, after storming into the phone for several minutes: "Oh,

Señor, a thousand pardons. How unfortunate that I neglected to tell you sooner. For three days that telephone doesn't work!"

F. Postlude.

A group of assembly line workers, spending their day of rest in the State Museum (of the future), as all good workers should do, passing before the painting shown in the prelude, smile all gone now, significantly and sadly reading the words (now *all* the workers can read):

> *"La verdadera civilizacion sera la harmonia de los*
> *hombres in la tierra y de los hombres entre se."*